The Poets' Corner

The Poets' Corner

The One-and-Only Poetry Book for the Whole Family

John Lithgow

lithgow
palooza

A Lark Production

GC
GRAND CENTRAL
PUBLISHING

New York   Boston

Grand Central Publishing
Hachette Book Group USA
237 Park Avenue
New York, NY 10017

Visit our Web site at www.HachetteBookGroupUSA.com.

Printed in the United States of America

First Edition: November 2007
10 9 8 7 6 5 4 3 2 1

Grand Central Publishing is a division of Hachette Book Group USA, Inc.
The Grand Central Publishing name and logo is a trademark of Hachette Book Group
USA, Inc.

Library of Congress Cataloging-in-Publication Data
The poets' corner : the one and only poetry book for the whole family / [selected by]
John Lithgow. — 1st ed.
     p. cm.
     Summary: "John Lithgow has hand-picked some of the best poems ever written in
this quintessential collection for the whole family to treasure"—Provided by publisher.
     ISBN-13: 978-0-446-58002-1
     ISBN-10: 0-446-58002-3
  1. English poetry. 2. American poetry. I. Lithgow, John, 1945-
  PR1175.L514 2007
  821.008—dc22   2006100805

*The photograph on the front of the book jacket was taken at
William Andrews Clark Memorial Library, UCLA.*

To Mary

Acknowledgments

Thanks, first of all, to Robin Dellabough, Lisa DiMona, and Flynn Berry at Lark Productions and especially Karen Watts for their tireless efforts on *The Poets' Corner*. Thanks to Nancy Cushing-Jones, Barbara Weller, and Cynthia Cleveland—the women of Broadthink—for the original instinct to create the book. Additional thanks to Les Pockell for his editorial insights. Thanks, too, to Linda Korn, John McEroy, and Karen Goldstein for the enormous task of organizing and producing the accompanying CD of the book's fifty poems. The voices heard on the CD belong to some of the best, most celebrated actors of our day, who lent their services with generosity and enthusiasm. Each of them is a former colleague and friend and I am deeply grateful to all of them.

Contents

Contents

Contents

Contents

Contents

Introduction:
To Readers, Young and Old

I grew up with poems.

All of us did, whether we realize it or not. Poetry is in our bloodstream: nursery rhymes, schoolyard chants, song lyrics, limericks, jingles, rap. But not many of us think of ourselves as poetry lovers. The very question "Do you love poetry?" makes most of us nervous. It shouldn't. Poetry is a part of us. The purpose of this book is to remind people, young and old, of that simple fact.

The fifty poets I've chosen for the book are vastly different from one another. Indeed, they have only two things in common: they wrote in English and their work survives them. They lived on different continents, in different eras, their work is old and new, romantic and savage, comic and gloomy, orderly and chaotic, long and short. The poems are presented alphabetically, by their authors' last names. If you read them in sequence, you'll travel a crazy, unpredictable journey, lurching back and forth through the centuries. My brief comments reflect what the poems have meant to me, but they speak far more resonantly for themselves.

Oh, yes. The poets have one other thing in common. I love them all.

I can trace my love of poetry back to my childhood, and to my grandmother, Ina B. Lithgow. Grammy was born late in the nineteenth century and grew up on the island of Nantucket. Hers was one of the last generations to make the memorization and recitation of poems an integral part of a child's education. In her late eighties she could still remember all the words to countless epic poems, such as Longfellow's "The Wreck of the

Hesperus." My brother, my sisters, and I would sit at her feet and beg her to recite. Her dark brown eyes would twinkle, she would tilt her head back, fold her hands in her lap, and begin to speak in a gentle, even voice. She would recite for as long as forty minutes. Incredibly, I never remember her missing a syllable.

One of our favorites was "The Deacon's Masterpiece or, the Wonderful One-hoss Shay," by Oliver Wendell Holmes. It is a saga about a deluxe horse-drawn buggy, made of the finest leather, wood, and brass, built to last. Not a thing goes wrong with it until the exact day, hour, minute, and second that it turns one hundred years old. All at once and without warning, the wonderful one-hoss shay flies into a million pieces. I can still hear my Grammy's voice reciting the last stanza:

> What do you think the parson found,
> When he got up and stared around?
> The poor old chaise in a heap or mound,
> As if it had been to the mill and ground!
> You see, of course, if you're not a dunce,
> How it went to pieces all at once,—
> All at once, and nothing first,—
> Just as bubbles do when they burst.
>
> End of the wonderful one-hoss shay.
> Logic is logic. That's all I say.

Oh, how I loved the story, the rhymes, the meter, that accent, and that voice! And, although I can't say for sure, my seven-year-old brain must have had some inkling of the metaphorical power of the moment. Here was my elderly grandmother performing mental feats that I would never be capable of. I must have been aware that I would lose her soon, but surely I did not imagine her razor-sharp mind ever failing her—not until the very end. Perhaps it was my first poetic insight: my Grammy was the wonderful one-hoss shay!

Introduction

Then there was my dad. Grammy must have passed on her poetry-loving genes to my father, for he devoted half of his professional life to producing Shakespeare's plays in a succession of theater festivals in Ohio. As a result, my own childhood was awash in Elizabethan verse. And although my dad poured most of his energy into rehearsals and performances, we usually had him to ourselves at bedtime. He would read aloud to us from either the funny papers, from a fat collection of stories called *Tellers of Tales*, from Kipling's *Jungle Book*, or, best of all, from a series of bright orange volumes for kids called *Childcraft*.

One of the *Childcraft* books was a collection of poems. It mostly featured loopy verse by doggerel poets such as Edward Lear and Lewis Carroll. None of the poems was especially complex or challenging, but we would request them over and over again. I can still rattle off several lines from memory:

> Once there was an elephant
> Who tried to use the telephant;
> No no, I mean an elephone
> Who tried to use the telephone. . . .

Or my favorite:

> I never saw a purple cow,
> I never hope to see one;
> But I can tell you anyhow:
> I'd rather see than be one.

I remember my father's exact inflections, his husky smell, the scratchy wool of our burnt orange couch. My father was a genial man, but slightly abstracted. He lived his life with his head halfway in the clouds. But when my sibs and I cuddled up to him and listened to those poems, we were never closer.

Those bedtime hours primed me for all the poetry I encountered later

Introduction

on, in high school and college English classes. Nonsense verses gave way to the metaphysical poets, the cavalier poets, the Romantic poets. Instead of telephants and purple cows, I discovered Donne, Herrick, Coleridge, Poe. I embraced these poets with a swoony, youthful exuberance. I felt as if they were speaking directly to me from centuries past. I remember declaiming Walt Whitman to my first girlfriend, pronouncing Marvell's "To His Coy Mistress" the perfect poem, memorizing Keats's ode "To Autumn" on a golden fall day in New England. As a student actor, I appeared in plays by T. S. Eliot, Dylan Thomas, and William Butler Yeats, drunk with the power of their words.

None of this made me an authority on poetry, nor even much of a scholar. But it made me a poetry lover, a lifelong seeker of poetic experience, whether reading, reciting, or listening to great poems.

I once witnessed firsthand just how intense the experience of poetry can be. The story bears repeating, because it partly inspired this book.

Ten years ago, a married couple asked me to host a benefit for a non-profit organization they had founded in a town eighty miles from my home. The request came at a time when I was busy and overextended, so I hesitated. But when my wife told me that these people were good friends of hers, I accepted their invitation. A few days later, the couple called again, asking me to recite some poems during the benefit. They said they would choose them for me. Once again I dutifully agreed. When the evening arrived, I quickly skimmed the poems they had chosen before setting off with my wife.

The fund-raiser was for an organization that fostered creative approaches to educating autistic children. Every single person at the event was the parent of at least one autistic child. The couple themselves had had three, one of whom had died young. Considering these poignant facts, the atmosphere at the banquet was amazingly lighthearted and festive. Everyone was cheerful and energized, none more so than my two new friends.

After dinner, I launched into my recitation. The couple had selected a dozen poems. As I read them, I began to realize why each poem had been chosen. Each had something to say about the plight of the parents in the audience and the struggles of their children. The first few were familiar poems by the likes of Emily Dickinson, W. H. Auden, and Robert Frost. Gradually the poems began to cut closer to the bone. Late in the sequence there were two written by the mother of an autistic boy. The final one was by a twenty-two-year-old woman, writing with heartbreaking clarity about her own autism. By the time I finished, everyone in the hall was in tears, myself included.

I had never performed for an audience like that. These people came from all walks of life. The only thing they had in common was the sad fact of their children's condition. Until this occasion, very few of them had had any experience of poetry. And yet, as I read aloud to them, I could sense a kind of electricity in the air. Every word of these poems was intensely meaningful to them, speaking to their deepest feelings. That night they felt connected to twelve poets whom they had never met nor perhaps even heard of. And as they never had before, they felt connected to one another. That connection was startling, exhilarating, and comforting to them.

Poetry can do that.

All the poets in this volume (including every name mentioned in this introduction) have made that kind of connection with their readers over time. Turn these pages, read these words, and see if you make the connection too. For those of you who already know the following poems, my hope is that they strike you as familiar strains of music, experienced in a fresh, vivid way. If the poems are new to you, grab on to them, wrestle with them, fall in love with them, make them a part of you, and grow up with them.

The Poets' Corner

Matthew Arnold

The Serious Poet

(1822–1888)

Among the Victorian poets of England, Matthew Arnold was not as famous as Tennyson and Robert Browning. Unlike them, he did not have the luxury of being able to devote himself full-time to writing. Arnold, the son of a clergyman and private-school headmaster, worked for a living his entire life. A ten-year appointment at Oxford University as a poetry professor, combined with his job as a government school inspector, meant he had to squeeze in his poetry on his own time. He wrote most of his poems before he was forty years old, when family life and work were less demanding. After that, he concentrated on writing essays about culture, religion, and literature, and his prose was better received than his poetry, at least during his lifetime. Some say it was his literary criticism that elevated criticism to an art form in its own right. Here is Arnold on poetry: "I think it will be found that grand style arises in poetry, when a noble nature, poetically gifted, treats with simplicity or with severity a serious subject."

To Arnold, no matter how beautiful its language or imagery, if a poem lacked an important subject, he found it unworthy of his attention. Serious and austere himself, he chose lofty subjects for his own poems—faith or the absence of faith, how to live in a meaningful way, politics, the individual in relation to society. He believed his work would endure because it reflected the period's big themes. "For the creation of a masterwork of literature two powers must concur," wrote Arnold, "the power of the man and the power of the moment, and the man is not enough without the moment." Arnold's moment in history happened to be one of great change and flux. You could say all his poetry was about coming to terms with the Victorian age of industrialism and the weakening of religion.

➹ Favorite Poems ➷

"Shakespeare" ❧ "The Scholar-Gipsy" ❧ "To Marguerite"

"Thyrsis" ❧ "The Forsaken Merman"

Dover Beach

The sea is calm to-night.
The tide is full, the moon lies fair
Upon the straits;—on the French coast, the light
Gleams and is gone; the cliffs of England stand,
Glimmering and vast, out in the tranquil bay.
Come to the window, sweet is the night-air!
Only, from the long line of spray
Where the sea meets the moon-blanch'd land,
Listen! you hear the grating roar
Of pebbles which the waves draw back, and fling,
At their return, up the high strand,
Begin, and cease, and then again begin,
With tremulous cadence slow, and bring
The eternal note of sadness in.

Sophocles long ago
Heard it on the Aegean, and it brought
Into his mind the turbid ebb and flow
Of human misery; we
Find also in the sound a thought,
Hearing it by this distant northern sea.

The Sea of Faith
Was once, too, at the full, and round earth's shore
Lay like the folds of a bright girdle furled.
But now I only hear
Its melancholy, long, withdrawing roar,
Retreating, to the breath
Of the night-wind, down the vast edges drear
And naked shingles of the world.

Ah, love, let us be true
To one another! for the world, which seems
To lie before us like a land of dreams,
So various, so beautiful, so new,
Hath really neither joy, nor love, nor light,
Nor certitude, nor peace, nor help for pain;
And we are here as on a darkling plain
Swept with confused alarms of struggle and flight,
Where ignorant armies clash by night.

There's just no way around it, this is a downbeat poem. I hear in it a desperate, yearning gloom, a sense of despair about the Victorian world and a personal crisis of faith. But despite the poet's melancholy, the poem is quite beautiful in its specificity. Arnold reveals his feelings very directly and openly. As the American novelist Henry James said, Arnold's poetry appeals to those who "like their pleasures rare" and who like to hear the poet "taking breath." The "breath" of the sea, its ebb and flow, in and out, reverberates throughout the lines, creating a kind of wavelike music. There is some hope in beauty—"a land of dreams / So various, so beautiful, so new"—and the potential to regain happiness and faith if his beloved can hang in there with him. For Arnold, this was the answer to emotional and spiritual isolation. For me, reading an exquisite, powerful poem such as "Dover Beach" is an antidote to a moody moment.

Read contemporary poet Anthony Hecht's
"The Dover Bitch" for a wonderful modern take on the
emotional landscape of "Dover Beach."

W. H. Auden

The High/Low Poet

(1907–1973)

W. H. Auden was the furthest thing from the sensitive poet holed up in a garret. He was a writer who lived enthusiastically in the midst of his time, and wove pop culture, current events, and everyday speech into his poems. He was also decidedly *not* a snob. Auden loved to mix the highbrow and the lowbrow: he worshiped opera as much as he enjoyed cheap cabarets. He also had a prankish sense of humor; sometimes he included private symbols that only a few close friends could discover and decipher, and he intended some of his poems to be sung to the tune of popular songs. It certainly changes the meaning to learn that the poem "James Honeyman" (about the scientist inventor of poison gas) was meant to be sung to the tune of "Stagolee," or that "Victor" (about a religious murderer) was set to the tune of "Frankie and Johnny." Auden was playful, but he was also very aware of what he was doing: shocking the stodgy and jauntily blasphemizing somber subjects.

Auden was offensive and devout, intellectual and silly, disillusioned and hopeful. He was a cranky, egotistical, precocious young man who churned out hundreds of poems, and he was also a playful old fellow who was crazy about Broadway shows and Gershwin tunes. Auden could write dense essays using a term like "consupponible" without bothering to define it, but he also wrote about manners for *Mademoiselle* and famous last words for *Harper's Bazaar*. He loved nursery rhymes, folk verse, and doggerel. He believed that "Sing a song of sixpence, a pocket full of rye" was pretty nearly "pure poetry."

"Why do you want to write poetry?" If the young man answers, "I have important things I want to say," then he is not a poet. If he answers, "I like hanging around words listening to what they say," then maybe he is going to be a poet.

—W. H. Auden

Along with contemporaries Stephen Spender, Christopher Isherwood, and Louis MacNeice, Auden wrote dazzling poems and won great fame. His *Age of Anxiety*, a long poem that takes place in a New York City bar, won him the 1948 Pulitzer Prize and provided an apt name for his time. Auden often wrote about journeys or quests, and his personal life provided him with plenty of material: he traveled to Germany, Iceland, and China, served in the Spanish civil war, and moved to the United States, where he became an American citizen. I've always thought it interesting how T. S. Eliot brought his Americanness to England and Auden brought his Englishness to America, each to such different effect.

Musée des Beaux Arts

About suffering they were never wrong,
The Old Masters; how well they understood
Its human position; how it takes place
While someone else is eating or opening a window or just walking
    dully along;
How, when the aged are reverently, passionately waiting
For the miraculous birth, there always must be
Children who did not specially want it to happen, skating
On a pond at the edge of the wood:
They never forgot
That even the dreadful martyrdom must run its course
Anyhow in a corner, some untidy spot
Where the dogs go on with their doggy life and the torturer's horse
Scratches its innocent behind on a tree.

In Breughel's *Icarus*, for instance: how everything turns away
Quite leisurely from the disaster; the ploughman may
Have heard the splash, the forsaken cry,
But for him it was not an important failure; the sun shone
As it had to on the white legs disappearing into the green
Water; and the expensive delicate ship that must have seen
Something amazing, a boy falling out of the sky,
had somewhere to get to and sailed calmly on.

The "musée" in the title is the Museum of Fine Arts in Brussels, which Auden visited in 1938 and viewed the painting *Fall of Icarus*, by Pieter Brueghel. Icarus, a character from Greek mythology, was trapped in Crete with his father, Daedalus, who made wings for both of them and fastened them onto their shoulders with wax. He explained to his son that if they flew too close to the sea, the water would soak their wings, and if they flew too high, the sun would melt the wax. Like many a stubborn young man ignoring his father's warnings, Icarus soared too close to the sun, the wax that held the wings to his body melted, and he crashed into the sea.

⟫ Favorite Poems ⟪

"As I walked out one evening" ∾ "The Unknown Citizen"

"Funeral Blues" ∾ "September 1, 1939"

"In Memory of W. B. Yeats"

The many artists who have painted the fall of Icarus—"an important failure"—usually show Icarus front and center. But to Brueghel, the significant point of view is the ploughman's. The only sign of Icarus is a splash in the bright harbor water, and a pair of legs disappearing. The ploughman, painted in the foreground, is perfectly indifferent and never looks up from his work, while beautiful ships sail serenely on. Auden is struck by the apathy of people toward suffering. His poem juxtaposes miraculous, fantastical events with commonplace, everyday ones: the ordinariness of plowing alongside the enormity of disaster. Gigantic catastrophes happen on a minute scale, and everyone goes on with their animal lives. And yet Auden continued to believe in the hope at the heart of human existence, saying, "We must love one another or die."

John Berryman

The Alter Ego

(1914–1972)

C haos was a large and natural part of Berryman's own life," explained the poet Robert Dana, who was once John Berryman's student. It was also very much a part of his poetry. Although he had a formal education in poetry from Columbia and Cambridge universities, as he matured he broke away from classical forms to the point of inventing his own form, a deceptively loose, seemingly random association of words and phrases that thrilled and mystified readers and fellow poets alike. In truth, there was nothing at all random about his work; having lost his father at a young age, he spent his lifetime carefully honing a style that expressed his sense of tragic disorder. His poems weren't all tragedy and sadness, though. He had a sharp sense of humor and a vast literary knowledge that made even his darkest poems twinkle with color and light.

Berryman's most distinguished work was *77 Dream Songs*, which reflected the perfection of his original poetic form and set tongues wagging in poetry circles ever since. What's to wag about? To start with, the length. Berryman described *77 Dream Songs* as one long poem, in the vein of Walt Whitman's "Song of Myself." So while at first there seems to the reader to be seventy-seven individual poems, it quickly becomes clear that these overlap and lean in on each other in ways not easily understood. Not that the poems themselves are easy to understand either. No less a poet than Robert Lowell admitted to being perplexed by their "disorder and oddness." But Lowell and most everyone else couldn't resist the buoyant, "racy jabber" that propelled the poems, nor the irresistible characters of Henry and Mr Bones, who are the protagonists (and the poet's presumed alter egos) of *77 Dream Songs*.

The artist is extremely lucky who is presented with the worst possible ordeal which will not actually kill him. At that point, he is in business.

—John Berryman

John Berryman enjoyed the public debate over his style and meaning. While he denied that the character Henry was himself, he seemed to cheerfully encourage the scholarly and popular chatter on the subject. He was a poet through and through—he idolized Yeats, rigorously taught and challenged a generation of poets that followed him, and matter-of-factly gave himself over to the truth of being a poet: "Well, being a poet is a funny kind of jazz. It doesn't get you anything. It doesn't get you any money, or not much, and it doesn't get you any prestige, or not much. It's just something that you *do*."

Dream Song 76: Henry's Confession

Nothin very bad happen to me lately.
How you explain that? —I explain that, Mr Bones,
terms o' your bafflin odd sobriety.
Sober as a man can get, no girls, no telephones,
what could happen bad to Mr Bones?
—*If* life is a handkerchief sandwich,

in a modesty of death I join my father
who dared so long ago to leave me.
A bullet on a concrete stoop
close by a smothering southern sea
spreadeagled on an island, by my knee.
—You is from hunger, Mr Bones,

I offers you this handkerchief, now set
your left foot by my right foot,
shoulder to shoulder, all that jazz,
arm in arm, by the beautiful sea,
hum a little, Mr Bones.
—I saw nobody coming, so I went instead.

From the start of this poem, you find yourself in the riddle of the relationship between Henry and Mr Bones. You want to know more about them—who are they and how do they know each other? You want to understand the dynamic between them, which seems to be a sad Mr Bones and a comforting Henry. And what awful thing happened to Mr Bones that calls for Henry's consoling words?

Well, it helps to know that Henry and Mr Bones are one and the same. Throughout *77 Dream Songs*, Henry often talks to himself in the voice of Mr Bones, who is a kind of sorrowful, minstrel-show twist on himself. So Henry is telling his own story here, of the harsh loss of his father, and of the one-foot-in-front-of-the-other sense of purpose required to keep on going. This poem paints such a vivid narrative picture—it's packed with story, but the story just suggests itself, never making clear its context. While you read, your brain is trying hard to place this story in a familiar context, but it's almost impossible to do. That's a neat trick, the poet smudging the edges just enough that you can't bring the whole of it into focus, and you're forced to look at the details instead. A bullet on a concrete stoop. A smothering southern sea. Spreadeagled on an island. Those are bleak impressions—no wonder Mr Bones (or Henry—or Berryman!) needs a reassuring hug.

⇶ Favorite Poems ⇷

"Dream Song 1" ❧ "Dream Song 29"

"Dream Song 263" ❧ "Homage to Mistress Bradstreet"

"The Ball Poem"

I like the rhythm of conversation between Henry and Mr Bones in Berryman's poems. The last stanza in "Henry's Confession" is like a song, and you can't help but be uplifted yourself. "Hum a little, Mr Bones"—what a sweet bit of encouragement that is. And, tell me, where can I get a handkerchief sandwich?

Elizabeth Bishop

The Poet's Poet

(1911–1979)

I had never heard of Elizabeth Bishop until thirty years ago when a poet friend said she was his favorite twentieth-century poet. Despite winning the Pulitzer Prize and many other literary awards, Bishop never achieved the fame of some of her more high-profile peers. During her lifetime, however, she was highly respected and well-known by other poets such as Marianne Moore, Robert Lowell, and John Ashbery, who said Bishop was "a writer's writer's writer." They appreciated her exquisitely precise descriptions of the natural world, whether a single fish, a cold spring, or the seascape, and how geography affects, forms, and reflects human beings. "All my life," wrote Bishop, "I have lived and behaved very much like the sandpiper—just running down the edges of different countries and continents, 'looking for something.'"

Bishop's perpetual travel was in large part forced on her by circumstance. After her father's death, before she was even a year old, her mother became mentally unstable. Bishop was sent to live with one set of grandparents in Nova Scotia, then another set in Worcester, Massachusetts, until she finally settled with an aunt in South Boston for the remainder of her childhood. She never saw her mother again. Little wonder many of her poems are filled with loss, displacement, and isolation.

⤜ Favorite Poems ⤛

"Sestina" ❦ "In the Waiting Room" ❦ "The Armadillo"

"One Art" ❦ "At the Fishhouses"

Yet she also has a wonderfully dry, subtle sense of humor, which weaves throughout her small body of work. Bishop was a perfectionist who loved to challenge herself by writing in strict forms such as *sestinas* and *villanelles*. She was a master of creating the most vivid, true miniature worlds within a single poem: a dentist's waiting room, washing hair in a basin. "I'm not interested in big-scale work as such," she once told Robert Lowell. "Something needn't be large to be good."

Filling Station

Oh, but it is dirty!
—this little filling station,
oil-soaked, oil-permeated
to a disturbing, over-all
black translucency.
Be careful with that match!

Father wears a dirty,
oil-soaked monkey suit
that cuts him under the arms,
and several quick and saucy
and greasy sons assist him
(it's a family filling station),
all quite thoroughly dirty.

Do they live in the station?
It has a cement porch
behind the pumps, and on it
a set of crushed and grease-
impregnated wickerwork;
on the wicker sofa
a dirty dog, quite comfy.

Some comic books provide
the only note of color—
of certain color. They lie
upon a big dim doily
draping a taboret
(part of the set), beside
a big hirsute begonia.

Why the extraneous plant?
Why the taboret?
Why, oh why, the doily?
(Embroidered in daisy stitch
with marguerites, I think,
and heavy with gray crochet.)

Somebody embroidered the doily.
Somebody waters the plant,
or oils it, maybe. Somebody
arranges the rows of cans
so that they softly say:
ESSO—SO—SO—SO
to high-strung automobiles.
Somebody loves us all.

What a fantastic, vivid description Bishop has written! It's like the verbal equivalent of an Edward Hopper painting. You feel as if you are right inside the poem, the filling station, because she makes it so immediate and clear. I can sense the poet coming upon the scene, like a still life, stopping to absorb the details, the flecks of color in this commonplace setting—the kind of beauty that is often invisible to us because we move through these ordinary moments unaware, not paying attention, not noticing the way Bishop does. As Randall Jarrell, the most important poetry critic in America at the time, pointed out, "All her poems have written underneath, *I have seen it.*"

I feel her surprise at discovering the individual effort and attempt at some kind of loveliness in such an unlikely place, amongst all the filth. She uses words so deliciously to help us appreciate the station's small touches—"taboret," "doily," "hirsute begonia." But then there is an echo of loneliness, of longing, just below the surface. The last line is almost like a prayer or a plea, and reminds me of the last line in another Bishop poem, "The Bight," which was the epitaph she chose for herself: "All the untidy activity continues, / awful but cheerful."

Listen to the audio recording *The Voice of the Poet: Elizabeth Bishop* to hear her reading twenty-three poems from six live appearances.

William Blake

The Mystical Visionary

(1757–1827)

William Blake first saw visions of God and angels as a child, which set him off as an odd bird throughout his life. He went to art school when he was ten; at twelve, he began to write poetry, and at fourteen he was apprenticed to an engraver. A homeschooled youngster who would later study at the Royal Academy, Blake never became a part of the artist and literati "in crowd"—he had more in common with fellow nonconformists such as Thomas Paine and Mary Wollstonecraft than with literary peers such as Coleridge. Blake worked throughout his life as an engraver, illustrator, and printmaker in order to support himself and his wife, whom he taught to read and write and make prints. As an engraver, he had the skills and tools to print his own poetry, and as an artist, he was inspired to invent a visual style for his work that became his signature—something similar to the illuminated manuscripts created by monks centuries earlier. He also illustrated or finished many pieces by his own hand in watercolors.

Blake's industriousness was legendary; he was constantly working, getting up in the middle of the night to write and then lighting the fire for breakfast before his wife was awake. Commissioned to illustrate Dante's

Divine Comedy, he taught himself Italian at the age of sixty-three so he could fully appreciate the work. An eighteenth-century radical and revolutionary and a true individualist, Blake heralded creativity and imagination over the tides of reason and rationalism that prevailed at the time. He was thought of as a genius, if a bit of a madman, by contemporaries such as Coleridge, Charles Lamb, and Robert Southey. He died in 1827, singing about what he saw in heaven.

The Tyger

Tyger! Tyger! burning bright,
In the forests of the night,
What immortal hand or eye
Could frame thy fearful symmetry?

In what distant deeps or skies
Burnt the fire of thine eyes?
On what wings dare he aspire?
What the hand dare seize the fire?

And what shoulder, & what art,
Could twist the sinews of thy heart?
And when thy heart began to beat,
What dread hand? & what dread feet?

What the hammer? what the chain?
In what furnace was thy brain?
What the anvil? what dread grasp
Dare its deadly terrors clasp?

When the stars threw down their spears,
And water'd heaven with their tears,
Did he smile his work to see?
Did he who made the Lamb make thee?

Tyger! Tyger! burning bright
In the forests of the night,
What immortal hand or eye
Dare frame thy fearful symmetry?

"The Tyger" was the most popular of all the poems William Blake published in his lifetime, and scholars have since ranked it the number one poem anthologized in English. There are so many reasons for this! First, it is just made to be read aloud. By speaking this poem, you can't help but be swept up in Blake's awe and fear of this powerful and mysterious animal. Although critics often point to this and other of his *Songs of Experience* as a metaphor for his condemnation of the Industrial Revolution, the Tyger surely represents the power of creation itself—the beauty, the terror, and the wonder of it. Words like "sinews" and "dread grasp" remind me of Blake's prints and watercolor paintings, which are so strange and curiously vivid.

Favorite Poems

"London" ❧ "The Garden of Love" ❧ "And did those feet"

"Infant Joy" ❧ "To the Evening Star"

Notice all the question marks—these are the universal questions we have when we try to make sense of our place in the natural world. Where do we come from? Who or what made us the way we are? He asks the Tyger, who could "frame thy fearful symmetry?" In other words, how did that Tyger get its stripes? This is about God and the whole wonderful, terrifying spectrum between great strength and tenderness, the Tyger and the Lamb.

I love the bravura of this muscular poem, which truly has a sense of its own power—this is the secret to why it's so satisfying to read aloud.

The Lamb

Little Lamb, who made thee?
Dost thou know who made thee?
Gave thee life & bid thee feed
By the stream & o'er the mead;
Gave thee clothing of delight,
Softest clothing woolly, bright;
Gave thee such a tender voice,
Making all the vales rejoice!
Little Lamb, who made thee?
Dost thou know who made thee?

Little Lamb, I'll tell thee,
Little Lamb, I'll tell thee!
He is called by thy name,
For He calls Himself a Lamb.
He is meek & He is mild,
He became a little child.
I a child & thou a lamb,
We are called by His name.
Little Lamb, God bless thee!
Little Lamb, God bless thee!

I must create a system or be enslaved by another man's. I will not reason and compare: my business is to create.

—William Blake

Gwendolyn Brooks

The Visionary

(1917–2000)

When Gwendolyn Brooks began writing at age seven, her mother predicted, "You are going to be the *lady* Paul Laurence Dunbar." She was first published at age eleven, and by sixteen was contributing weekly poetry to the *Chicago Defender* newspaper. The precociously talented Brooks went on to exceed her mother's prophecy and became a great poet in her own right.

Gwendolyn Brooks was born in Topeka, Kansas, and raised in Chicago. She lived through the aftermath and disillusionment of World War I, the Great Depression, World War II, and the tumultuous civil rights movement. Poetry for Brooks was always a social act. Tackling tough issues head-on, she used her verse to address segregation, postwar bitterness, and the enormity of the civil rights movement. She traveled all over the country, giving talks and workshops in schools, libraries, and prisons. She was the first black writer to receive the Pulitzer Prize, for *Annie Allen* in 1949. In 1968 she was named poet laureate for the state of Illinois, and from 1985 to 1986 was the Consultant in Poetry to the Library of Congress. As a leader in the Black Arts movement in Chicago in the 1960s and

'70s, Brooks encouraged black poets to find their voice—and who could help but be inspired by the piercing clarity of her own?

⇒ Favorite Poems ⇐

"the sonnet-ballad" ❧ "do not be afraid of no"

"The Bean Eaters" ❧ "kitchenette building"

"Speech to the Young: Speech to the Progress-Toward"

We Real Cool

The Pool Players.
Seven at the Golden Shovel.

We real cool. We
Left school. We

Lurk late. We
Strike straight. We

Sing sin. We
Thin gin. We

Jazz June. We
Die soon.

Gwendolyn Brooks

I love how spare and lean this poem is. What a perfect example of the powerful punch within something so simple—it's a downright scary poem. At a reading at the Guggenheim Museum in 1983, Brooks said, "I wrote it because I was passing by a pool hall in my community one afternoon during schooltime and I saw therein a little bunch of boys . . . and they were shooting pool. But instead of asking myself, 'Why aren't they in school?' I asked myself, 'I wonder how they feel about themselves.'" Brooks listened to people: their inflections, their favorite words, the way they seemed to want to portray themselves.

Brooks's style is distinctive. She took the sermons she heard at church, the blues, jazz, and black spirituals and melded them with traditional forms like the ballad and the sonnet. In a priceless recording of "We Real Cool," Brooks recites like a Beat poet. Her old voice warbles from word to word at a syncopated rhythm. She stays on the "We," then jumps down to the next line suddenly. The alliteration moves it along like a blues song, making the abrupt ending that much more powerful. There is not one word in "We Real Cool" that is unnecessary—every single one belongs and does a whole lot of work for the poem.

Brooks showed the courage of ordinary people in the face of hardship, at a time when America badly needed her gutsy and compassionate voice.

❧•❧

Listen to Gwendolyn Brooks read "We Real Cool"

(recorded May 3, 1983, at the Guggenheim Museum) at

http://poets.org/viewmedia.php/prmMID/15433.

❧•❧

Elizabeth Barrett Browning

The Beloved

(1806–1861)

Elizabeth Barrett Browning was one of the most cherished poets—male or female—of her time. Her poems are powerful and gripping, and her personal life was like a Lifetime drama. Educated at home, as a child she borrowed her brother's tutor and studied Latin, history, philosophy, and literature. She "ate and drank Greek" and even taught herself Hebrew so she could read the Old Testament. She was writing epic poems by the time she was twelve.

Barrett Browning struggled with debilitating illness throughout her early life, though she wrote steadily and gained popularity in the 1830s. At the age of thirty-nine, she was living an invalid's life of seclusion in her father's house. She received visitors, but almost never left her bedroom. Still, her life had a second act waiting to unfold.

Her 1844 volume, entitled simply *Poems*, established her as one of Britain's most popular and revered poets. She received buckets of fan mail, including one letter from a Mr. Robert Browning. He wrote, "I do, as I say, love these books with all my heart—and I love you too." Her severe father had forbidden all eleven of his children ever to marry, but Elizabeth and Robert quietly exchanged some 574 letters over twenty months and fell head over heels in love. One morning, Robert came to Elizabeth's room, and, with him, she shed what she called her "graveclothes" and walked out of the bedroom on her own two feet for the first time in six years. The lovers eloped and settled in Florence, Italy, where Barrett Browning regained her strength, wrote feverishly, and raised a son, the aptly nicknamed Pen.

> ⇒ **Favorite Poems** ⇐
>
> "A Musical Instrument" ∞ "Change Upon Change"
> "A Man's Requirements" ∞ "Irreparableness" ∞ "Grief"

Barrett Browning wrote the *Sonnets from the Portuguese*, of which the following poem is number 43, between when she met Robert Browning in 1845 and when they were married in 1846. She chose the title because of her husband's nickname for her: his "Portuguese," due to her tan skin. It is this mixture of private and public, of strong intellectual force and mysterious winks, that keeps readers rummaging through Barrett Browning's lovely poems today.

How do I love thee?
Let me count the ways
(Sonnet 43)

How do I love thee? Let me count the ways.
I love thee to the depth and breadth and height
My soul can reach, when feeling out of sight
For the ends of being and ideal grace.
I love thee to the level of every day's
Most quiet need, by sun and candle-light.
I love thee freely, as men strive for right.
I love thee purely, as they turn from praise.
I love thee with the passion put to use
In my old griefs, and with my childhood's faith.
I love thee with a love I seemed to lose
With my lost saints! I love thee with the breath,
Smiles, tears, of all my life; and, if God choose,
I shall but love thee better after death.

Elizabeth Barrett Browning

The *Sonnets from the Portuguese* are some of the most famous love poems in English. "How do I love thee? Let me count the ways" is one of the most recognizable lines in the English canon. In the words of her husband, Elizabeth Barrett Browning's poems were strong with "the fresh strange music, the affluent language, the exquisite pathos and true new brave thought."

I think when you read this you naturally think of the person you love the most—if you're lucky enough to love someone that much. Browning deals with every aspect of love: simple love ("most quiet need"), complicated love ("the breath / Smiles, tears, of all my life"), and sacred love ("my childhood's faith"). She helps you understand love at the same time that you are enveloped in its mystery. Her own life and love echo familiar fairy tales and myths. Her forbidden courtship casts her as a Juliet, her invalid status makes her a sort of Sleeping Beauty, and, of course, she had a Cinderella-story happy ending, complete with prince, casa, if not castle, and fame. In *The Ring and the Book*, Browning himself compared their courtship to the legends of Andromeda and Perseus and Saint George and his maiden.

Luckily, Barrett Browning's work is as strong as her myth. She was England's most famous woman poet during her lifetime. Her fans included John Ruskin, Emily Dickinson, and Algernon Charles Swinburne, and mobs of other people admired her for her strong morality and passion. Barrett Browning wrote about causes that moved her: everything from the exploitation of children in coal mines to the *risorgimento*, the movement to unify Italy as a nation-state. She felt for those who were unjustly held back or discriminated against, perhaps having developed that sympathy from living a stalled life until she claimed it for her own.

The Best Thing in the World

What's the best thing in the world?
June-rose, by May-dew impearled;
Sweet south-wind, that means no rain;
Truth, not cruel to a friend;
Pleasure, not in haste to end;
Beauty, not self-decked and curled
Till its pride is over-plain;
Love, when, *so*, you're loved again.
What's the best thing in the world?
—Something out of it, I think.

What is genius but the power of expressing a new individuality?

—Elizabeth Barrett Browning

Robert Burns

The Ploughman Poet

(1759–1796)

alt Whitman once wrote that no man who ever lived was so beloved as Robert Burns. He explained why: "He had a real heart of flesh and blood beating in his bosom; you could almost hear it throb. The gods, indeed, made him poetical, but Nature had a hand in him first. His heart was in the right place."

And so was his intellect and compassion and abiding affection for the land and his country. The Scots loved him for his rowdy, playful way and for his deep fondness for rural Scottish life. I love him best for his ferocious wit and his boisterous use of language—clearly, his language and his country are inextricably bound. Writing in his wild Scottish dialect, he goosed traditional English poetry like a mischievous prankster. And reading Burns aloud, you feel wonderfully as if you're in on the whole happy song.

To a Mouse

(On turning her up in her nest with the plough, November, 1785)

Wee, sleekit, cow'rin, tim'rous beastie,
O, what a panic's in thy breastie!
Thou need na start awa sae hasty,
Wi' bickering brattle!
I wad be laith to rin an' chase thee,
Wi' murd'ring pattle!

I'm truly sorry man's dominion
Has broken Nature's social union,
An' justifies that ill opinion,
Which makes thee startle
At me, thy poor, earth-born companion.
An' fellow mortal!

I doubt na, whyles, but thou may thieve:
What then? poor beastie, thou maun live!
A daimen icker in a thrave
'S a sma' request;
I'll get a blessin wi' the lave,
An' never miss't!

Thy wee-bit housie, too, in ruin!
It's silly wa's the win's are strewin!
An' naething, now, to big a new ane,
O' foggage green!
An' bleak December's win's ensuin.
Baith snell an' keen!

Thou saw the fields laid bare an' waste,
An' weary winter comin fast.
An' cozie here, beneath the blast,
Thou thought to dwell,
Till crash! the cruel coulter past
Out thro' thy cell.

That wee bit heap o' leaves an' stibble,
Has cost thee mony a weary nibble!
Now thou's turn'd out, for a' thy trouble.
But house or hald,
To thole the winter's sleety dribble,
An' cranreuch cauld!

But Mousie, thou art no thy lane,
In proving foresight may be vain:
The best-laid schemes o' mice an' men
Gang aft agley,
An' lea'e us nought but grief an' pain,
For promis'd joy!

Still thou art blest, compar'd wi' me!
The present only toucheth thee:
But och! I backward cast my e'e,
On prospects drear!
An' forward, tho' I canna see,
I guess an' fear!

It's a very simple notion that a mouse has a more uncomplicated life than a man because a man has memories and the mouse does not. But the little tragedy of its unwittingly being upended by a plough puts mouse and man very much in the same boat—who of us doesn't feel from time to time upended by fate or circumstance or plain bad luck? And a little fearful of more of the same to come. You're a mouse, I'm a mouse; only Burns could reach out to such a creature with such vivid and utterly convincing empathy.

Robert Burns, like Shakespeare, is one of those poets whose use of language is so original that you feel you might want to have a special dictionary handy so you don't miss any of the good jokes. Indeed, Burns aficionados have long compiled glossaries of his words to help themselves and others decipher the dialect and turns of phrase. The lists are loaded with fabulous words like *cankrie* (grumpy), *drouthy* (thirsty), and *creepie chair* (which is essentially where you go when you have a time-out). Go to www.worldburnsclub.com to view a terrific and extensive online Burns dictionary.

Robert Burns was a man who had calluses on his hands, dirt under his fingernails, and was deeply connected to the earth. And his language was as true as the soil under his feet—when he wrote this poem in 1785, did he have any notion that he would dazzle people from other centuries with words like "snell" or "foggage" or "coulter"? He was an educated man—he could have written "You small, glossy-coated, shy beast" but chose the words of his native land on purpose. With plough in hand and these marvelous words on his tongue, he plumbed the depths of human experience, all within the universe of a single poem, as "To a Mouse." To give Whitman the last word on why we should turn our ear to the poems of Robert Burns, "He held the plough or the pen with the same firm, manly grasp. And he was loved."

⇒ Favorite Poems ⇐

"Auld Lang Syne" ∝ "Holy Willie's Prayer" ∝ "Tam O' Shanter"

"The Jolly Beggars" ∝ "Afton Water"

A Red, Red Rose

O my luve's like a red, red rose,
   That's newly sprung in June;
O my luve's like the melodie
   That's sweetly played in tune.

As fair art thou, my bonnie lass,
   So deep in luve am I;
And I will luve thee still, my dear,
   Till a' the seas gang dry.

Till a' the seas gang dry, my dear,
   And the rocks melt wi' the sun:
O I will luve thee still, my dear,
   While the sands o' life shall run.

And fare thee weel, my only luve,
   And fare thee weel awhile!
And I will come again, my luve,
   Though it were ten thousand mile.

George Gordon, Lord Byron

The Romantic

(1788–1824)

Byron was an aristocrat by title but a scalawag by reputation. He may not have had any choice in the matter, as the son of a man known as Captain "Mad Jack" Byron, the grandson of Vice Admiral "Foul-weather Jack" Byron, and the brother of William "the Wicked Lord" Byron. These folks probably weren't members of the church choir!

Byron was the personification of the romantic adventurer. Born in London and raised in Scotland, he was plagued from birth by lameness in one leg. He struggled with this handicap his whole life, as much emotionally as physically. Some might argue that his disability was a hindrance to his heroic aspirations, but I'm inclined to guess it challenged him to pursue his boundless passions.

He became "Lord Byron" at the age of ten, on the death of a great-uncle who passed on the title and an inheritance that enabled Byron's proper education and culminated in his attending Trinity College at Cambridge. After university, his Grand Tour of Asia and Europe set him on his lifelong path of adventure.

Byron was the very definition of an independent spirit. He spoke his mind and was well-known for his sharp political opinions and rough but intelligent criticism of his political opponents. At the age of twenty-four, he became famous for the first of his narrative poems in *Childe Harold's Pilgrimage*. And he quickly became infamous for his various affairs and social misdoings, which caused him to leave England forever to be free of its judgment of his conduct.

The Byronic hero is a brooding, moody literary type associated with Lord Byron's poetry and the influence of his persona. This hero is flawed, rebellious, passionate, antisocial, disdainful of the privileged classes, and usually self-destructive. He also is often miserably thwarted in love and must hide an unsavory past. Think of the character of Heathcliff in *Wuthering Heights* or Mr. Rochester in *Jane Eyre*.

I imagine Byron as the Mick Jagger of his time. Famous the world over, he left a swath of passion and creativity and scandalous relationships in his wake. One of his paramours, Lady Caroline Lamb, notably described him as "mad, bad, and dangerous to know." People cheered him, shook their fists at him, even followed him into battle. In 1824, out of sympathy for the movement for Greek independence from Turkey, Byron spent his own money to outfit the Greek naval fleet and set off to fight alongside the Greek rebels. On the way, he fell ill and died a couple of months later. This was the essence of Byron, to throw himself headlong into a rebellious, romantic endeavor, no matter how self-destructive it might ultimately prove to be. Just like a rock star.

I would I were a careless child

I would I were a careless child,
Still dwelling in my highland cave,
Or roaming through the dusky wild,
Or bounding o'er the dark blue wave;
The cumbrous pomp of Saxon pride
Accords not with the freeborn soul,
Which loves the mountain's craggy side,
And seeks the rocks where billows roll.

Fortune! Take back these cultured lands,
Take back this name of splendid sound!
I hate the touch of servile hands,
I hate the slaves that cringe around.
Place me among the rocks I love,
Which sound to Ocean's wildest roar;
I ask but this—again to rove
Through scenes my youth hath known before.

Few are my years, and yet I feel
The world was ne'er designed for me:
Ah! Why do dark'ning shades conceal
The hour when man must cease to be?
Once I beheld a splendid dream,
A visionary scene of bliss:
Truth!—wherefore did thy hated beam
Awake me to a world like this?

I loved—but those I loved are gone;
Had friends—my early friends are fled:
How cheerless feels the heart alone

When all its former hopes are dead!
Though gay companions o'er the bowl
Dispel awhile the sense of ill;
Though pleasure stirs the maddening soul,
The heart—the heart—is lonely still.

How dull! to hear the voice of those
Whom rank or chance, whom wealth or power,
Have made, though neither friends nor foes,
Associates of the festive hour.
Give me again a faithful few,
In years and feelings still the same,
And I will fly the midnight crew,
Where boist'rous joy is but a name.

And woman, lovely woman! thou,
My hope, my comforter, and my all!
How cold must be my bosom now,
When e'en thy smiles begin to pall!
Without a sigh I would resign
This busy scene of splendid woe,
To make that calm contentment mine,
Which virtue knows, or seems to know.

Fain would I fly the haunts of men—
I seek to shun, not hate mankind;
My breast requires the sullen glen,
Whose gloom may suit a darken'd mind.
Oh! that to me the wings were given
Which bear the turtle to her nest!
Then would I cleave the vault of heaven,
To flee away and be at rest.

What a painful longing to be a child again, carefree and without adult concerns. Not long before my own dad died, he would share vivid, fleeting memories of perfect moments from his childhood, say, standing atop a snowy hill on a perfect winter day before heading down the hill on a sled. I understand how captivating these childhood memories can be when recalled in later years, as you face the whole big snowball of your life—where you've been, what you've done, whom you've known. These moments seem clear and true and they're like bright little beacons of light that keep you going. But this poem was written early in Byron's life ("Few are my years"), so I wonder, why would such a young man pine for his carefree childhood?

For one thing, he seems weary of the trappings of his class—the "cultured lands," the "servile hands." He complains, "How dull!" to listen to the chatter of wealthy or powerful people who aren't really his friends, but with whom he must attend parties and dinners. Byron thinks of himself as a "freeborn soul" who relates more to the wild and craggy mountainside. And though he has friends around the world, he feels lonely for the pure love and friendships he enjoyed in his youth, the "faithful few."

✦ Favorite Poems ✦

"Prometheus" ✦ "So we'll go no more a-roving"

"When we two parted" ✦ "Love's Last Adieu" from *Don Juan*, Canto I

If Byron complained of the stiff reality of his aristocratic existence, he more than made up for it with bohemian escapades that took him around the globe. Byron was a poet who lived his life unapologetically with the pedal to the metal—the English tabloids would have *loved* him.

She walks in beauty

She walks in beauty, like the night
   Of cloudless climes and starry skies;
And all that's best of dark and bright
   Meet in her aspect and her eyes:
Thus mellowed to that tender light
   Which heaven to gaudy day denies.

One shade the more, one ray the less,
   Had half impaired the nameless grace
Which waves in every raven tress,
   Or softly lightens o'er her face;
Where thoughts serenely sweet express
   How pure, how dear their dwelling place.

And on that cheek, and o'er that brow,
   So soft, so calm, yet eloquent,
The smiles that win, the tints that glow,
   But tell of days in goodness spent,
A mind at peace with all below,
   A heart whose love is innocent!

Lewis Carroll

The Storyteller

(1832–1898)

O ne lazy summer day, on a rowing trip from Folly Bridge to God-
stow, England, Lewis Carroll began telling a story to amuse three
bored little girls—Lorina, Alice, and Edith Liddell. He started by
tossing "my heroine straight down a rabbit-hole, to begin with, without
the least idea what was to happen afterwards." It was July 4, 1862, and
the story would become *Alice's Adventures in Wonderland* and its sequel
Through the Looking-Glass.

Lewis Carroll's Wonderland is entirely and abundantly imagined. Car-
roll (whose real name was Charles Lutwidge Dodgson) was a deacon in
the Anglican Church, a lecturer in mathematics at Oxford, and an experi-
mental portrait photographer, and he used all of his varied talents to con-
jure up a complete and completely madcap world for his heroine. It is a
bright place filled with gryphons, croquet played with flamingos, sleepy
dormice, grinning Cheshire cats, and rabbits wearing pocket-watches. In
Victorian England, children were warned against idleness and mischief,
but Carroll cheerfully encouraged daydreaming and childlike curiosity—
he liked the idea of the kind of kid who would peer down a rabbit-hole
and chat with a bespectacled caterpillar. Carroll had a rebellious streak

that is reflected in his language: words are not proper and never trustworthy; they are constantly slipping and shape-shifting into nonsense verse and puns. In "Jabberwocky," he revels in his mathematician's fondness for puzzles and word games and his defense of creativity above all else.

"Jabberwocky" is from *Through the Looking-Glass*. Alice picks up a book but cannot read the language, until she realizes, "Why, it's a Looking-glass book, of course! And, if I hold it up to a glass, the words will all go the right way again."

⤜ Favorite Poems ⤛

From *Alice's Adventures in Wonderland*, "You are old, Father William"

From *Through the Looking-Glass*, Epilogue

"The Mad Gardener's Song" ⤬ "Phantasmagoria"

The Hunting of the Snark

Jabberwocky

'Twas brillig, and the slithy toves
Did gyre and gimble in the wabe;
All mimsy were the borogoves,
And the mome raths outgrabe.

"Beware the Jabberwock, my son!
The jaws that bite, the claws that catch!
Beware the Jubjub bird, and shun
The frumious Bandersnatch!"

He took his vorpal sword in hand:
Long time the manxome foe he sought—
So rested he by the Tumtum tree,
And stood awhile in thought.

And as in uffish thought he stood,
The Jabberwock, with eyes of flame,
Came whiffling through the tulgey wood,
And burbled as it came!

One, two! One, two! And through and through
The vorpal blade went snicker-snack!
He left it dead, and with its head
He went galumphing back.

"And hast thou slain the Jabberwock?
Come to my arms, my beamish boy!
O frabjous day! Callooh! Callay!"
He chortled in his joy.

'Twas brillig, and the slithy toves
Did gyre and gimble in the wabe;
All mimsy were the borogoves,
And the mome raths outgrabe.

Lewis Carroll kindly provided a note on pronunciation for
"Jabberwocky": "The 'i' in 'slithy' is long, as in 'writhe'; and 'toves'
is pronounced so as to rhyme with 'groves.' Again, the first 'o' in
'borogroves' is pronounced like the 'o' in 'borrow.' I have heard people
try to give it the sound of the 'o' in 'worry.' Such is Human Perversity."

What took Tolkien four fat books to tell, all happens within the book-ends of this one short poem. A satire of a heroic, epic story, it's a fabulous combination of serious high adventure and the completely ridiculous. The poem is silly and goofy, but Carroll seems to be winking at you a little. He knows that silliness, in a world so focused on strict practicality, is no trifling matter. It's as if he set out to use the most delicious words, relishing them and making us love every one. He challenges us to throw out the dictionary and make up our own words. What kind of awful monster is a Jabberwock? And the Jubjub bird or the frumious Bandersnatch? Carroll uses familiar sounds that trick you into thinking, just for a minute, that you have heard the word before and know what it means. If you think of it, when you're four years old, half the words you hear you don't understand anyway. So it's how they *sound* that leaves an impression.

After reading the poem, Alice turns to Humpty Dumpty (of course!) to ask what it all means. Humpty Dumpty explains,

> "'Brillig' means four o'clock in the afternoon—the time when you begin *broiling* things for dinner . . . 'slithy' means 'lithe and slimy.' You see it's like a portmanteau—there are two meanings packed up into one word . . . 'toves' are something like badgers—they're something like lizards—and they're something like corkscrews . . . also they make their nests under sundials—and they live on cheese . . . 'mimsy' is 'flimsy and miserable' . . . and a 'borogove' is a thin shabby-looking bird with its feathers sticking out all round—something like a live mop . . . 'mome' I'm not certain about. I think it's short for 'from home'—meaning that they'd lost their way, you know."

Humpty's not a bad translator, but these words are only from the first stanza—what do you suppose the others mean? What exactly is a *beamish* boy or a *frabjous* day or a *manxome* foe? Have you ever been lost in *uffish* thought or wanted to *gyre and gimble* down the street? Would a *vorpal* sword stand you in good stead in a battle with a Jabberwock? I'd say Dr. Seuss owes a lot to Lewis Carroll.

Carroll's work is bittersweet. His beloved children cannot stay young forever, and he feels gloomy that they will one day give up their daydreams and fancies. Still, he writes hopefully to a young friend, "Some children have a most disagreeable way of getting grown-up. I hope you won't do anything of that sort before we meet again."

Geoffrey Chaucer

The Knight Poet

(circa 1342–1400)

Chaucer was born sometime around 1342 in London. The son of a vintner, he was sent as a teenager to be a page for the Countess of Ulster. Chaucer was bright and capable and made friends with his noble employers. He was sent into France in 1359 on one of the many expeditions of the Hundred Years' War, and was captured while fighting. King Edward III paid a part of his ransom in 1360 to get him safely back to England. Being a prisoner of war was not all bad, though—it was in France that Chaucer began to appreciate poetry. He was smitten with the poems of *amour courtois*, or courtly love, which is the idealized ardor of a man for an unattainable maiden. When he returned to England, he translated the *Roman de la Rose*, the bible of courtly love. Although Chaucer's own relationships were far more run-of-the-mill (he married Philippa de Roet, a lady in attendance for the queen, in what seemed to have been an ordinary and comfortable union), every one of his heroes sees love as an exquisite calamity.

The job of the poet in the 1300s was not to invent stories: it was to find stories, borrow them, and twist them into new and entertaining shapes. Chaucer purloined stories everywhere, from the *fabliaux*, which were common yarns that traveled around town, to ancient classical myths, to the lives of saints, to tales from the Orient. He found stories that were spellbinding and that often had a moral buried in their ending, then spun them into pure gold.

Chaucer's epic poem *The Canterbury Tales* is unlike anything that came before it—or after it, for that matter. It is rowdy and funny and raunchy—fart jokes and snappy insults abound. It is also one of the most lyrical and lovely poems in the English language. The poem rollicks through a pilgrimage to Canterbury in which thirty pilgrims are to entertain one another by telling tales. Chaucer never finished *The Canterbury Tales*, so vast was the undertaking. After his death, he was buried in Westminster Abbey, the first of the literary luminaries laid to rest in what's now known as "Poets' Corner."

Geoffrey Chaucer is often referred to as the "father of English literature," as he is considered the first to legitimize the use of the ordinary spoken style of English in writing, rather than formal Latin or French, which had previously been used. In popularizing what is now known as Middle English, Chaucer is credited with introducing hundreds, if not thousands, of now-common words to the English language.

from The General Prologue

Whan that Aprill with his shoures soote
The droghte of March hath perced to the roote,
And bathed every veyne in swich licour
Of which vertu engendred is the flour;
Whan Zephirus eek with his sweete breeth
Inspired hath in every holt and heeth
The tendre croppes, and the yonge sonne
Hath in the Ram his halve cours yronne,
And smale foweles maken melodye,
That slepen al the nyght with open ye
(So priketh hem Nature in hir corages);
Thanne longen folk to goon on pilgrimages,
And palmeres for to seken straunge strondes,
To ferne halwes, kowthe in sondry londes;
And specially from every shires ende
Of Engelond to Caunterbury they wende,
The hooly blisful martir for to seke,
That hem hath holpen whan that they were seeke.
    Bifil that in that seson on a day,
In Southwerk at the Tabard as I lay
Redy to wenden on my pilgrymage
To Caunterbury with ful devout corage,
At nyght was come into that hostelrye
Wel nyne and twenty in a compaignye,
Of sondry folk, by aventure yfalle
In felaweshipe, and pilgrimes were they alle,
That toward Caunterbury wolden ryde.
The chambres and the stables weren wyde,
And wel we weren esed atte beste.
And shortly, whan the sonne was to reste,

So hadde I spoken with hem everichon
That I was of hir felaweshipe anon,
And made forward erly for to ryse,
To take oure wey ther as I yow devyse.
    But nathelees, whil I have tyme and space,
Er that I ferther in this tale pace,
Me thynketh it acordaunt to resoun
To telle yow al the condicioun
Of ech of hem, so as it semed me,
And whiche they weren, and of what degree,
And eek in what array that they were inne;
And at a knyght than wol I first bigynne.

❧ Favorite Poems ❦

From *The Legend of Good Women,* "Balade"

From *The Canterbury Tales*, "The Knight's Tale"

From *The Legend of Good Women*, "The Legend of Cleopatra"

"Merciles Beaute" ❧ "Lak of Stedfastnesse"

Geoffrey Chaucer

I think of this poem as a fantastic piece of time travel. It sort of hurls you back across generations and continents—we don't really know exactly how the language sounded because the accents were different. My father often explained to his students the mystery of how language evolves using Chaucer and other writers of that period. He'd teach a brief history of the evolution of the English language simply by showing how a simple phrase from Middle English turned into plain modern English. For example, he would declaim a phrase that sounded like, "Tess fahss a koat kyningen!" He would say it about eight times and every time the sounds would change slightly until he ended up with the phrase, "This was a good king!"

The "Prologue" is utterly unique, both for its time and even now, some 600 years later. It has a wonderful innocence to it and a compelling direct-ness and simplicity. It sets us down in the month of April, with its fruit and flowers, very much an example of the *reverdie* poetic tradition—*reverdie* means "regreening," and is a kind of poem that celebrates spring and all that comes with it.

The first lines of the "Prologue" are a perfect setup for the tales to follow. Using lush words of spring, it describes the coming of Zephyrus, the west wind, the "tender shoots and buds" and the "young sun." The narrator and twenty-nine others are crowded into an inn, all of them on a pilgrimage to Canterbury, quickly getting to know each other, and the narrator eager to describe every one of them. So begins the introduction to one of the all-time great poems in the English language. It grabs you and makes you as impatient to hear the pilgrims' stories as they are to share them. How ready are *we* to meet the Knight?

Like many people of my generation, I had to memorize the first eigh-teen lines of the "Prologue." I still find myself saying bits of it—but I can't think of anything wrong with a little Chaucer rattling around inside my head!

Samuel Taylor Coleridge

The Imagineer

(1772–1834)

Coleridge, Wordsworth. Wordsworth, Coleridge. You hardly hear of one of these British Romantic poets without mention of the other. They were great friends and giants among poets of this period, and perhaps did as much to define Romanticism as any artists of the time. The Mickey Mantle and Roger Maris of the Romantic period, they enjoyed five intense years of friendship and an incredible creative collaboration that produced *Lyrical Ballads*, a collection of both of their poems, which are some of the finest in the English language. They inspired each other to greater poetic feats, Coleridge inventing the conversational poem, which Wordsworth famously adopted and refined, Wordsworth's friendship giving Coleridge the confidence and security he needed to write.

When Coleridge developed a debilitating addiction to opium, his work declined and his relationship with Wordsworth grew strained. He went off to travel and lecture, spending the last years of his life bunking with a physician friend, worn out by marital problems, debt, illness, and addiction.

Coming to the end of life in less than triumphant circumstances isn't unusual for poets and writers and artists of all stripes. Many seem to burn through years on the fumes of their own curiosity and creativity, some of them creating their finest work in the most difficult times of their lives, others succumbing to the furies of the lives they led. I think Coleridge probably falls somewhere in the middle. He wrote his best poems early on in his career, but late in life also turned out *Biographia Literaria*, a volume of literary criticism that is considered one of his most valuable contributions to the Romantic dialogue, especially on the subject of imagination. I think Coleridge is the most revolutionary and inspiring to the creative mind in those essays.

➤ **Samuel Taylor Coleridge's epitaph reads:** ◀

Stop, Christian passer-by!—Stop, child of God,

And read with gentle breast. Beneath this sod

A poet lies, or that which once seem'd he.

O, lift one thought in prayer for S. T. C.;

That he who many a year with toil of breath

Found death in life, may here find life in death!

Mercy for praise—to be forgiven for fame

He ask'd, and hoped through Christ. Do thou the same!

Kubla Khan

In Xanadu did Kubla Khan
A stately pleasure-dome decree:
Where Alph, the sacred river, ran
Through caverns measureless to man
   Down to a sunless sea.
So twice five miles of fertile ground
With walls and towers were girdled round:
And here were gardens bright with sinuous rills,
Where blossomed many an incense-bearing tree;
And here were forests ancient as the hills,
Enfolding sunny spots of greenery.

But oh! that deep romantic chasm which slanted
Down the green hill athwart a cedarn cover!
A savage place! as holy and enchanted
As e'er beneath a waning moon was haunted
By woman wailing for her demon-lover!
And from this chasm, with ceaseless turmoil seething,
As if this earth in fast thick pants were breathing,
A mighty fountain momently was forced:
Amid whose swift half-intermitted burst
Huge fragments vaulted like rebounding hail,
Or chaffy grain beneath the thresher's flail:
And 'mid these dancing rocks at once and ever
It flung up momently the sacred river.
Five miles meandering with a mazy motion
Through wood and dale the sacred river ran,
Then reached the caverns measureless to man,
And sank in tumult to a lifeless ocean:
And 'mid this tumult Kubla heard from far

Ancestral voices prophesying war!
    The shadow of the dome of pleasure
    Floated midway on the waves;
    Where was heard the mingled measure
    From the fountain and the caves.
It was a miracle of rare device,
A sunny pleasure-dome with caves of ice!

    A damsel with a dulcimer
    In a vision once I saw:
    It was an Abyssinian maid,
    And on her dulcimer she played,
    Singing of Mount Abora.
Could I revive within me
Her symphony and song,
To such a deep delight 'twould win me,
That with music loud and long,
I would build that dome in air,
That sunny dome! those caves of ice!
And all who heard should see them there,
And all should cry, Beware! Beware!
His flashing eyes, his floating hair!
Weave a circle round him thrice,
And close your eyes with holy dread,
For he on honey-dew hath fed,
And drunk the milk of Paradise.

The story goes that Coleridge published "Kubla Khan" at the request of fellow poet Lord Byron, who had heard him recite it aloud and found it mesmerizing. With it, Coleridge published a note explaining that he'd written the poem after a deep sleep, in which he had dreamed it in fantastic, vivid detail. After he awoke, with a clear vision and perfect memory of the dream, he wrote down the words of the poem. He also suggested that he'd been interrupted in this effort by a visitor from the village of Porlock in southwestern England, and when he returned to his writing, he was unable to remember the details of the rest of his dream. So "Kubla Khan" is a "fragment" of a poem, according to Coleridge, but, oh, what a fragment!

⟩⟩ Favorite Poems ⟨⟨

"The Rime of the Ancient Mariner" ✧ "Christabel"

"Frost at Midnight" ✧ "The Nightingale" ✧ "Fears in Solitude"

"Dejection: An Ode"

This poem is considered one of Coleridge's "mystery poems," so described by critics for its otherworldly imagery and language, and for the puzzling, mysterious nature of the poem itself. I think of it as a hallucination in which the poet finds himself the narrator *and* a character.

There really was a Kubla Khan who built himself a Xanadu in China. The poet tells this story in careful detail, describing the folly of a man deluding himself, pursuing a path of impossible immortality. Then the poem splits in half and the poet turns himself into Kubla Khan, a terrifying figure who has tasted magic and would do anything to taste it again. Kubla Khan (and the poet) are doomed; no matter what humans do to isolate themselves from age or mortality, war or danger, these things will come. No fortress of Paradise can protect from that eventuality,

This poem may reveal a cold, hard truth, but I'm still crazy about the language. This is Coleridge the imagineer at his finest, describing a "savage place" with "caverns measureless to man," a "sunny pleasure-dome with caves of ice." You know he's never actually seen these places but he enlists his imagination to give brilliantly detailed shape to this story he has to tell. Where Wordsworth and company deferred to reason and common language, Coleridge fired up his imagination and used "the best words in the best order," no matter how uncommon they might be. "His flashing eyes, his floating hair!" is certainly an image from a dream, but there are no better words, in Coleridge's mind, to convey the terror and the truth of Kubla Khan.

Coleridge, who was a wonderful reader of his own work, would entrance an audience with a deep-toned, droning reading of this poem that would send chills down the spine. Said his lifelong friend Charles Lamb, "His face when he repeats his verses hath its ancient glory, an archangel a little damaged."

A poet ought not to pick nature's pocket. Let him borrow, and so borrow as to repay by the very act of borrowing. Examine nature accurately, but write from recollection, and trust more to the imagination than the memory.

—Samuel Taylor Coleridge

Hart Crane

The Lost Optimist

(1899–1932)

In the summer of 1924, a friend told Hart Crane about an apartment that was available at 110 Columbia Heights in Brooklyn. Crane moved in and began writing poetry from his room above the harbor. As he worked at a table underneath the flat's rear window, he could see Gothic arches and formidable steel cables soaring across the East River. This is how Hart Crane met the Brooklyn Bridge. He wrote to his friend, "I am living in the shadow of that bridge. There is all the glorious dance of the river directly beyond the back window . . . the ships, the harbor, the skyline of Manhattan . . . it is everything from mountains to the walls of Jerusalem and Nineveh."

Crane was a high school dropout from Ohio, the son of the successful candy wizard who invented Life Savers. When he came to the big city to make a life for himself, he dropped his first name, Harold, in favor of Hart, his mother's maiden name. Crane was perpetually broke, but in the most glamorous sense of the word—he stomped around his crumbling apartment playing the same jazz record over and over on his old Victrola; he lived on small grants, bits of prize money, and fellowships; he crashed at the houses of cosmopolitan friends like the playwright Eugene O'Neill and the photographer Walker Evans; and he was photographed by Man Ray for *Vanity Fair* magazine.

His first poem, "C-33," was published in an experimental magazine, *Bruno's Weekly*, when he was just seventeen. Crane devoured Sherwood Anderson, Ezra Pound, T. S. Eliot, Rimbaud, and Laforgue, but he also loved Webster, Donne, and Marlowe ("dear olde Kit," as Crane called him). It was this eclectic collection of influences that brought out Crane's style, which mixed modern images with dashing Elizabethan language. He skipped through the halls of Elizabethan poetry, picking and plundering what he liked best. His first volume of poetry, *White Buildings*, was published in 1926. *The Bridge* (1930), his epic poem, won the annual Poetry award in 1930. E.E. Cummings called him a "born poet."

Crane was a card-carrying member of the Lost Generation—those beautiful and tragic souls who haunted Paris and New York in the 1920s. But he was also brightly optimistic about the modern world. In so many of his poems, he considered the city, his times, and impressions from incidents in his own life. He wanted his epic poem, *The Bridge*, of which "To Brooklyn Bridge" was a part, to portray a "mystic synthesis of America." He embraced the modern city—he didn't see it as some kind of failure or symbol of a grim future. He contemplated urban space—subways, tunnels, bridges, cityscapes—in a way no other has written of it before or since.

⇒ Favorite Poems ⇐

"The Broken Tower" ❧ "At Melville's Tomb" ❧ "Voyages" I–VI

"For the Marriage of Faustus and Helen" ❧ "The River"

To Brooklyn Bridge

How many dawns, chill from his rippling rest
The seagull's wings shall dip and pivot him,
Shedding white rings of tumult, building high
Over the chained bay waters Liberty—

Then, with inviolate curve, forsake our eyes
As apparitional as sails that cross
Some page of figures to be filed away;
—Till elevators drop us from our day . . .

I think of cinemas, panoramic sleights
With multitudes bent toward some flashing scene
Never disclosed, but hastened to again,
Foretold to other eyes on the same screen;

And Thee, across the harbor, silver-paced
As though the sun took step of thee, yet left
Some motion ever unspent in thy stride,—
Implicitly thy freedom staying thee!

Out of some subway scuttle, cell or loft
A bedlamite speeds to thy parapets,
Tilting there momently, shrill shirt ballooning,
A jest falls from the speechless caravan.

Down Wall, from girder into street noon leaks,
A rip-tooth of the sky's acetylene;
All afternoon the cloud-flown derricks turn . . .
Thy cables breathe the North Atlantic still.

And obscure as that heaven of the Jews,
Thy guerdon . . . Accolade thou dost bestow
Of anonymity time cannot raise:
Vibrant reprieve and pardon thou dost show.

O harp and altar, of the fury fused,
(How could mere toil align thy choiring strings!)
Terrific threshold of the prophet's pledge,
Prayer of pariah, and the lover's cry,—

Again the traffic lights that skim thy swift
Unfractioned idiom, immaculate sigh of stars,
Beading thy path—condense eternity:
And we have seen night lifted in thine arms.

Under thy shadow by the piers I waited;
Only in darkness is thy shadow clear.
The City's fiery parcels all undone,
Already snow submerges an iron year . . .

O Sleepless as the river under thee,
Vaulting the sea, the prairies' dreaming sod,
Unto us lowliest sometime sweep, descend
And of the curveship lend a myth to God.

From a report by engineer John A. Roebling to the New York Bridge Company on September 1, 1867:

> The contemplated work, when constructed in accordance with my design, will not only be the greatest bridge in existence, but it will be the great engineering work of the Continent and of the age. Its most conspicuous feature—the great towers—will serve as landmarks to the adjoining cities, and they will be entitled to be ranked as national monuments. As a great work of art, and a successful specimen of advanced bridge engineering, the structure will forever testify to the energy, enterprise, and wealth of that community which shall secure its erection.

Besides being a tremendous portrait of a bridge, I think this poem has all the clamor of a city. The elements—a river, the night, city shapes and sights—come into focus, as soft as a dream and as spare and metallic as a nightmare. Tough, breathless, dangerous imagery contrasts with a delicate strength of almost godlike proportion. Crane paints a word picture of a huge, powerful, looming object that happens to be beautiful. The poem reminds me a lot of the early-twentieth-century Ashcan School of painting, a group of artists in New York City who portrayed urban street life in a gritty, unromanticized style.

Crane addresses the Brooklyn Bridge as "thee," in a nod to Elizabethan sonnets. He uses unexpected phrases—"elevators drop us from our day," "noon leaks" onto the street. He mixes his impressive intellect with the earnest heart of a boy from Ohio. Underneath his difficult constructions and words like "acetylene" and "guerdon" (a colorless, highly explosive gas, and a reward, respectively), it's not hard to see the yearnings and wonder of a small-town kid.

Crane's hopeful poems did not always match up with the tenor of his life. He hurled his typewriter out of his apartment window during more than one bout of writer's block. He was incredibly hard on himself, ignoring the praise that *The Bridge* won and drinking heavily. The Mexican painter David Siqueiros painted a portrait of Crane showing the poet looking down—it seems that when Crane looked directly up, there was too much pain in his eyes.

Crane won a Guggenheim Fellowship and moved to Mexico in 1931 to work on an epic about the conquistadors. When his grant was up, however, he only had a handful of poems. He boarded the SS *Orizaba* in April of 1932, but he never made it back to New York. Crane jumped from the steamship to his death, in an echo of words he once wrote: "This fabulous shadow only the sea keeps."

Chaplinesque

We will make our meek adjustments,
Contented with such random consolations
As the wind deposits
In slithered and too ample pockets.

For we can still love the world, who find
A famished kitten on the step, and know
Recesses for it from the fury of the street,
Or warm torn elbow coverts.

We will sidestep, and to the final smirk
Dally the doom of that inevitable thumb
That slowly chafes its puckered index toward us,
Facing the dull squint with what innocence
And what surprise!

And yet these fine collapses are not lies
More than the pirouettes of any pliant cane;
Our obsequies are, in a way, no enterprise.
We can evade you, and all else but the heart:
What blame to us if the heart live on.

The game enforces smirks; but we have seen
The moon in lonely alleys make
A grail of laughter of an empty ash can,
And through all sound of gaiety and quest
Have heard a kitten in the wilderness.

E. E. Cummings

The Rule-Breaker

(1894–1962)

Many years ago, a friend gave me a worn paperback collection of E. E. Cummings's poems with the inscription, "Read all of these in spring." There is no other season that reminds me more strongly of Cummings: reading his poems is like opening a window and breathing in the spring air after a long, stuffy winter.

E. E. Cummings took all the customs of poetry and the conventions of proper English and turned them on their head. He created his own rules for titles, punctuation, form, and grammar, and not for a lack of education: Cummings grew up in Cambridge, Massachusetts, and attended Harvard, where he was an extraordinary student but rebelled against its conservative, academic atmosphere. His fascination with modern art, impressionism, post-impressionism, cubism, and futurism inspired a poetry style all his own, a kind of written cubism in which he chops up lines and carefully arranges words and phrases on the page. Cummings's playfulness and lyricism make words shine. When reading his poems, it is easy to skip from line to line like stones on the bed of a stream, hopping from one to the next.

if everything happens that can't be done

if everything happens that can't be done
(and anything's righter
than books
could plan)
the stupidest teacher will almost guess
(with a run
skip
around we go yes)
there's nothing as something as one

one hasn't a why or because or although
(and buds know better
than books
don't grow)
one's anything old being everything new
(with a what
which
around we come who)
one's everyanything so

so world is a leaf so tree is a bough
(and birds sing sweeter
than books
tell how)
so here is away and so your is a my
(with a down
up
around again fly)
forever was never till now

now i love you and you love me
(and books are shuter
than books
can be)
and deep in the high that does nothing but fall
(with a shout
each
around we go all)
there's somebody calling who's we

we're anything brighter than even the sun
(we're everything greater
than books
might mean)
we're everyanything more than believe
(with a spin
leap
alive we're alive)
we're wonderful one times one

Almost anybody can learn to think or believe or know, but not a single human being can be taught to feel . . . the moment you feel, you're nobody-but-yourself. To be nobody-but-yourself—in a world which is doing its best, night and day, to make you everybody else—means to fight the hardest battle which any human being can fight; and never stop fighting.

—E. E. Cummings

What an absolutely ecstatic poem. When you read "if everything happens that can't be done," your voice does exactly what Cummings describes: you leap, you spin, you fly. Your mouth moves quickly, contorting and bouncing onto the next word. I love how Cummings creates a delirium of excitement; it's almost a doggerel, with its loopiness and crazy contradictions. Cummings has a great ear for rhythm: the poem reads at times like a playground chant or a song. He is intimate and chummy, confiding in the reader in those parentheses. He shatters every notion that poems are dusty tomes of iambic pentameter and flawless rhyme schemes. He plays with ideas in this poem, tossing them up like pickup sticks—how well they land in a pattern that's all about the glorious state of love.

Cummings detested conformity and artificiality, and often poked sharply at American society in his poems. While he was working in the Norton-Harjes Ambulance Corps in World War I, his pacifist beliefs even led to him being thrown into a French prison camp under suspicion of espionage, an experience Cummings molded into a novel, *The Enormous Room*. Throughout his career, he was criticized for his fragmented writing and individualistic style. But by the time he died in 1962, he was one of the most widely read and beloved poets in America. In a 1925 poem to Picasso, to whom he felt a kinship and admiration, Cummings says, "you hew form truly." I say it takes one to know one.

➤ Favorite Poems ◆

"my father moved through dooms of love"

"maggie and millie and molly and may"

"All in green went my love riding" ❧ "Spring is like a perhaps hand"

"since feeling is first"

Emily Dickinson

The Cloistered Poet

(1830–1886)

A young Emily Dickinson was so pleased with one of her school compositions that she described it in a letter to a friend as "exceedingly edifying to myself as well as everybody else." She was witty and even wrote the humor column for the Amherst Academy newspaper. But the funny schoolgirl who was in love with her own words at fifteen would not grow up to be a celebrated writer of prose. She would always love words—and her mid-nineteenth-century New England was a literary hive—but Dickinson withdrew entirely from the outside world, living her adult life in seclusion in her family's home in Amherst, Massachusetts. Her companions, she once wrote to an editor, were "hills . . . and the sundown, and a dog large as myself, that my father bought me. They are better than beings because they know, but do not tell." Holed up in Amherst, she nevertheless carried on a voluminous personal correspondence with friends, family, and publishing acquaintances. Her letters reveal an engaging young woman who cared and thought deeply about people, literature, religion, and other concerns of the day. But she preferred time with books, certainly her easiest friends, and poetry was her chosen mode of transport.

Dickinson was extremely prolific and often included poems in the letters she wrote to friends. But her greatness as a poet was not recognized in her lifetime. Upon her death in 1886, her family discovered more than 800 of her poems, handwritten and bound in small booklets. Her first volume of poems was not published until 1890.

⇒ Favorite Poems ⇐

"The Mystery of Pain" ∞ "I cannot live with You" (640)

"Because I could not stop for Death" (712)

"I heard a Fly buzz—when I died" (465)

"A Bird came down the Walk" (328)

There is no Frigate like a Book (1263)

There is no Frigate like a Book
To take us Lands away
Nor any Coursers like a Page
Of prancing Poetry—
This Traverse may the poorest take
Without oppress of Toll—
How frugal is the Chariot
That bears the Human soul.

The Poets' Corner

There's usually no mistaking an Emily Dickinson poem—the dashes, the capitalization, the distinct vocabulary. I've always admired her choice of nouns and verbs over adjectives and adverbs. The emphasis is on the idea the words are expressing more than the words themselves. (Although how often is it that we get to roll a "frigate" off the tongue?) I also love how this poem, in so few words, reflects the joy of creating on the one hand, and savoring on the other. A librarian's favorite, this famous Dickinson poem is a perfect example of her elegant and spare work. Her poems are deceptively simple—this one is a celebration of the fact that written words can carry emotion and that the comfort of language is free to all of us.

If I read a book and it makes my whole body so cold no fire can ever warm me, I know that is poetry.

—Emily Dickinson

The most triumphant Bird I ever knew or met (1265)

The most triumphant Bird I ever knew or met
Embarked upon a twig today
And till Dominion set
I famish to behold so eminent a sight
And sang for nothing scrutable
But intimate Delight.
Retired, and resumed his transitive Estate—
To what delicious Accident
Does finest Glory fit!

John Donne

The Metaphysical Poet

(1572–1631)

Although Donne cleaved to love, death, and religion as the great themes in his work, the forms in which he wrote were far-ranging. He was equally eloquent in any genre, from songs, sonnets, and love poetry to sermons, religious poems, Latin translations, elegies, and epigrams. Hallmarks of his writing are startling extended metaphors, inventive wordplay, clever and indirect argument, and unusual syntax. His education in secular and religious law, his experience in the navy, his membership in Parliament, and his appointment as royal chaplain and dean of Saint Paul's Cathedral all contributed to his poetry's remarkable imagery: *rags of time; the round earth's imagin'd corners; our eyebeams twisted, and did thread our eyes upon one double string.*

Donne's deeply personal and ambivalent relationship to religion was illuminated in his brilliant, entertaining sermons, for which he was famous. In fact, one of his most quoted phrases is from a sermon, not a poem: "No man is an island, entire of itself; every man is a piece of the continent, a part of the main." He also struggled with a profound, unresolved fear of death, especially after his wife died at age thirty-three after the birth of their twelfth child. (Only seven children survived.)

But Donne was a master of paradox, and even as he wrestled with mortality and physical and spiritual disease, he was capable of witty investigations of lighter subjects, such as the poem that follows. For Donne, the world was always there waiting for his exploration.

➤ **"On Donne's Poetry," by Samuel Taylor Coleridge** ◀

With Donne, whose muse on dromedary trots,

Wreathe iron pokers into truelove knots;

Rhyme's sturdy cripple, fancy's maze and clue,

Wit's forge and fire-blast, meaning's press and screw.

Song

Go and catch a falling star,
   Get with child a mandrake root,
Tell me where all past years are,
   Or who cleft the devil's foot,
Teach me to hear mermaids singing,
Or to keep off envy's stinging,
      And find
      What wind
Serves to advance an honest mind.

If thou be'st born to strange sights,
   Things invisible to see,
Ride ten thousand days and nights,
   Till age snow white hairs on thee,
Thou, when thou return'st, wilt tell me,
All strange wonders that befell thee,
      And swear,
      No where
Lives a woman true and fair.

If thou find'st one, let me know,
   Such a pilgrimage were sweet;
Yet do not, I would not go,
   Though at next door we might meet,
Though she were true, when you met her,
And last, till you write your letter,
      Yet she
      Will be
False, ere I come, to two, or three.

John Donne

I think it's fitting that this poem is simply called "Song" because it has all the humor and coldhearted truth of a great country music song. With its laundry list of fantastical things that are impossible to achieve, the poem is a wonderful, playful joke about never trusting a woman. The vivid imagery and musical rhythm contrast with the cynical attitude of the narrator and create a terrific tension. Although the poem is 400 years old, when you read it aloud it sounds as fresh and modern as if it had been written today—a testimony to the inherent magic contained in the words themselves.

The poem reflects familiar symbols of the seventeenth century, which Donne loved to twist and turn into his own private universe, not caring particularly whether it was popular. In fact, John Dryden, an English poet of the next generation, described Donne's secular poetry this way: "He affects the metaphysics, not only in his satires, but in his amorous verses, where nature only should reign; and perplexes the minds of the fair sex with nice speculations of philosophy, when he should engage their hearts, and entertain them with the softnesses of love." Certainly this particular "Song" would not exactly engage any woman's heart!

Metaphysics: the branch of philosophy concerned with the study of the nature of being and beings, existence, time and space, and causality.

The Sun Rising

Busy old fool, unruly Sun,
  Why dost thou thus,
Through windows, and through curtains call on us?
Must to thy motions lovers' seasons run?
  Saucy pedantic wretch, go chide
  Late school-boys and sour prentices,
Go tell court-huntsmen that the king will ride,
Call country ants to harvest offices;
Love, all alike, no season knows nor clime,
Nor hours, days, months, which are the rags of time.

  Thy beams so reverend, and strong
  Why shouldst thou think?
I could eclipse and cloud them with a wink,
But that I would not lose her sight so long.
  If her eyes have not blinded thine,
  Look, and to-morrow late tell me,
Whether both th' Indias of spice and mine
Be where thou left'st them, or lie here with me.
Ask for those kings whom thou saw'st yesterday,
And thou shalt hear, "All here in one bed lay."

  She's all states, and all princes I;
  Nothing else is;
Princes do but play us; compared to this,
All honour's mimic, all wealth alchemy.

Thou, Sun, art half as happy as we,
    In that the world's contracted thus;
Thine age asks ease, and since thy duties be
    To warm the world, that's done in warming us.
Shine here to us, and thou art everywhere;
This bed thy centre is, these walls thy sphere.

➤ Favorite Poems ◄

"Break of Day" ❧ "Death, be not proud" (Holy Sonnet 10)

"Air and Angels" ❧ "The Ecstasy" ❧ "Love's Growth"

T. S. Eliot

The Modernist

(1888–1965)

Though Thomas Stearns Eliot once said that growing up in St. Louis, Missouri, "beside the big river" influenced his poetry, he was no Mark Twain. His family had deep roots in that Mississippi River town, but Eliot left St. Louis after high school and never looked back. A brilliant student, he attended Harvard and Oxford, traveled in Europe, and settled in to a high literary life in London, where in 1925 he became a director of the publishing firm Faber and Faber, a position he held for the next forty years. He became a British citizen in 1927 and seemed to embody more of an English sensibility than an American one.

Eliot is considered by many to be the most influential poet of the twentieth century. In 1915, when he was only twenty-two years old, the poet Ezra Pound nudged him onto the public stage by arranging for his poem "The Love Song of J. Alfred Prufrock" to be published in *Poetry* magazine. The stream-of-consciousness style and stark imagery of this poem upset both readers and critics, who were still caught up in the idyll of late Romantic–style poetry. Pound recognized that at first Eliot would "puzzle many and delight a few," but that his long-term contribution would be tremendous. World War I had arrived, and the harsh truth of this first modern war would sweep away Romantic notions forever, leaving artists and writers like Eliot to invent a new vocabulary for this terrible new world.

Eliot's *The Waste Land*, which was published in 1922, is considered the anthem of disillusionment of the postwar generation. "The Hollow Men" and *Four Quartets* continued to forge a new poetic form and reflected Eliot's vast knowledge of literature, philosophy, religion, and culture. T. S. Eliot was a scholar and a critic whose opinion was highly influential and whose work inspired a whole generation of poets after him. A serious, religious man, he surprised readers with his playful *Old Possum's Book of Practical Cats*, which would become the basis for the long-playing Broadway musical *Cats*. And it tickles me that one of Eliot's favorite possessions was a portrait of Groucho Marx, whom he befriended through correspondence later in life. Maybe deep inside, Eliot was just a fun-loving American after all!

Modernist: one who deliberately departed from traditional forms of expression and adopted the innovative forms that distinguish the arts and literature of the twentieth century.

Rhapsody on a Windy Night

Twelve o'clock.
Along the reaches of the street
Held in a lunar synthesis,
Whispering lunar incantations
Dissolve the floors of memory
And all its clear relations,
Its divisions and precisions,
Every street-lamp that I pass
Beats like a fatalistic drum,
And through the spaces of the dark
Midnight shakes the memory
As a madman shakes a dead geranium.

Half-past one,
The street-lamp sputtered,
The street-lamp muttered,
The street-lamp said, "Regard that woman
Who hesitates toward you in the light of the door
Which opens on her like a grin.
You see the border of her dress
Is torn and stained with sand,
And you see the corner of her eye
Twists like a crooked pin."

The memory throws up high and dry
A crowd of twisted things;
A twisted branch upon the beach
Eaten smooth, and polished
As if the world gave up
The secret of its skeleton,

Stiff and white.
A broken spring in a factory yard,
Rust that clings to the form that the strength has left
Hard and curled and ready to snap.

Half-past two,
The street-lamp said,
"Remark the cat which flattens itself in the gutter,
Slips out its tongue
And devours a morsel of rancid butter."
So the hand of the child, automatic,
Slipped out and pocketed a toy that was running along the quay.
I could see nothing behind that child's eye.
I have seen eyes in the street
Trying to peer through lighted shutters,
And a crab one afternoon in a pool,
An old crab with barnacles on his back,
Gripped the end of a stick which I held him.

Half-past three,
The lamp sputtered,
The lamp muttered in the dark.
The lamp hummed:
"Regard the moon,
La lune ne garde aucune rancune,
She winks a feeble eye,
She smiles into corners.
She smoothes the hair of the grass.
The moon has lost her memory.
A washed-out smallpox cracks her face,
Her hand twists a paper rose,
That smells of dust and eau de Cologne,
She is alone

With all the old nocturnal smells
That cross and cross across her brain."
The reminiscence comes
Of sunless dry geraniums
And dust in crevices,
Smells of chestnuts in the streets,
And female smells in shuttered rooms,
And cigarettes in corridors
And cocktail smells in bars.

The lamp said,
"Four o'clock,
Here is the number on the door.
Memory!
You have the key,
The little lamp spreads a ring on the stair,
Mount.
The bed is open; the tooth-brush hangs on the wall,
Put your shoes at the door, sleep, prepare for life."

The last twist of the knife.

T. S. Eliot

Although Eliot is thought of as such an intellectual poet—and indeed, some of his major poems are intellectual touchstones of the modern era—this poem is not intellectual. It's as universal and accessible as it can be because it's about the sensuality of memory. As you read, you feel the flickers of memory are familiar to you, in part because Eliot evokes a familiar, dreamy semiconscious state we've all experienced. This stroll in the middle of the night features a woman, a child, a cat, a dead geranium, and many other sights and sounds and smells that are snips of the memories of wakefulness. These may not be the exact images that would appear in *your* mind-wandering late-night stroll, but they still feel perfectly familiar.

The poem also shows what a wonderful dramatist Eliot is. It has a very specific shape and drama to it. He even creates a main character in the street-lamp. The sharp images contribute to the sense of drama—the corner of the woman's eye "twists like a crooked pin"; "a twisted branch upon the beach eaten smooth"; "the smallpox cracks" on the face of the moon; and finally, to end the story, "the last twist of the knife." That's high drama, and yet the whole poem still manages to feel like a dream or a sleepwalk.

The poems for which Eliot is best known, such as *The Waste Land* and the *Four Quartets*, are hard work, worth the effort for all they reveal, but deeply challenging and hard to just dip into. I like this poem because it allows me a wonderful taste of Eliot's intelligence, his keen eye for detail and his storytelling skill, without the hard climb of some of his other work.

> ### ❧ Favorite Poems ❦
>
> "The Love Song of J. Alfred Prufrock" ❧ "The Hollow Men"
> "Whispers of Immortality" ❧ "Sweeney Among the Nightingales"
> "The Naming of Cats"

Robert Frost

The Naturalist

(1874–1963)

R obert Frost penned perhaps the most quoted lines of American poetry ever written: "Two roads diverged in a wood, and I— / I took the one less traveled by, / And that has made all the difference." *The road less traveled* is a catchphrase now, a motto for mavericks, risk-takers, and rugged individualists. Frost was all of these, of course. A free spirit to his bones, he attended both Dartmouth and Harvard, but did not graduate from either, leaving instead to follow his own path. He loved his New England home, but when his farm in New Hampshire failed, he moved to England with his wife, Elinor Miriam White, in 1912. While in England, he wrote about his New England and met other poets such as Robert Graves, Rupert Brooke, and Ezra Pound, who took a particular interest in his work. His second collection of poems, *North Boston*, brought him international recognition. He returned to the United States in 1915, and by the 1920s, he was the most celebrated poet in America until his death in 1963.

Frost believed in writing in language that was actually spoken; he loved the sound of the human voice and claimed that "all poetry is a reproduction of the tones of actual speech." Although he avoided experimenting in contemporary forms of the time, he was a thoroughly modern poet who explored complex universal themes.

For a farmer-poet, Frost walked in some tall cotton: he won four Pulitzer Prizes in his career, a mountain in Vermont was named after him in 1955, and he read a poem, "The Gift Outright," at John F. Kennedy's presidential inauguration in 1961.

A poem begins as a lump in the throat, a sense of wrong, a homesickness, a lovesickness.

—Robert Frost

Birches

When I see birches bend to left and right
Across the lines of straighter darker trees,
I like to think some boy's been swinging them.
But swinging doesn't bend them down to stay.
Ice-storms do that. Often you must have seen them
Loaded with ice a sunny winter morning
After a rain. They click upon themselves
As the breeze rises, and turn many-colored
As the stir cracks and crazes their enamel.
Soon the sun's warmth makes them shed crystal shells
Shattering and avalanching on the snow-crust—
Such heaps of broken glass to sweep away
You'd think the inner dome of heaven had fallen.
They are dragged to the withered bracken by the load,
And they seem not to break; though once they are bowed
So low for long, they never right themselves:
You may see their trunks arching in the woods
Years afterwards, trailing their leaves on the ground
Like girls on hands and knees that throw their hair
Before them over their heads to dry in the sun.
But I was going to say when Truth broke in
With all her matter-of-fact about the ice-storm
I should prefer to have some boy bend them
As he went out and in to fetch the cows—
Some boy too far from town to learn baseball,
Whose only play was what he found himself,
Summer or winter, and could play alone.
One by one he subdued his father's trees
By riding them down over and over again
Until he took the stiffness out of them,

And not one but hung limp, not one was left
For him to conquer. He learned all there was
To learn about not launching out too soon
And so not carrying the tree away
Clear to the ground. He always kept his poise
To the top branches, climbing carefully
With the same pains you use to fill a cup
Up to the brim, and even above the brim.
Then he flung outward, feet first, with a swish,
Kicking his way down through the air to the ground.
So was I once myself a swinger of birches.
And so I dream of going back to be.
It's when I'm weary of considerations,
And life is too much like a pathless wood
Where your face burns and tickles with the cobwebs
Broken across it, and one eye is weeping
From a twig's having lashed across it open.
I'd like to get away from earth awhile
And then come back to it and begin over.
May no fate willfully misunderstand me
And half grant what I wish and snatch me away
Not to return. Earth's the right place for love:
I don't know where it's likely to go better.
I'd like to go by climbing a birch tree,
And climb black branches up a snow-white trunk
Toward heaven, till the tree could bear no more,
But dipped its top and set me down again.
That would be good both going and coming back.
One could do worse than be a swinger of birches.

Every time I read this poem, I have a very vivid memory of an incident from my childhood when I was about ten. My family was taking a long drive in the western Massachusetts countryside. We stopped the car to walk in the woods and I went wandering off on my own. I came upon a rotting block and tackle and a piece of rope. I tied the rope around my feet, threw the end of the rope over a limb of the tree, and pulled myself upside down so I was hanging suspended by my own hold on the rope. I was about six feet up when I saw that the rope was going to break—I was terrified. Eventually it did break and I had a nasty fall that took the wind right out of me. It was thrilling but scary, a hair-raising moment that totally embodied the breathless thrill of being a child. When Frost writes, "One could do worse than be a swinger of birches," I think he's saying, what is a life without thrill? And perhaps his reference to love toward the end is the ultimate thrill, the heady sensation of falling in love like falling to earth.

⤜ Favorite Poems ⤛

"Mending Wall" ✑ "Stopping by Woods on a Snowy Evening"

"The Road Not Taken" ✑ "Design" ✑ "To Earthward"

The storyteller in the poem feels in his bones the outdoors and the seasons. You feel the poet amiably, gently twisting this deep sense into a wonderful metaphor. Frost knew of the literary trends of the day—the experiments, radical new poems—but he continually wrote in straight-forward, everyday speech. Not that he was a simple man—he had a razor-sharp mind—but he chose his own path. Frost never shied away from the hard stuff; he used the landscape to explore the depths of his feelings. His poems are full of the quiet Vermont mountains, stacked one upon the other, the ferns in the woods, the dark night. Frost saw everything, and his deep love and respect for nature showed him entire worlds inside of snowdrops or the nests of birds. He took his beautiful America and gave it back to his readers not idealized as much as fully appreciated.

When Robert Frost was invited to recite a poem at President John F. Kennedy's inauguration in 1961, he intended to read a poem called "Dedication," which he had written for the occasion. But when he stood to speak, he discovered he couldn't read his notes and didn't know the poem well enough yet to recite it from memory, so he did a quick switch and recited a poem he *could* remember—"The Gift Outright." This short poem, which speaks of America as the land that "was ours before we were the land's," was an instant sensation.

William S. Gilbert

The Topsy-Turvy Poet

(1836–1911)

William S. Gilbert is acknowledged to be the great-granddaddy of song lyricists. With his collaborator, the composer Arthur Sullivan, he created a beloved repertoire of fourteen comic operettas, which are still performed with an almost religious fidelity to their first nineteenth-century London productions. These "Savoy Operas" include *The Mikado*, *The Pirates of Penzance*, and *H.M.S. Pinafore*. My guess is that all the great lyricists—Loranz Hart, Dorothy Fields, Cole Porter, Ira Gershwin, Noel Coward, Oscar Hammerstein, Stephen Sondheim, et al.—were surely Gilbert and Sullivan fans in their formative years.

Are lyricists poets? This is open to discussion. Where a poet writes for himself and his reader, a lyricist must serve the needs of composer, singer, plot, and audience. He must observe rhyme and meter far more rigorously than a poet. He must provide his singer with singable words and phrases. He must tell a story or shape a song with the skill of a fine cabinetmaker. And the songs must connect with an audience the moment they are sung: we can't linger over lyrics the way we might slowly savor a poem.

That said, Gilbert strikes me as a dazzling poet. "Love Unrequited," from the operetta *Iolanthe*, is a tour de force of comic rhymed verse. Better known as "The Nightmare Song," it is the best example of a Gilbert and Sullivan "patter song," to be sung at breakneck speed, one syllable per note, with lots of tongue-twisting and breathless pacing. Presented on the page, rather than sung, its wit leaps out at you.

A bit of context: like all Gilbert and Sullivan plots, *Iolanthe* is whimsical and convoluted. It is a satirical take on Britain's House of Lords, but also a fairy tale. After a series of absurd plot twists, the operetta ends when the Peers of the Realm run off with a whole bevy of fairies and the Lord Chancellor ends up marrying the Fairy Queen. As they hurtle to this ridiculous climax, the Lord Chancellor is tormented by a dream. When he awakens he sings "The Nightmare Song," appearing here without its brief introduction.

Love Unrequited, or the Nightmare Song

When you're lying awake with a dismal headache, and repose is
    taboo'd by anxiety,
I conceive you may use any language you choose to indulge in,
    without impropriety;
For your brain is on fire—the bedclothes conspire of usual slumber to
    plunder you:
First your counterpane goes, and uncovers your toes, and your sheet
    slips demurely from under you;
Then the blanketing tickles—you feel like mixed pickles—so terribly
    sharp is the pricking.
And you're hot, and you're cross, and you tumble and toss till there's
    nothing 'twixt you and the ticking.
Then the bedclothes all creep to the ground in a heap, and you pick
    'em all up in a tangle;
Next your pillow resigns and politely declines to remain at its usual
    angle!
Well, you get some repose in the form of a doze, with hot eye-balls and
    head ever aching.
But your slumbering teems with such horrible dreams that you'd very
    much better be waking;
For you dream you are crossing the Channel, and tossing about in a
    steamer from Harwich—
Which is something between a large bathing machine and a very small
    second-class carriage—
And you're giving a treat (penny ice and cold meat) to a party of
    friends and relations—
They're a ravenous horde—and they all came on board at Sloane
    Square and South Kensington Stations.
And bound on that journey you find your attorney (who started that
    morning from Devon);

He's a bit undersized, and you don't feel surprised when he tells you
    he's only eleven.
Well, you're driving like mad with this singular lad (by the by, the
    ship's now a four-wheeler),
And you're playing round games, and he calls you bad names when
    you tell him that "ties pay the dealer";
But this you can't stand, so you throw up your hand, and you find
    you're as cold as an icicle.
In your shirt and your socks (the black silk with gold clocks), crossing
    Salisbury Plain on a bicycle:
And he and the crew are on bicycles too—which they've somehow or
    other invested in—
And he's telling the tars all the particulars of a company he's interested
    in—
It's a scheme of devices, to get at low prices all goods from cough
    mixtures to cables
(Which tickled the sailors), by treating retailers as though they were all
    vegetables—
You get a good spadesman to plant a small tradesman (first take off his
    boots with a boot-tree).
And his legs will take root, and his fingers will shoot, and they'll
    blossom and bud like a fruit-tree—
From the greengrocer tree you get grapes and green pea, cauliflower,
    pineapple, and cranberries,
While the pastrycook plant cherry brandy will grant, apple puffs, and
    three corners, and Banburys—
The shares are a penny, and ever so many are taken by Rothschild and
    Baring,
And just as a few are allotted to you, you awake with a shudder
    despairing—
You're a regular wreck, with a crick in your neck, and no wonder you
    snore, for your head's on the floor, and you've needles and pins
    from your soles to your shins, and your flesh is a-creep, for your left

leg's asleep, and you've cramp in your toes, and a fly on your nose, and some fluff in your lung, and a feverish tongue, and a thirst that's intense, and a general sense that you haven't been sleeping in clover;

But the darkness has passed, and it's daylight at last, and the night has been long—ditto, ditto my song—and thank goodness they're both of them over!

William S. Gilbert

A cranky contemporary critic has said that Gilbert and Sullivan is more fun to perform than to actually watch. This may be true. I performed in five Gilbert and Sullivan operettas as a student, loving every minute. But I haven't seen one since.

I couldn't resist including "The Nightmare Song" in this volume. I suppose this is because I played the Lord Chancellor myself in two different college productions. I remember the crowd's clamorous response to my big number. But it was W. S. Gilbert, not I, who elicited that response. Nightmares are something we all have in common, and Gilbert's verbal and psychological pyrotechnics always stopped the show.

But aside from my own personal history with "The Nightmare Song," I fervently believe that great lyrics belong in the company of great poems, even if just for comic relief.

Allen Ginsberg

The Beat Poet

(1926–1997)

While Allen Ginsberg was studying at Columbia University in New York City in the 1940s, he became friends with Jack Kerouac, William S. Burroughs, and Neal Cassady (the real-life inspiration for the main character in Kerouac's *On the Road*). The tight-knit group spontaneously combusted, bursting out of New York, gathering other writers, poets, and artists, rolling into San Francisco, and founding the Beat movement. The Beats portrayed a shocking glimpse of the flip side of straight America—they revealed a world of spiritualism, drugs, and sexuality that seemed dangerous and unfamiliar. Like T. S. Eliot's grim reflection on the state of the world after World War I, the Beats—and Ginsberg especially—painted a dark picture of their truth about American life in the years after World War II. Still, Ginsberg and his friends believed that spiritual life was essential to a person's existence: "Beat" is short for "beatific," or "holy."

Ginsberg's *Howl and Other Poems* (which includes "A Supermarket in California") was published in 1956 in San Francisco to much clamor, positive and negative, and became the first widely read book of the Beat generation. Its publisher was actually brought to trial on charges of obscenity, and in spite of a firestorm of publicity and controversy over the book, the judge ruled that *Howl* was not obscene. It went on to become one of the most widely read of the twentieth century and has been translated into twenty-two languages—the "howl" heard round the world.

After living in California and traveling in India, meeting with spiritual gurus and speaking with the sharpest minds of his generation, and founding the Jack Kerouac School of Disembodied Poetics in Colorado, Ginsberg returned to New York and settled down in the East Village. His colorful life wrapped around him, he had many visitors and friends, and churned out a steady stream of poetry until his death.

Beat: Allen Ginsberg's pal Jack Kerouac claims to have coined the term to describe his generation of postwar down-and-outers. It was meant to suggest an overwhelming, worn-out disappointment. The term took on other meanings, as artists and writers came to identify themselves with Ginsberg, Kerouac, and others turning "beat" into a movement. Kerouac later said "beat" had an additional meaning—"beatific," or sacred and holy. This was particularly so for Kerouac, who frequently visited the theme of spirituality and holiness in his own work. In 1958, the *San Francisco Chronicle* columnist Herb Caen described the alienated young people who converged on San Francisco, inspired by Ginsberg and company, as "beatniks."

A Supermarket in California

What thoughts I have of you tonight, Walt Whitman, for I walked down the sidestreets under the trees with a headache self-conscious looking at the full moon.

In my hungry fatigue, and shopping for images, I went into the neon fruit supermarket, dreaming of your enumerations!

What peaches and what penumbras! Whole families shopping at night! Aisles full of husbands! Wives in the avocados, babies in the tomatoes!—and you, García Lorca, what were you doing down by the watermelons?

I saw you, Walt Whitman, childless, lonely old grubber, poking among the meats in the refrigerator and eyeing the grocery boys.

I heard you asking questions of each: Who killed the pork chops? What price bananas? Are you my Angel?

I wandered in and out of the brilliant stacks of cans following you, and followed in my imagination by the store detective.

We strode down the open corridors together in our solitary fancy tasting artichokes, possessing every frozen delicacy, and never passing the cashier.

Where are we going, Walt Whitman? The doors close in an hour. Which way does your beard point tonight?

(I touch your book and dream of our odyssey in the supermarket and feel absurd.)

Will we walk all night through solitary streets? The trees add shade to shade, lights out in the houses, we'll both be lonely.

Will we stroll dreaming of the lost America of love past blue automobiles in driveways, home to our silent cottage?

Ah, dear father, graybeard, lonely old courage-teacher, what

America did you have when Charon quit poling his ferry and you got out on a smoking bank and stood watching the boat disappear on the black waters of Lethe?

Berkeley, 1955

Listen to Ginsberg read "A Supermarket in California" at www.poetryarchive.org. It makes his imaginary conversation with Whitman quite real.

This Ginsbergian stream-of-consciousness account of a visit to the grocery store reminds me of T. S. Eliot's "Rhapsody on a Windy Night" in its dreamy, late-night, semiconscious mood. Ginsberg was a tremendous sensualist—what's more sensual than walking among peaches, melons, all the smells, color, juice, so full of life? No wonder he invokes the other great sensualist, Walt Whitman. I love Ginsberg's happy willingness to connect with the phantom of this poet (and another poet ancestor, Federico García Lorca) in the humble aisles of a grocery store.

Famous for his slightly kooky sense of humor, he could look at a supermarket and see the ridiculousness of it all—babies in the tomatoes! He both luxuriates in the abundance and is made uncomfortable by the embarrassment of riches. But he also delves into his own mind with stunning courage. He goes deep inside and hides nothing—even admitting that he feels "absurd" writing the poem. Fellow poet William Carlos Williams said of Ginsberg, "He avoids nothing but experiences it to the hilt. He contains it. Claims it as his own—and, we believe, laughs at it."

➤◄

Poetry is not an expression of the party line. It's that time of night, lying in bed, thinking what you really think, making the private world public, that's what the poet does.

—Allen Ginsberg

Robert Herrick

The Cavalier Poet

(1591–1674)

R obert Herrick is one of those literary figures about whom little is known, and not just because he was born more than 400 years ago. Details of his childhood are sketchy, though it is known that his father died when Herrick was quite young and he was apprenticed for some years before entering St. John's College at Cambridge. There he became known as one of the "Sons of Ben," popular young writers who idolized the poet Ben Jonson. Herrick and others in this crowd were criticized by the Puritans for writing about such frivolous subjects as romance. They were dubbed the "Cavalier poets" for their association with the court of King Charles I, and known for their saucy style, use of common language, and man-about-town manner. The Cavaliers were a bit of a literary Rat Pack, but they produced some of the most enjoyable and distinctive poems of the period, and were an important bridge between the poetic traditions that came before and after them.

Though Herrick was a fun-loving fellow who thoroughly enjoyed the social life in London, in 1623 he was ordained as an Episcopal minister and sent to the quiet countryside of Devon, where he settled into his life's work. I love that the unmarried Reverend Herrick went on to write hundreds of poems celebrating the feminine charms of lasses and ladies and mistresses, most famously a giant body of work devoted to someone named Julia, though there are plenty of others he toasts, including Sylvia, Anthea, Perilla, and Dianeme. Besides the fact that this man of the cloth spent so much of his free time daydreaming about women, it is also funny to consider that several literary historians believe that most of these ladies were fictional. In other words, for all the glorious detail he uses to describe them and his feelings for them, they were likely all in his head!

No matter. The rapture Herrick voices in a verse about Sylvia's bracelet or her petticoat or even her teeth—well, it's clear he had a wonderful appreciation of women that found its perfect expression in the Cavalier style. He wrote about flowers and poverty and fortune and family and mortality and royalty and even fairies with equal warmth and good humor.

The Beggar to Mab, the Fairy Queen

Please your Grace, from out your store,
Give an alms to one that's poor,
That your mickle may have more.
Black I'm grown for want of meat;
Give me then an ant to eat,
Or the cleft ear of a mouse
Over-sour'd in drink of souce;
Or, sweet lady, reach to me
The abdomen of a bee;
Or commend a cricket's hip,
Or his huckson, to my scrip.
Give for bread a little bit
Of a pease that 'gins to chit,
And my full thanks take for it.
Flour of fuzz-balls, that's too good
For a man in needy-hood;
But the meal of milldust can
Well content a craving man.
Any orts the elves refuse
Well will serve the beggar's use.
But if this may seem too much
For an alms, then give me such
Little bits that nestle there
In the prisoner's panier.
So a blessing light upon
You and mighty Oberon:
That your plenty last till when
I return your alms again.

This is a poem full of astounding notions, not the least the idea of a starving beggar pleading with a tiny fairy queen to fashion somehow a meal for him. Queen Mab is a fairy famous in Irish folklore as the bringer of dreams, whom Shakespeare first wrote about in a speech by Mercutio in *Romeo and Juliet*. And Oberon, mentioned near the end of the poem, is the king of the fairies in Shakespeare's *A Midsummer Night's Dream*.

It's quite captivating, combining talk of fairies and magic with the brutal reality of a wretchedly poor man, and mixing lighthearted fancy with something so grim and gruesome. "Black I'm grown for want of meat"— that's a stark and haunting image, especially right next to a line asking for an ant to eat or the ear of a mouse. But there's a hint of hope in it, and a heartening dollop of gratitude, as only could be expressed by someone who has absolutely nothing. The beggar asks the fairy for alms, a small bit of food, and by the end you feel sure he'll return the favor, if ever given the chance. This is the sort of matter-of-fact good nature that I have always loved about the Cavaliers.

❧ Favorite Poems ❧

"Delight in Disorder" ❧ "To Daffodils"

"To the Virgins, to Make Much of Time"

"The Argument of His Book" ❧ "To Sylvia, to Wed"

"Upon Julia's Clothes"

Sons of Ben: self-description of the dramatists and poets who proclaimed the ardent admiration for the poet Ben Jonson. Robert Herrick, who counted himself as a Son of Ben, wrote "His Prayer to Ben Jonson" to honor the influence Jonson had on his own work:

When I a verse shall make,
Know I have pray'd thee,
For old religion's sake,
Saint Ben, to aid me.

Make the way smooth for me,
When I, thy Herrick,
Honouring thee, on my knee
Offer my lyric.

Candles I'll give to thee,
And a new altar,
And thou, Saint Ben, shalt be
Writ in my Psalter.

Be my mistress short or tall

Be my mistress short or tall
And distorted therewithall
Be she likewise one of those
That an acre hath of nose
Be her teeth ill hung or set
And her grinders black as jet
Be her cheeks so shallow too
As to show her tongue wag through
Hath she thin hair, hath she none
She's to me a paragon.

Gerard Manley Hopkins

The Reluctant Poet

(1844–1889)

Gerard Manley Hopkins had one of the most important days of his literary career in 1918, twenty-nine years after he died. On that day, his friend and fellow poet Robert Bridges published a volume of Hopkins's work called *Poems*. During his lifetime, Hopkins only shared his poetry privately with a small circle of friends. He was a religious man, and he sacrificed fame as a poet in favor of becoming a Jesuit priest. In 1867, he swore to "write no more." He destroyed all of his poetry and did not write again until 1875.

It took a deeply moving tragedy to inspire Hopkins to take up writing again. In 1875, a German ship, the *Deutschland*, was shipwrecked during a storm near the Thames River and five nuns were among those who drowned. His poem "The Wreck of the Deutschland" introduced what he described as "sprung rhythm," a new form that gave room for more unaccented syllables. Hopkins said, "[I] had long had haunting my ear the echo of a new rhythm which now I realised on paper. . . . I do not say the idea is altogether new . . . but no one has professedly used it and made it the principle throughout, that I know of." This was a modest assessment—his new form was groundbreaking and enormously innovative.

Hopkins was aware of his otherness as a poet; he wrote in a letter to a chum, "No doubt, my poetry errs on the side of oddness." "The Wreck of the Deutschland" was so unconventional that the editor of a Jesuit magazine, the *Month*, according to Hopkins, "dared not print it." Hopkins was a champion of eccentricity and celebrated the unusual as a sign of the multitude and marvels of the world.

Sprung rhythm: a term coined by Gerard Manley Hopkins to describe a form of free verse that featured a regular rhythm intended to imitate the rhythm of natural speech.

Because Hopkins wasn't published until nearly thirty years after his death, he is often grouped with modern poets like W. H. Auden, Dylan Thomas, and T. S. Eliot, rather than the Victorian poets who were his contemporaries. Instead of going out of style along with the Victorians, Hopkins fit in with the modern crowd because of his experimental structure and quirky use of words—some say he was a tremendously important influence who paved the way for modernist poetry.

Pied Beauty

Glory be to God for dappled things—
    For skies of couple-colour as a brinded cow;
      For rose-moles all in stipple upon trout that swim;
Fresh-firecoal chestnut-falls; finches' wings;
    Landscape plotted and pieced—fold, fallow, and plough;
      And áll trádes, their gear and tackle and trim.

All things counter, original, spare, strange;
    Whatever is fickle, freckled (who knows how?)
      With swift, slow; sweet, sour; adazzle, dim;
He fathers-forth whose beauty is past change:
                Praise Him.

Just look at Hopkins's fantastic use of language and rhythm, his artful dexterity with alliteration and the coupling of words. He saw colors and patterns everywhere—even the land itself is patterned and divided into squares of different colors: dark and loamy where it has been ploughed and sown, green for pasture, or left fallow. Hopkins always had an eye out for the striking and unusual bits of natural phenomena: "pied" means having two or more colors, in patches or splotches. A "brinded" cow is one whose coat is brownish orange with bits of gray. In his *Journals*, Hopkins described "chestnuts as bright as coals or spots of vermilion." Like an impressionist painter, he also loved light playing on subjects. He cherished—worshiped—the glory of the natural world with all its unexpectedness. This poem is an homage to variety, unpredictability, irregularity . . . dappled things. The last line, "Praise Him," is perfect—it sounds just like a hymn.

⇝ Favorite Poems ⇜

"The Windhover" ∞ "Inversnaid" ∞ "The Habit of Perfection"

"I wake and feel the fell of dark, not day"

"As kingfishers catch fire"

God's Grandeur

The world is charged with the grandeur of God.
  It will flame out, like shining from shook foil;
  It gathers to a greatness, like the ooze of oil
Crushed. Why do men then now not reck his rod?
Generations have trod, have trod, have trod;
  And all is seared with trade; bleared, smeared with toil;
  And wears man's smudge and shares man's smell: the soil
Is bare now, nor can foot feel, being shod.

And for all this, nature is never spent;
  There lives the dearest freshness deep down things;
And though the last lights off the black West went
  Oh, morning, at the brown brink eastward, springs—
Because the Holy Ghost over the bent
  World broods with warm breast and with ah! bright wings.

A. E. Housman

The Scholar Poet

(1859–1936)

A. E. Housman was an enigma. In his personal life, he was unsociable, fiercely private, and very guarded in his interactions with others. But in his poems, he sheds his thick skin and reveals a sensitive soul in tune with the tenderness of lost love and youth. How to account for these two very different sides of a complicated man?

Housman was born in Fockbury, England. He attended St. John's College at Oxford, but shocked everyone—including himself—by failing his final exams. He left Oxford and worked as a clerk in the Patent Office in London for ten years, teaching himself Latin and Greek whenever he could find the time. He spent hours in the British Museum, reading ancient texts and translating classical poems and gaining a reputation as a scholar, which led to his appointment as a professor of Latin at University College in London. In 1911, he was appointed professor of Latin at Trinity College, Cambridge, where he stayed for the rest of his life.

His first collection of poems, *A Shropshire Lad* (1896), astounded his colleagues and students. The quite public laying bare of feeling and nostalgia shocked those who were acquainted with the gruff, often sarcastic scholar. *A Shropshire Lad* plumbed in deeply personal ways themes such as the loss of innocence, unrequited love, the cruel passage of time, and death. Yet all this is expressed through the fictional character of the Shropshire lad and takes place in a half-made-up place; Housman had never actually set foot in Shropshire; he had only seen its faraway hills as a boy ("blue remembered hills").

Listen to *A Shropshire Lad*, set to music by Samuel Barber, Sir Lennox Berkeley, and others on the CD *A. E. Housman: A Shropshire Lad, Complete in verse and song.*

Housman never attempted to reconcile his severe, academic side with the passionate poet that existed somewhere inside him. He was a loner by choice and lived a cold, sterile existence—someone once described his apartment at Trinity as a train station waiting room. Yet he was incredibly curious about the world and delved into ancient texts with passion and hunger. In a lecture, he once said, "At Easter time they hide coloured eggs about the house and the garden that the children may amuse themselves in hunting after them and finding them. It is to some such game of hide-and-seek that we are invited by that power which planted in us the desire to find out what is concealed, and stored the universe with hidden things that we might delight ourselves in discovering them. . . . The sum of things to be known is inexhaustible, and however long we read we shall never come to the end of our story-book."

When I was one-and-twenty

When I was one-and-twenty
   I heard a wise man say,
"Give crowns and pounds and guineas
   But not your heart away;
Give pearls away and rubies
   But keep your fancy free."
But I was one-and-twenty,
   No use to talk to me.

When I was one-and-twenty
   I heard him say again,
"The heart out of the bosom
   Was never given in vain;
'Tis paid with sighs a plenty
   And sold for endless rue."
And I am two-and-twenty
And oh, 'tis true, 'tis true.

A. E. Housman

I can hear the swooning sigh of a young man, the almost theatrical regret of love and loss, in this poem. In Housman's *Last Poems*, he says mournfully, "May will be fine next year as like as not: / Oh ay, but then we shall be twenty-four." When you're young, it can all seem so dramatically melancholy, until the weight and passage of time puts age and experience into perspective. And a young man can't hear that from an older man, no matter how wise—he has to go through it himself. This young man speaks for every young man or woman teetering on the edge between youth and maturity—old enough to feel the very real pain of a broken heart, but young enough to make the mistake of not listening to someone who probably knows better.

❧ Favorite Poems ❧

"To An Athlete Dying Young" ❧ "Terence, this is stupid stuff"

"Wenlock Edge" ❧ "Stars, I have seen them fall"

"White in the moon the long road lies"

Housman was never entirely comfortable in his own skin, which is sad. But the window he opened to his heart and soul in his poetry reflects a stunning compassion for the universal aspects of human experience. His work and his life continue to intrigue and inspire—*A Shropshire Lad* is still one of the best-selling books of English verse of all time. Dozens of composers, from Arthur Somervell to Samuel Barber, have set his poems to music. The famous playwright Tom Stoppard's *The Invention of Love* deals with Housman looking back at his life and loves. In 1996, a window in Poets' Corner in Westminster Abbey was dedicated to him.

Reveille

Wake: the silver dusk returning
    Up the beach of darkness brims,
And the ship of sunrise burning
    Strands upon the eastern rims.

Wake: the vaulted shadow shatters,
    Trampled to the floor it spanned,
And the tent of night in tatters
    Straws the sky-pavilioned land.

Up, lad, up, 'tis late for lying:
    Hear the drums of morning play;
Hark, the empty highways crying
    "Who'll beyond the hills away?"

Towns and countries woo together,
    Forelands beacon, belfries call;
Never lad that trod on leather
    Lived to feast his heart with all.

Up, lad: thews that lie and cumber
    Sunlit pallets never thrive;
Morns abed and daylight slumber
    Were not meant for man alive.

Clay lies still, but blood's a rover;
    Breath's a ware that will not keep.
Up, lad: when the journey's over
    There'll be time enough to sleep.

Langston Hughes

The Jazz Poet

(1902–1967)

One of Langston Hughes's favorite ways to pass time was sitting in a jazz club and writing poetry. I think the melodies, the stop-time rhythms, and the trembling trumpet solos found their way inside his words. Hughes is 1920s Harlem personified, with all its life and movement, its bustling theaters and smoky blues clubs, and even its frustration with the present and hope for a brighter future.

Hughes left his hometown of Joplin, Missouri, and went to Columbia University in New York to study engineering, as his father worried that he wouldn't be able to support himself through writing. He dropped out of the program, but continued to write poetry—and managed not only to support himself through his writing, but also to earn a place as one of the most influential American poets of the century.

Throughout his life, Hughes was exposed to discrimination and segregation, but he wrote, he says, "without fear or shame." As a cultural beacon and a mentor for young black writers, he showed America a new vision for hope and justice. He traveled on the SS *Malone* headed for Africa in 1923, stopping in more than thirty ports; he lived in Paris, Venice, and Genoa before settling in New York. In Harlem, he discovered the bright society and the dazzling literature of the "New Negro Renaissance" writers: Zora Neale Hurston, Wallace Thurman, Countee Cullen, and Eric Walrond. Hughes loved Harlem and was at the center of it all, pen in hand, capturing what he saw. And Harlem loved him back: the block where he lived, on East 127th Street, was renamed Langston Hughes Place after he died.

I tried to write poems like the songs they sang on Seventh Street . . . [that] had the pulse beat of the people who keep going.

—Langston Hughes

The Weary Blues

Droning a drowsy syncopated tune,
Rocking back and forth to a mellow croon,
   I heard a Negro play.
Down on Lenox Avenue the other night
By the pale dull pallor of an old gas light
   He did a lazy sway. . . .
   He did a lazy sway. . . .
To the tune o' those Weary Blues.
With his ebony hands on each ivory key
He made that poor piano moan with melody.
   O Blues!

Swaying to and fro on his rickety stool
He played that sad raggy tune like a musical fool.
   Sweet Blues!
Coming from a black man's soul.
   O Blues!
In a deep song voice with a melancholy tone
I heard that Negro sing, that old piano moan—
   "Ain't got nobody in all this world,
   Ain't got nobody but ma self.
   I's gwine to quit ma frownin'
   And put ma troubles on the shelf."

Thump, thump, thump, went his foot on the floor.
He played a few chords then he sang some more—
   "I got the Weary Blues
   And I can't be satisfied.
   Got the Weary Blues
   And can't be satisfied—

          I ain't happy no mo'
          And I wish that I had died."
And far into the night he crooned that tune.
The stars went out and so did the moon.
The singer stopped playing and went to bed
While the Weary Blues echoed through his head.
He slept like a rock or a man that's dead.

Langston Hughes

> ### ❧ Favorite Poems ❧
>
> "Dream Variations" ❧ "Harlem" ❧ "Night Funeral in Harlem"
> "I, Too, Sing America" ❧ "The Negro Speaks of Rivers"

When "The Weary Blues" was published in 1926, Harlem was enjoying a renaissance: its theater was thriving, and jazz was beginning to give America a brand-new tune. This is a fabulous blues poem that evokes a very vivid, specific time and place. Hughes writes with a mixture of hot and cold, fast and slow, just like jazz. Can you hear the onomatopoetic "thump thump thump" in this poem, the rhymes holding it together, the cadence like a syncopated bass line? Once the singer gets it out of his system, he sleeps like the dead. To me the blues is all about the comfort of expression, the catharsis that allows us to move on.

Randall Jarrell

The War Poet

(1914–1965)

Randall Jarrell was born in Nashville, Tennessee, and graduated from Vanderbilt University, where he was a student in the company of literary luminaries such as Robert Penn Warren, John Crowe Ransom, and Allen Tate. His first job after graduating was teaching at Kenyon College in Ohio, where he befriended fellow poet Robert Lowell. He taught for a while at the University of Texas, during which time his first book of poems, *Blood for a Stranger*, was published.

In 1942, Jarrell enlisted in the Air Force, where he became an aviation instructor for his entire stint in the military. It was this experience that turned his steady eye to the subject of war. What distinguished him from the war poets before him was his unique, bird's-eye perspective on modern war, or more precisely, on what would become the future of war. When he trained young men to fly in battle, he saw them as innocent children about to become entangled in the least innocent of human endeavors. His war poems reflect the machinery and precision and professional nature of war, along with its violent, senseless outcome on the most human levels. Lowell called him "the most heartbreaking poet of our time."

Jarrell wrote about more than war. He was a terrific scholar and enthusiast of modern poetry, and was as well-known for his brilliant literary criticism as for his own verse. Shortly before he died, he published a final book of poetry, *The Lost World*, that left a bright and creative last impression.

War poets: a term that came into use during World War I to describe soldier-poets who wrote of their terrible and demoralizing experiences on the battlefield.

The Death of the Ball Turret Gunner

From my mother's sleep I fell into the State,
And I hunched in its belly till my wet fur froze.
Six miles from earth, loosed from its dream of life,
I woke to black flak and the nightmare fighters.
When I died they washed me out of the turret with a hose.

⤜ Favorite Poems ⤛

"Well Water" ❧ "Next Day" ❧ "Eighth Air Force"

"Hope" ❧ "The Breath of Night"

Randall Jarrell

This is a very short poem with tremendous, permanently haunting impact. It features a vivid, horrific image of death in the air. A ball turret gunner was the person who sat inside a little bubble at the bottom of a bomber airplane and shot at enemy planes in order to protect his own. It was among the most dangerous jobs on a bomber, because you were out there in a very open, visible, and vulnerable spot, cramped up in a fetal position for up to ten hours on a mission. And you were situated right next to the fuselage of the plane, which meant that if the plane was hit there, you would not survive. This was the grimmest of scenarios for a soldier.

I think this is why the feeling of helplessness is so clear in the poem. The man has nowhere to go, nowhere to hide from his fate in this war. The action here happens to him—it's as if he has no control from start to finish. He is unavoidably one with the machine that takes him to his death, "Six miles from earth, loosed from its dream of life."

I am moved by the imagery of a mother's womb, and that in the moment before death the gunner reflects on the very beginning of life. The poem gives the distinct sense of a dead man talking, as if the poet was right there in that ball turret. It is the ultimate close-up view of war, as the last line simply and horribly defines. This short poem alone should be enough to cure us of war, as if our daily newspaper headlines aren't enough.

Ben Jonson

The Passionate Poet

(1572–1637)

en Jonson was bigger than life. An actor, playwright, and poet, he was a notorious character who ruled the literary roost in early-seventeenth-century London. With a legion of young followers known as the Sons of Ben (later known as the Cavalier poets), he cavorted and opined, dueled and argued, spending more than a few nights in jail over various royal controversies he instigated. And what an extraordinary time to be alive—William Shakespeare himself was in the cast of Jonson's second play, *Every Man in His Humour*! At the time, though, Jonson was the man—Shakespeare wouldn't become a literary hero until later.

Jonson introduced a clear, classical form that harkened to the ancient Roman poets, such as Horace and Catullus, but that featured colloquial language that was different from the flowery, ornamental diction used by Edmund Spenser, the reigning dean of English poetry who preceded him. Jonson's work reflected English life in a realistic vein, which was also quite different from the Spenserian approach.

Jonson had a volatile temperament that seemed to create more devotees than detractors. In 1605, he was appointed court poet to King James I, which is a testament to his popularity at the highest level. He was probably his own best fan, though; he was not shy about expressing his high regard for his own talent. Friend and fellow poet William Drummond of Hawthornden wrote of Jonson, "He is a great lover and praiser of himself; a condemner and scorner of others; given rather to lose a friend than a jest; . . . he is passionately kind and angry." Friends and admirers were forgiving of his flaws. When he died, he was buried in Westminster Abbey, under a marker that reads, "O Rare Ben Jonson!" Rare indeed.

➻ Favorite Poems ❧

"His Excuse for Loving" ❧ "An Elegy"

"To the Memory of My Beloved, the Author Mr. William Shakespeare"

"An Ode to Himself" ❧ "My Picture Left in Scotland"

Inviting a Friend to Supper

Tonight, grave sir, both my poor house and I
Do equally desire your company;
Not that we think us worthy such a guest,
But that your worth will dignify our feast
With those that come, whose grace may make that seem
Something, which else could hope for no esteem.
It is the fair acceptance, sir, creates
The entertainment perfect; not the cates.
Yet shall you have, to rectify your palate,
An olive, capers, or some better salad
Ushering the mutton; with a short-legged hen,
If we can get her, full of eggs, and then
Lemons and wine for sauce; to these, a coney
Is not to be despaired of, for our money;
And though fowl, now, be scarce, yet there are clerks,
The sky not falling, think we may have larks.
I'll tell you of more, and lie, so you will come:
Of partridge, pheasant, woodcock, of which some
May yet be there; and godwit, if we can,
Knat, rail, and ruff, too. Howsoe'er, my man
Shall read a piece of Virgil, Tacitus,
Livy, or of some better book to us,
Of which we'll speak our minds, amidst our meat;
And I'll profess no verses to repeat;
To this, if ought appear which I know not of,
That will the pastry, not my paper, show of.
Digestive cheese, and fruit there sure will be;
But that which most doth take my Muse, and me
Is a pure cup of rich Canary wine,
Which is the Mermaid's now, but shall be mine;

Of which had Horace or Anacreon tasted,
Their lives, as do their lines, till now had lasted.
Tobacco, nectar, or the Thespian spring
Are all but Luther's beer to this I sing.
Of this we shall sup free, but moderately,
And we will have no Pooly, or Parrot by;
Nor shall our cups make any guilty men,
But at our parting we shall be as when
We innocently met. No simple word
That shall be uttered at our mirthful board
Shall make us sad next morning, or affright
The liberty that we'll enjoy tonight.

Language most shows a man, speak that I may see thee.

—Ben Jonson

This is one of my favorite kinds of poems, the occasional poem. Jonson wrote this on the occasion of having a friend to dinner, and it reads like an invitation to a fabulous evening's entertainment that would be hard to resist. Where Robert Herrick wrote of the beggar's hope of a meal of crumbs, Jonson writes about the bounty of the table. Even though this poem is 400 years old, you can still enjoy the rollicking descriptions of the extraordinary food! Mutton and a short-legged hen. Partridge, pheasant, and woodcock. Knat, rail, and ruff—what's that? I can only guess what Pooly, Parrot, and Canary wine might be like. You can't help but be attracted to his portrayal of an evening rich in the finest poetry, the most wonderful food, and the liveliest conversation. I know I'd show up with bells on if I received this invitation!

To Celia

Drinke to me, only, with thine eyes,
  And I will pledge with mine;
Or leave a kiss but in the cup,
  And I'll not looke for wine.
The thirst that from the soul doth rise,
  Doth ask a drink divine;
But might I of Jove's nectar sup,
  I would not change for thine.

I sent thee, late, a rosy wreath,
  Not so much honoring thee,
As giving it a hope that there
  It could not withered be.
But thou thereon did'st only breathe,
  And sent'st it back to me;
Since when it grows, and smells, I sweare,
  Not of itself, but thee.

John Keats

The Tragic Romantic

(1795–1821)

John Keats came from humble beginnings as the son of a London stablekeeper. His father died when he was a boy, followed by his mother's death when he was a young teenager, after which he and his siblings were tended by his grandmother. Despite his rough start in life, Keats got an excellent education and showed an early love of literature. He became a surgeon's apprentice and was on a path to becoming a doctor when he quit his medical studies to devote himself to writing.

Keats's family was plagued by illness, in particular the tuberculosis that killed his mother, his brother Tom, and eventually Keats himself. He began showing signs of his infection as early as 1818, and by the following year he felt so ill and sure of his imminent decline that he began referring to his life as his "posthumous existence." In 1820, his doctors advised him to leave England and go to Italy, where the warm, dry climate might improve his health.

By this time, Keats had published many individual poems and two volumes of poetry, most of which were not well received. These were lively times and there were critics and poets and artists aplenty, all cued up to criticize each other, jockeying for a slightly higher step on the literary ladder. Keats's friendships with the editor Leigh Hunt and the poets Percy Bysshe Shelley and William Wordsworth gave him valuable artistic support, but could not protect him from the critics.

Keats published what is considered his best work, *Lamia, Isabella, The Eve of St. Agnes, and Other Poems* in 1820. This volume featured several poems that came to be known as some of the finest ever written in English, including "Ode to a Nightingale," "Ode on a Grecian Urn," "Ode on Melancholy," and "To Autumn." It is this work that gave him his place in the pantheon of great Romantic poets.

John Keats died at the age of twenty-five in Rome, just months after finally achieving critical success. Besides his rich, deeply felt, beautifully crafted poetry, he left behind the legend of the tragic artist, gone too soon, like a nineteenth-century James Dean. Percy Bysshe Shelley wrote an exquisite tribute to his friend, a poem called *Adonais*, that set that legend in stone forever. Every year, millions of Keats fans make a pilgrimage to his house on the Piazza di Spagna, right next to the Spanish Steps.

❧ Favorite Poems ❧

"Ode to a Nightingale" ❦ "Ode on a Grecian Urn"

"Bright Star" ❦ "On the Grasshopper and the Cricket"

"This Living Hand"

To Autumn

Season of mists and mellow fruitfulness,
  Close bosom-friend of the maturing sun;
Conspiring with him how to load and bless
  With fruit the vines that round the thatch-eves run;
To bend with apples the moss'd cottage-trees,
  And fill all fruit with ripeness to the core;
    To swell the gourd, and plump the hazel shells
With a sweet kernel; to set budding more,
  And still more, later flowers for the bees,
  Until they think warm days will never cease,
    For Summer has o'er-brimm'd their clammy cells.

Who hath not seen thee oft amid thy store?
  Sometimes whoever seeks abroad may find
Thee sitting careless on a granary floor,
  Thy hair soft-lifted by the winnowing wind;
Or on a half-reap'd furrow sound asleep,
  Drowsed with the fume of poppies, while thy hook
    Spares the next swath and all its twined flowers:
And sometimes like a gleaner thou dost keep
  Steady thy laden head across a brook;
  Or by a cider-press, with patient look,
    Thou watchest the last oozings hours by hours.

Where are the songs of Spring? Ay, where are they?
  Think not of them, thou hast thy music too,—
While barréd clouds bloom the soft-dying day,
  And touch the stubble-plains with rosy hue;
Then in a wailful choir the small gnats mourn
  Among the river sallows, borne aloft

Or sinking as the light wind lives or dies;
And full-grown lambs loud bleat from hilly bourn;
  Hedge-crickets sing; and now with treble soft
The red-breast whistles from a garden-croft;
    And gathering swallows twitter in the skies.

The great beauty of Poetry is that it makes everything, every place interesting.

—John Keats

Keats wrote this poem after enjoying a glorious autumn day, which he described to a friend as warm and "better than the chilly green of spring." And how vivid his depiction, in the first stanza especially, with the feeling of ripening to the point of bursting, the trees bent with apples, swollen gourds, an overflowing of honey. What a wonder, these sensuous, glowing images of the sights and sounds and smells of ripeness in the season of harvest.

Ode: an elaborate form of lyrical verse with classical Greek origins. The English ode generally takes a serious, meditative approach to subjects such as nature or art.

When autumn itself becomes a character in the second stanza, we see it as we've never seen it before, dozing and lazily watching the season come to its end. The poem personifies autumn and the autumnal moment in the cycles of life, which Keats appreciated perhaps more than any other. He accepted how life and death mix, spring bringing new life, summer the fullness of life, and autumn the inevitable conclusion.

We're all a part of the passing of seasons and the passing of time, from youth to our elder years. When Keats asks, "Where are the songs of Spring? . . . Think not of them, thou hast thy music too," he reminds us that age has its music, to be savored and experienced as richly as youth. He seems to be expressing a joyous gratitude, even in the face of his own death.

The noted critic Harold Bloom called "To Autumn" one of the "most beautiful of all Keats's odes, and as close to perfect as any shorter poem in the English language." I'm inclined to agree.

La Belle Dame Sans Merci

Ah, what can ail thee, Knight at arms,
    Alone and palely loitering;
The sedge is wither'd from the lake,
    And no birds sing.

Ah, what can ail thee, Knight at arms,
    So haggard and so woe-begone?
The squirrel's granary is full,
    And the harvest's done.

I see a lily on thy brow,
    With anguish moist and fever dew;
And on thy cheek a fading rose
    Fast withereth too.

I met a lady in the meads
    Full beautiful, a faery's child;
Her hair was long, her foot was light,
    And her eyes were wild.

I set her on my pacing steed,
    And nothing else saw all day long;
For sideways would she lean, and sing
    A faery's song.

I made a garland for her head,
    And bracelets too, and fragrant zone;
She look'd at me as she did love,
    And made sweet moan.

She found me roots of relish sweet,
    And honey wild, and manna dew;
And sure in language strange she said,
    I love thee true.

She took me to her elfin grot,
    And there she gaz'd and sighed deep,
And there I shut her wild sad eyes—
    So kiss'd to sleep.

And there we slumber'd on the moss,
    And there I dream'd, ah woe betide,
The latest dream I ever dream'd
    On the cold hill side.

I saw pale kings, and princes too,
    Pale warriors, death-pale were they all;
Who cry'd—"La belle Dame sans merci
    Hath thee in thrall!"

I saw their starv'd lips in the gloam
    With horrid warning gaped wide,
And I awoke, and found me here
    On the cold hill side.

And this is why I sojourn here
    Alone and palely loitering,
Though the sedge is wither'd from the lake,
    And no birds sing.

Philip Larkin

The Librarian

(1922–1985)

P hilip Larkin was one of the most acclaimed English poets of the second half of the twentieth century, and for good reason. He had a uniquely modern yet straightforward voice and wrote of scenes and people that rang remarkably true.

Larkin was born in Coventry, England, and educated at St. John's College at Oxford. Biographers and critics have speculated that he had an unhappy childhood, which contributed to his often gloomy perspective. After graduating from Oxford, he became a librarian at a municipal library, then assistant librarian at a university, and finally the head librarian at the University of Hull, a position he held until his death.

His first book of poetry, *The North Ship*, was published in 1945, but his later work, *The Whitsun Weddings*, for which he won the Queen's Gold Medal for Poetry, established his reputation as a premier English poet. The title poem is an extraordinary representation of England from the window of a train on Whitsunday, a very old Christian holiday celebrated by the Church of England. This holiday features festivals, weddings, baptisms, processional walks, even the occasional rolling of a wheel of cheese around town—quite a lot to witness from a train. What a clever way to capture so many aspects of postwar English life, almost like a documentary.

But this was no ordinary documentary. Larkin was a bit of a hard case—unsentimental, antisocial, sometimes bitingly critical of the modern world. Besides the vividly detailed scenes, the poems in this volume also reflected Larkin's particular worldview, a somewhat glum, fatalistic outlook, tempered with a love of country, and presented in a brilliantly inclusive, accessible way.

❧ Favorite Poems ❧

"The Whitsun Weddings" ❧ "Church Going"

"Home Is so Sad" ❧ "This Be the Verse" ❧ "Going, Going"

Besides being a librarian and poet, Larkin was a novelist, essayist, and jazz critic. He cited as his greatest influence the novelist and poet Thomas Hardy, which might explain his affection for colloquial language and the English countryside.

Days

What are days for?
Days are where we live.
They come, they wake us
Time and time over.
They are to be happy in:
Where can we live but days?

Ah, solving that question
Brings the priest and the doctor
In their long coats
Running over the fields.

I love the structure and pace of this poem. It is obviously very carefully crafted, but at the same time it feels light and airy. It sounds almost like a conversation with a child, in the first stanza especially, though it touches on one of the most timeless and compelling of the universal questions—why are we here? But couched in the context of a day, the answer is quite hopeful and cheery. We're here to be and to be happy.

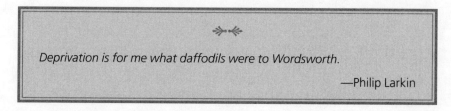

Deprivation is for me what daffodils were to Wordsworth.

—Philip Larkin

Then comes the satirical adult reality, the harsh truth of it. It *should* be as simple as just being happy in a day, but humankind is inclined always to try to explain things (the priest) and fix them (the doctor), mucking up the simplicity of being happy to be here on earth.

The image of the priest and the doctor in their long coats is terrific. You can just see them frantically running across the field of history, waving their arms, making a commotion, doing their best to make it impossible to be happy in a day. It seems to me that the question "Where can we live but days?" doesn't need an answer. That may be because I *do* think days are to be happy in.

Edward Lear

The Trickster

(1812–1888)

Edward Lear described his own poems as "nonsense pure and abso-lute," but that was the highest and truest compliment anyone could give his work. Lear invented nonsense as a literary form, amusing his Victorian contemporaries at the same time he was challenging them to consider a less rigid way of viewing the world. Nonsense is the opposite of sense and order and reveals the contradictions and absurdities of things that are otherwise familiar to us. In 1888, Sir Edward Strachey called non-sense a "true work of the imagination, a child of genius, and its writing one of the fine arts." With his delicious wit and his wonderful visual ca-pacity, Lear was the master of nonsense.

Lear was the twentieth born in his family, and was raised by his eldest sister in a suburb of London. He was artistically gifted and began working as an illustrator at the age of fifteen, drawing birds, flowers, and butter-flies. In 1832, the London Zoological Society commissioned him to cre-ate bird illustrations, the same year the Earl of Denby invited him to live on his estate. Lear wrote his first volume of verse, *A Book of Nonsense*, for Denby's grandchildren. A serious artist who wanted to devote himself to landscape painting, he became popular as a poet almost instantaneously and the call to write more and more of his wonderful nonsense continued throughout his life.

Lear was a lifelong traveler, making many trips through Europe, Asia, and the Middle East and spending considerable time in Italy, where he died. Every single thing he saw along the journey of his life, including his own face in the mirror, was fodder for his irreverent, preposterous rhymes. In a poem titled "How Pleasant to Know Mr. Lear," he writes, "How pleasant to know Mr. Lear! / Who has written such volumes of stuff! / Some think him ill-tempered and queer, / But a few think him pleasant enough. / His mind is concrete and fastidious, / His nose is remarkably big, / His visage is more or less hideous, / His beard it resembles a wig."

⇌ Favorite Poems ⇌

"The Daddy Long-legs and the Fly"

"The Courtship of the Yonghy-Bonghy-Bo"

"The Dingle Bank" ⋙ "The Quangle Wangle's Hat"

"There was an old man with a beard"

The Owl and the Pussy-Cat

The Owl and the Pussy-Cat went to sea
   In a beautiful pea-green boat:
They took some honey, and plenty of money
   Wrapped up in a five-pound note.
The Owl looked up to the stars above,
   And sang to a small guitar,
"O lovely Pussy, O Pussy, my love,
   What a beautiful Pussy you are,
     You are,
     You are!
   What a beautiful Pussy you are!"

Pussy said to the Owl, "You elegant fowl,
   How charmingly sweet you sing!
Oh! let us be married; too long we have tarried,
   But what shall we do for a ring?"
They sailed away, for a year and a day,
To the land where the Bong-tree grows;
And there in a wood a Piggy-wig stood,
   With a ring at the end of his nose,
     His nose,
     His nose,
   With a ring at the end of his nose.

"Dear Pig, are you willing to sell for one shilling
   Your ring?" Said the Piggy, "I will."
So they took it away, and were married next day
   By the turkey who lives on the hill.
They dined on mince and slices of quince,
   Which they ate with a runcible spoon;

And hand in hand, on the edge of the sand,
   They danced by the light of the moon,
      The moon,
      The moon,
   They danced by the light of the moon.

Lear's limericks: Edward Lear's trademark free-form limericks, which were as long or as short as he felt like making them, usually (though not always) featured first and last lines that ended in the same word. Even though at the time they weren't yet known as limericks, Lear is known for turning them into a favorite form of light verse. The following limerick was typeset on the cover of the first edition of *A Book of Nonsense*, and referred to Derry Down Derry, the pseudonym he used for that book:

There was an Old Derry down Derry,
   who loved to see little folks merry,
So he made them a book, and with laughter they shook
   at the fun of that Derry down Derry.

Edward Lear

I consider Edward Lear, along with A. A. Milne, to be the most important influence on my own writing for children. His kind of doggerel—so musical and sayable and quotable—is dear to my heart and is my favorite way to reach readers of all ages. There are few poems in the world that are as fun to recite as "The Owl and the Pussy-Cat."

The poem is merry and silly, yet absolutely beautiful: you can see Lear's painterly eye in the vivid, unforgettable, utterly credible images. The "pea-green boat," the "five-pound note," and singing under the stars to "a small guitar." And there is a childlike sensibility to the telling, though it is about a very grown-up thing, running off to get married—the couple being an owl and a pussycat, no less!

The unlikely mix of animals of all shapes and sizes is everywhere in Lear's work. He gets us to look at all kinds of unlikely relationships and scenarios and to consider that not everything has to make sense to be true. What's more wonderfully real than two lovers, hand in hand, dancing by the light of the moon?

Lear never for a minute disbelieves his poems; he is never self-conscious or winking at his own jokes. Sure, he's a trickster and a show-boat—how else to explain the audacity to make up a word like "runcible" just to complete the meter! But now the phrase "runcible spoon" has entered the lexicon to describe a forklike spoon. Nonsense? I don't think so!

The Jumblies

I

They went to sea in a Sieve, they did,
  In a Sieve they went to sea:
In spite of all their friends could say,
On a winter's morn, on a stormy day,
  In a Sieve they went to sea!
And when the Sieve turned round and round,
And every one cried, "You'll all be drowned!"
They called aloud, "Our Sieve ain't big,
But we don't care a button! we don't care a fig!
  In a Sieve we'll go to sea!"
    Far and few, far and few,
      Are the lands where the Jumblies live;
      Their heads are green, and their hands are blue,
      And they went to sea in a Sieve.

II

They sailed in a Sieve, they did,
  In a Sieve they sailed so fast,
With only a beautiful pea-green veil
Tied with a ribbon by way of a sail,
  To a small tobacco-pipe mast;
And every one said, who saw them go,
"O won't they be soon upset, you know!
For the sky is dark, and the voyage is long,
And happen what may, it's extremely wrong
  In a Sieve to sail so fast!"
    Far and few, far and few,

Are the lands where the Jumblies live;
Their heads are green, and their hands are blue,
And they went to sea in a Sieve.

III

The water it soon came in, it did,
The water it soon came in;
So to keep them dry, they wrapped their feet
In a pinky paper all folded neat,
And they fastened it down with a pin.
And they passed the night in a crockery-jar,
And each of them said, "How wise we are!
Though the sky be dark, and the voyage be long,
Yet we never can think we were rash or wrong,
While round in our Sieve we spin!"
Far and few, far and few,
Are the lands where the Jumblies live;
Their heads are green, and their hands are blue,
And they went to sea in a Sieve.

IV

And all night long they sailed away;
And when the sun went down,
They whistled and warbled a moony song
To the echoing sound of a coppery gong,
In the shade of the mountains brown.
"O Timballo! How happy we are,
When we live in a Sieve and a crockery-jar,
And all night long in the moonlight pale,
We sail away with a pea-green sail,
In the shade of the mountains brown!"

Far and few, far and few,
 Are the lands where the Jumblies live;
Their heads are green, and their hands are blue,
 And they went to sea in a Sieve.

V

They sailed to the Western Sea, they did,
 To a land all covered with trees,
And they bought an Owl, and a useful Cart,
And a pound of Rice, and a Cranberry Tart,
 And a hive of silvery Bees.
And they bought a Pig, and some green Jack-daws,
And a lovely Monkey with lollipop paws,
And forty bottles of Ring-Bo-Ree,
 And no end of Stilton Cheese.
 Far and few, far and few,
  Are the lands where the Jumblies live;
 Their heads are green, and their hands are blue,
  And they went to sea in a Sieve.

VI

And in twenty years they all came back,
In twenty years or more,
And every one said, "How tall they've grown!
For they've been to the Lakes, and the Torrible Zone,
 And the hills of the Chankly Bore!"
And they drank their health, and gave them a feast
Of dumplings made of beautiful yeast;
And every one said, "If we only live,
We too will go to sea in a Sieve,—
 To the hills of the Chankly Bore!"

Far and few, far and few,
    Are the lands where the Jumblies live;
Their heads are green, and their hands are blue,
    And they went to sea in a Sieve.

Henry Wadsworth Longfellow

The Fireside Poet

(1807–1882)

Henry Wadsworth Longfellow was the most popular American poet of the nineteenth century. Born in Portland, Maine, he was the grandson of a Revolutionary War hero and a descendant of John Alden from the *Mayflower*. A bookworm from a very early age, he was entranced with epic tales from other lands, like *Robinson Crusoe* and *The Arabian Nights*. He had an ear for languages, and after graduating from Bowdoin College he went to Europe for three years to study. He returned to become a professor at Bowdoin and eventually at Harvard, where he spent the rest of his teaching career.

What could turn this straight-arrow academic into the heartfelt voice of an entire country? Heartache, in part. His first wife died traveling with him in Europe, and his second wife (the mother of his six children) died from injuries suffered in a fire. He was a family man through and through, and these losses were deeply felt. He published poetry over the course of a forty-year writing career that put the myth of America—its drive, its fortitude, its independence—into words. Poems like "The Village Blacksmith," "The Song of Hiawatha," "Paul Revere's Ride," and "The Children's Hour" plumbed themes that were simple but resonated profoundly with Americans worn down by dissent and civil war who needed very much to hear their own ennobling story.

Longfellow, who is considered rather formal and sentimental by today's measure, was an all-out idol in his time. Bona fide best sellers, his books were embraced around the world, where the legend of America was growing by the minute. He became known as the first among the Fireside Poets, so named for their huge popularity in homes across the country, as popular as any English poet of the time. Five years after his death, a marble bust of Longfellow was placed in Poets' Corner in Westminster Abbey in London—he was the first American to be honored there.

In a speech he gave at his and his dear friend Nathaniel Hawthorne's graduation from Bowdoin in 1825, Longfellow said, "Already has a voice been lifted up in this land,—already a spirit and a love of literature are springing up in the shadows of our free political institutions." Longfellow's poetry caused this spirit to come alive in America, which is a truly remarkable legacy.

❧ Favorite Poems ❧

"Paul Revere's Ride" ❧ "Snowflakes" ❧ "Hymn to the Night"

"Christmas Bells" ❧ "The Village Blacksmith"

A Psalm of Life

What the Heart of the Young Man Said to the Psalmist

Tell me not, in mournful numbers,
    "Life is but an empty dream!"
For the soul is dead that slumbers,
    And things are not what they seem.

Life is real! Life is earnest!
    And the grave is not its goal;
"Dust thou art, to dust returnest,"
    Was not spoken of the soul.

Not enjoyment, and not sorrow,
    Is our destined end or way;
But to act to each to-morrow
    Finds us farther than to-day.

Art is long, and Time is fleeting,
    And our hearts, though stout and brave,
Still, like muffled drums, are beating
    Funeral marches to the grave.

In the world's broad field of battle,
    In the bivouac of Life,
Be not like dumb, driven cattle!
    Be a hero in the strife!

Trust no Future, howe'er pleasant!
    Let the dead Past bury its dead!

Act,—act in the living Present!
    Heart within, and God o'erhead!

Lives of great men all remind us
    We can make our lives sublime,
And, departing, leave behind us
    Footprints on the sands of time;

Footprints, that perhaps another,
    Sailing o'er life's solemn main,
A forlorn and shipwrecked brother,
    Seeing, shall take heart again.

Let us, then, be up and doing,
    With a heart for any fate;
Still achieving, still pursuing,
    Learn to labor and to wait.

This is such an American poem, so reflective of our unique kind of activism, positivism, faith, and belief in the result of our labors. It has a rigid meter that reminds me of a call to action before a march into battle. He's encouraging us to live beyond the plodding march from the cradle to the grave, to live well, to live now. Full of the hardy ego—as well as the innocence and naiveté—of a still-young America, the poem says that we can lift ourselves up "with a heart for any fate."

Longfellow's images are so descriptive that you can't help but be swept up in the message. "The soul is dead that slumbers"—that's a wake-up call! He urges us to be inspired by our forefathers to "make our lives sublime" and leave "footprints on the sands of time." The poem is truly a sacred song to come back to for inspiration again and again.

Look, then, into thine heart, and write!

—Henry Wadsworth Longfellow

The Children's Hour

Between the dark and the daylight,
    When the night is beginning to lower,
Comes a pause in the day's occupations,
    That is known as the Children's Hour.

I hear in the chamber above me
    The patter of little feet,
The sound of a door that is opened,
    And voices soft and sweet.

From my study I see in the lamplight,
    Descending the broad hall stair,
Grave Alice, and laughing Allegra,
    And Edith with golden hair.

A whisper, and then a silence:
    Yet I know by their merry eyes
They are plotting and planning together
    To take me by surprise.

A sudden rush from the stairway,
    A sudden raid from the hall!
By three doors left unguarded
    They enter my castle wall!

They climb up into my turret
    O'er the arms and back of my chair;
If I try to escape, they surround me;
    They seem to be everywhere.

They almost devour me with kisses,
    Their arms about me entwine,
Till I think of the Bishop of Bingen
    In his Mouse-Tower on the Rhine!

Do you think, O blue-eyed banditti,
    Because you have scaled the wall,
Such an old mustache as I am
    Is not a match for you all!

I have you fast in my fortress,
    And will not let you depart,
But put you down into the dungeon
    In the round-tower of my heart.

And there will I keep you forever,
    Yes, forever and a day,
Till the walls shall crumble to ruin,
    And moulder in dust away!

Robert Lowell

The Confessional Poet

(1917–1977)

Robert Lowell was born into a prominent old Boston family that arrived in America in 1639 and forged long associations in the fields of education, law, banking, shipping, and literature. More than 300 years' worth of Lowells attended Harvard, though this staid family tradition—along with many others—would end with Robert. Lowell dropped out of Harvard after two years to attend Kenyon College, where he studied with the poet Allen Tate and the critic John Crowe Ransom, and later at Lousiana State University with Robert Penn Warren.

His early work was crafted in a formal style, many poems touching on subjects associated with his New England heritage and God, but moving over time toward an outright rejection of the Puritan values at the heart of American identity. He had brilliant mechanics as a poet, a command of the form and the language that was simply outstanding. An early volume, *Lord Weary's Castle*, won the Pulitzer Prize for Poetry in 1947. Randall Jarrell praised him as "a talent whose ceiling is invisible."

Sometime in his forties, Lowell's style began to change to a more personal approach, largely due to the affairs of his own complicated day-to-day existence. He had followed a path far from his Brahmin roots—he lived a regular rumpus of a life, fraught with antiwar protests, messy marriages, religious crises, bouts of mental illness, and the draw of literary celebrity that put him in the company of Jackie Kennedy and other famous luminaries of the 1960s and '70s. He forged a distinct confessional style that was looser in form than his earlier work and sometimes shockingly laid bare the details of his private life. This new style, marked by the publication of his *Life Studies* in 1959, changed modern poetry permanently. Poets such as John Berryman, Sylvia Plath, Allen Ginsberg, and Anne Sexton adopted the confessional form, fearlessly exposing themselves through their writing. You don't need to read a biography of Robert Lowell for a portrait of his life; you just need to read his poetry from beginning to end. It forms a kind of autobiography, revealing more truth about the poet than any biography could.

You can obtain an audio recording of Robert Lowell and John Berryman reading selections from their works *Life Studies* and *77 Dream Songs* respectively at www.poets.org/viewmedia.php/prmMID/17047. It's amazing.

The Public Garden

Burnished, burned-out, still burning as the year
you lead me to our stamping ground.
The city and its cruising cars surround
the Public Garden. All's alive—
the children crowding home from school at five,
punting a football in the bricky air,
the sailors and their pick-ups under trees
with Latin labels. And the jaded flock
of swanboats paddles to its dock.
The park is drying.
Dead leaves thicken to a ball
inside the basin of a fountain, where
the heads of four stone lions stare
and suck on empty fawcets. Night
deepens. From the arched bridge, we see
the shedding park-bound mallards, how they keep
circling and diving in the lanternlight,
searching for something hidden in the muck.
And now the moon, earth's friend, that cared so much
for us, and cared so little, comes again—
always a stranger! As we walk,
it lies like chalk
over the waters. Everything's aground.
Remember summer? Bubbles filled
the fountain, and we splashed. We drowned
in Eden, while Jehovah's grass-green lyre
was rustling all about us in the leaves
that gurgled by us, turning upside down . . .
The fountain's failing waters flash around
the garden. Nothing catches fire.

This is an immensely evocative poem for me, especially as I remember spending many childhood Thanksgivings with relatives in Boston, walking in the Public Garden after dinner, soaking up the last bits of autumn. I know the Garden well in every season, from my years at college in Cambridge, and there isn't a detail Lowell touches that isn't absolutely, precisely so. This is a "place" poem that does its job, like William Blake's "London" or even Matthew Arnold's "Dover Beach." The poets want you to close your eyes and see it and smell it, relying on the particular details they suggest.

❧ Favorite Poems ❧

"The Quaker Graveyard in Nantucket" ❧ "Skunk Hour"

"The Lesson" ❧ "For the Union Dead" ❧ "Dolphin"

In the course of the poem day ends, night comes, the moon rises, and most every image of the life of the Garden—schoolchildren, sailors, mallards, the stone lions, the fountain—is exquisitely invoked. If you'd never laid eyes on the Public Garden you could still paint a picture in your mind that is instantly familiar. "Punting a football in the bricky air" and sailors under "trees with Latin labels"—this is a communal gathering place of extraordinary beauty, as it was the first botanical garden in the country, which explains the Latin labels on the trees.

"Burnished, burned-out, still burning"—what a description of a particular moment of the spent season, with its shining, autumnal glow. The drying up of leaves and fountains, the closing down of activities. Then "Remember summer?" when water flowed and gurgled and splashed. And that stunning final line, harkening back to the burning in the first line: "Nothing catches fire."

I feel for the tortured soul of Lowell, the New England Puritan. He's full of joys to express, joys to be denied, and a sense of predestined finality, even within the confines of this short poem. But I can't help enjoying my own experience of "The Public Garden," far more in the vein of Keats's "To Autumn"—I relish the fact that summer passes and autumn comes, bringing its own culminating beauty.

Andrew Marvell

The Posthumous Poet

(1621–1678)

Andrew Marvell came to be known as one of the greatest poets of the seventeenth century, but not until long after his death. His collected poetry, *Miscellaneous Poems*, was not published until three years after he died. In his lifetime, he mainly published political pamphlets and satires and was deeply involved in English politics during the Cromwell years and beyond.

Marvell grew up the son of a minister in Yorkshire, England. He attended Trinity College at Cambridge, where he studied for seven years. After leaving Cambridge, he traveled in Europe, worked as a tutor, and eventually became involved in government service and politics after befriending the influential writer John Milton. Due to his political skill, he managed to keep his head—literally!—when the monarchy was restored after the Oliver Cromwell republican period. He served as a member of Parliament from 1659 until his death, and was a model of conscientious leadership and public service.

It was Marvell's nephew who put together the collection of poems he found after his uncle's death, many of which are believed to have been written decades earlier. On publication of his poetry, Marvell became known as one of the Metaphysical poets, along with contemporaries John Donne and George Herbert, though the term was only applied many decades after their time. As he is one of my favorite poets, I think it's wonderful that the appreciation of Andrew Marvell's poetry grew over the centuries—many modern poets attest to the influence of his work, and no less than T. S. Eliot references Marvell's "To His Coy Mistress" in his own "The Love Song of J. Alfred Prufrock" and *The Waste Land*. What a terrific testament to 400-year-old, just plain good poetry.

⋙ Favorite Poems ⋘

"The Nymph Complaining of the Death of Her Fawn"

"A Dialogue Between the Soul and Body"

"The Definition of Love" ∾ "The Garden" ∾ "Upon Appleton House"

To His Coy Mistress

Had we but world enough, and time,
This coyness, Lady, were no crime.
We would sit down and think which way
To walk and pass our long love's day.
Thou by the Indian Ganges' side
Shouldst rubies find: I by the tide
Of Humber would complain. I would
Love you ten years before the Flood,
And you should, if you please, refuse
Till the conversion of the Jews.
My vegetable love should grow
Vaster than empires, and more slow;
An hundred years should go to praise
Thine eyes and on thy forehead gaze;
Two hundred to adore each breast,
But thirty thousand to the rest;
An age at least to every part,
And the last age should show your heart;
For, Lady, you deserve this state,
Nor would I love at lower rate.
   But at my back I always hear
Time's wingèd chariot hurrying near;
And yonder all before us lie
Deserts of vast eternity.
Thy beauty shall no more be found,
Nor, in thy marble vault, shall sound
My echoing song: then worms shall try
That long preserved virginity,
And your quaint honour turn to dust,
And into ashes all my lust:

The grave's a fine and private place,
But none, I think, do there embrace.
    Now therefore, while the youthful hue
Sits on thy skin like morning dew,
And while thy willing soul transpires
At every pore with instant fires,
Now let us sport us while we may,
And now, like amorous birds of prey,
Rather at once our time devour
Than languish in his slow-chapt power.
Let us roll all our strength and all
Our sweetness up into one ball,
And tear our pleasures with rough strife
Thorough the iron gates of life:
Thus, though we cannot make our sun
Stand still, yet we will make him run.

This is one of the poems I love the most in the whole wide world of poetry. It's a ravishing poem of love and desire. It's also a classic carpe diem poem, urging us to seize the day and make the most of life while we can. Although that is usually good advice, in this case the poet is using the argument to convince his reluctant lover to abandon her chasteness and join him in a frolic before time runs out. Sly of him? Yes, but also irresistibly seductive.

I appreciate the three very different attacks of this poem. At first the poet suggests that it is great to love, and if there was all the time in the world to watch love grow and ripen, he would be patient enough to do that. The second part states the fact that, unfortunately, time is always chasing us swiftly to our end, and what a waste of his lady's beauty and "quaint honour" when they'll both soon be "dust." Finally, the conquest—the celebration of his longing and his closing argument, if you will, that instead of letting time chase them, they should chase time right back by living their lives with urgency and vigor. How to argue with that reasoning?

"To His Coy Mistress" is filled with quotable turns of phrase, not the least, "Had we but world enough, and time," which is a poignant notion that most people use to express regret, even though Marvell means for it to help us avoid regret. Marvell is also known as a gardening poet, whose love of nature, ripening to the bursting point, weaves itself like a subtle green thread through his work. "My vegetable love should grow / Vaster than empires"—what a glorious image.

To me, this poem is like the dish you have to have every time you go to your favorite restaurant. You know you should try something else, but each time you can't resist your favorite. Call it a guilty pleasure.

The Mower's Song

My Mind was once the true survey
Of all these Meadows fresh and gay;
And in the greenness of the Grass
Did see its Hopes as in a Glass;
When Juliana came, and She
What I do to the Grass, does to my Thoughts and Me.

But these, while I with Sorrow pine,
Grew more luxuriant still and fine;
That not one Blade of Grass you spy'd,
But had a Flower on either side;
When Juliana came, and She
What I do to the Grass, does to my Thoughts and Me.

Unthankful Meadows, could you so
A fellowship so true forego,
And in your gawdy May-games meet,
While I lay trodden under feet?
When Juliana came, and She
What I do to the Grass, does to my Thoughts and Me.

But what you in Compassion ought,
Shall now by my Revenge be wrought:
And Flow'rs, and Grass, and I and all,
Will in one common Ruine fall.
For Juliana comes, and She
What I do to the Grass, does to my Thoughts and Me.

And thus, ye Meadows, which have been
Companions of my thoughts more green,

Shall now the Heraldry become
With which I shall adorn my Tomb;
For Juliana comes, and She
What I do to the Grass, does to my Thoughts and Me.

Edna St. Vincent Millay

The Bohemian

(1892–1950)

Edna St. Vincent Millay did it her way. Known for her artistic independence, her pointed political positions, her eclectic relationships, and her unconventional lifestyle, she could easily have alienated a conservative public. Her poetry spoke louder than her wild-child ways, though, and she became one of the most beloved poets of her time.

Raised with her two sisters by a single mother, Millay lived in a variety of homes shared by friends and relatives in Maine. Although they had little money, her mother introduced her daughters to classic literature and fine music and encouraged them to be independent-minded and self-sufficient. Vincent, as she was known to her friends, took this encouragement to heart. She was a precocious student who began writing poetry as a teenager. In 1912, her poem "Renascence" won her a literary prize and a scholarship to Vassar College, where she wrote poetry and plays and cultivated a variety of relationships with women there. Her first book of poetry, *Renascence and Other Poems*, was published in 1917, the year she graduated and moved to Greenwich Village in New York.

Here began the legend of Edna St. Vincent Millay's bohemian life. A freer spirit never lived, and Greenwich Village was the perfect place for her to express her freedom. She lived in an attic apartment, wrote anything someone would pay her for, and feverishly cavorted with fellow writers and artists who lived in the Village. She described herself and her friends as "very, very poor and very, very merry." She had many love affairs, she smoked cigarettes with shameless abandon, acted in a downtown theater group, and traveled to Europe. She also worked hard on her writing, publishing short stories and poems in magazines, and eventually her next books of poems, *A Few Figs from Thistles* and *Second April*. By this time, she'd become a literary celebrity and the symbol of the New Woman in America.

A great performer of her own poetry, Millay was enormously popular at lecture halls across the country, where tickets to her readings regularly sold out to audiences of thousands. She was tiny and fair-skinned, with a glorious head of red hair that matched the fire she breathed into her spoken poetry. Like an American Byron, she was adored for her gorgeous poetry and idolized for the myth of her extraordinary life. Women wanted to be her; men wanted to marry her.

The English novelist Thomas Hardy once said that there were only two great things in the United States—skyscrapers and the poetry of Edna St. Vincent Millay. Her work spoke of youth, love, change, death, and liberation, especially for women. She had a sensitivity and delicacy that gave her poems a distinctly seductive quality. In 1923 she became the first woman ever to be awarded the Pulitzer Prize for Poetry.

Love is not all

Love is not all: it is not meat nor drink
Nor slumber nor a roof against the rain;
Nor yet a floating spar to men that sink
And rise and sink and rise and sink again;
Love can not fill the thickened lung with breath,
Nor clean the blood, nor set the fractured bone;
Yet many a man is making friends with death
Even as I speak, for lack of love alone.
It well may be that in a difficult hour,
Pinned down by pain and moaning for release,
Or nagged by want past resolution's power,
I might be driven to sell your love for peace,
Or trade the memory of this night for food.
It well may be. I do not think I would.

This poem reminds me of what M. F. K. Fisher answered when she was asked why she kept writing about food. She said that it was because there were only two things that humans couldn't live without—food and love. It's true that humans have a natural hunger for both that drives us. You can refuse food and die. You can deny love and starve your soul.

> ### ➤ Favorite Poems ◄
>
> "Renascence"
>
> "What lips my lips have kissed, and where and why" (Sonnet XLIII)
>
> "Second Fig" ❧ "Euclid alone has looked on beauty bare"
>
> "The Ballad of the Harp-Weaver"

Millay makes a clever case for this truth. She notes from the start that love isn't everything. It won't sustain us as food and water does. It won't protect us from the elements, or save us when we're drowning, or fix what's wrong with us when we're ill. "Yet many a man is making friends with death / Even as I speak, for lack of love alone." Love isn't everything, but we cannot survive without it.

The first part of the poem is a list of all the things love is not, all the things love cannot do. Then it shifts into what love is, described not in a list, but in a sort of worst-case scenario, where the poet admits she could never be so desperate as to deny herself the love she cannot do without. This poem has everything a great Millay poem should—wit and truth and deeply personal resonance.

Marianne Moore

The Genuine Poet

(1887–1972)

Marianne Moore was born in Kirkwood, Missouri, spent most of her childhood in Carlisle, Pennsylvania, and eventually attended Bryn Mawr College. After college she took secretarial courses, then taught secretarial skills and English at the Indian school in Carlisle. She traveled to Europe in 1911 and in 1915 began publishing her poetry in journals and periodicals, to almost immediate acclaim by fellow poets and critics. In 1918, she moved to Greenwich Village in New York with her mother, with whom she lived for most of her adult life. In New York, she quickly began mixing with other poets such as Wallace Stevens and William Carlos Williams, as well as all the up-and-coming artists and intellectuals. She also was an enthusiastic baseball fan, especially of the Brooklyn Dodgers.

Marianne Moore saw beauty in all things well made, from the stitching on a baseball to the scales on an anteater, and she strived to create poetry that featured that same intricate precision. She worked with incredible discipline and attention to detail and structure, observing the world around her with a scientist's eye and a poet's heart. She was endlessly curious about the natural world; she took laboratory courses in biology while she was a college student, and her fascination with animals lasted all her life. She sought "enchantment" in her work and would settle for nothing less—she compares the pangolin (the aforementioned anteater) with Leonardo da Vinci and likens its scaly body to a spruce cone, an artichoke, and the ironwork at Westminster Abbey. Moore claimed to have wanted to be a painter, which might explain why she used such painterly precision in her work.

She played with language like a cubist, taking familiar structures and putting them back together in a slightly unexpected way, occasionally dropping quotes from other sources into her work, much the way Picasso and Juan Gris pasted scraps of newspaper onto some of their still lifes. Her original and detailed visual observations were like a breeze blowing through the poetry of the time.

Her first collection, *Poems*, was published in 1921 in England. Moore had a long, celebrated career, publishing poem after poem in periodicals like the *Kenyon Review*, the *Nation*, the *New Republic*, and the *Partisan Review*, as well as in celebrated volumes such as her 1951 *Collected Poems*, which won the Pulitzer Prize for Poetry and the National Book Award. She was esteemed and celebrated by her peers; William Carlos Williams admired "the edge-to-edge contact" between objects in her poems, while in the introduction to her *Selected Poems* in 1935, T. S. Eliot called her poetry "durable" and allowed she was one of the few writers of the time who had made a contribution to the language. Eliot was a notorious snob, so these were no small compliments.

Famous for her signature three-cornered hat and a dark cape, Moore was a celebrity even outside of poetry circles. When she accepted the National Book Award in 1951, she quipped that her work was called poetry because there was nothing else to call it, and described herself as "a happy hack."

Poetry

I, too, dislike it: there are things that are important beyond all this fiddle.
   Reading it, however, with a perfect contempt for it, one discovers in
   it after all, a place for the genuine.
      Hands that can grasp, eyes
      that can dilate, hair that can rise
         if it must, these things are important not because a

high-sounding interpretation can be put upon them but because they are
   useful. When they become so derivative as to become unintelligible,
   the same thing may be said for all of us, that we
      do not admire what
      we cannot understand: the bat
         holding on upside down or in quest of something to

eat, elephants pushing, a wild horse taking a roll, a tireless wolf under
   a tree, the immovable critic twitching his skin like a horse that feels
                             a flea, the base-
   ball fan, the statistician—
      nor is it valid
         to discriminate against "business documents and

school-books"; all these phenomena are important. One must make a
                                 distinction
   however: when dragged into prominence by half poets, the result is not
                                    poetry,
nor till the poets among us can be
   "literalists of
   the imagination"—above
      insolence and triviality and can present

for inspection, "imaginary gardens with real toads in them," shall we
  have it. In the meantime, if you demand on the one hand,
    the raw material of poetry in
      all its rawness and
      that which is on the other hand
        genuine, you are interested in poetry.

In a poem the excitement has to sustain itself. I am governed by the pull
of the sentence as the pull of fabric is governed by gravity.

—Marianne Moore

This is a wonderful, conversational poem about what she does and why she thinks it's important. I identify with this poem because as an actor, I ask myself all the time, "Why do I act? Why do they watch me? Why do I need to act? Why do they need to watch?" What I see in this poem is the answer that poetry (or art or acting) is not indispensable, but it is important. It reminds us of the inherent usefulness of art, and that like love in Edna St. Vincent Millay's poem "Love is not all," art may not be everything, but it is *necessary*.

Moore takes digs at poetry that is dishonest or "so derivative as to be unintelligible," so we can believe that not all poetry is useful. She sees poetry as a "place for the genuine," to be valued above all else. She insists on poetry containing "imaginary gardens with real toads in them"—I thrill to that phrase, for that is the essence of acting as well.

There's a wonderful, purposeful incongruity to this poem that is typical of Moore. She throws in little tidbits like quotes and unlikely references to the baseball fan or the statistician, and manages to bring the ordinary, grubby stuff of real life into an important conversation about poetry. She gives readers an intellectual and emotional exercise that puts them in touch with what's genuine in poetry and life.

In his 1925 essay, "Marianne Moore," William Carlos Williams describes how Moore could magnify a small object until it seemed to contain an entire world: "so that in looking at some apparently small object, one feels the swirl of great events." What a tremendous inspiration to a poet—or an actor!

⇒ Favorite Poems ⇐

"A Graveyard"   ∞   "An Octopus"   ∞   "Baseball and Writing"

"The Pangolin"   ∞   "No Swan So Fine"

Ogden Nash

The Worsifier

(1902–1971)

O gden Nash is another great hero of mine—he's the undisputed master of contemporary light verse. His is a great American story of an ordinary man accessing the extraordinary poet inside him.

Born in Rye, New York, Nash came from a prominent family after whom the city of Nashville, Tennessee, is named. He attended Harvard briefly, but dropped out for financial reasons and ventured into the working world. He taught school, gave Wall Street a try, and wrote advertising copy for a short time. In 1925, he landed a job at Doubleday as an editor and publicist. There he collaborated with the writer Christopher Morley on several books of humor, giving him a taste of being published.

In 1930, his first published poem appeared in the *New Yorker*, followed by a collection of poetry, *Hard Lines*, in 1931. The book was an instant success, going through seven printings in its first year of publication. Nash left Doubleday to work at the *New Yorker* for a short while, but soon quit to devote all his time to his own writing.

Nash was incredibly prolific, partly because he had a lot to say, and partly because he was just a hard worker. Over his lifetime, his poems were published in dozens of periodicals, including the *Saturday Evening*

Post, *Harper's*, *Life*, and, of course, the *New Yorker*. He published dozens of books of verse, humor, and essays and more than 1,500 individual poems; he cowrote a hit Broadway musical, *One Touch of Venus*; he wrote movie scripts and even song lyrics. He appeared on radio comedy and game shows in the 1940s, similar television shows in the 1950s, and was a popular lecturer across the United States and England.

Ogden Nash had a wit so sharp and quick, you feel if you met him you might have trouble keeping up. Yet that was his gift, to use every word as an opportunity to turn a notion upside down, to tickle, to tease, all in the most accessible way. Each line of each poem had something real to say, and he would invigorate and deliver his message with the tools of his wit. Like Lewis Carroll and Edward Lear before him, Nash was known to make up a word or two, or at least to manipulate the spelling of a word for his own cunning purposes. He even made up a word to describe himself and his way with words—he said he was a "worsifier." And like Marianne Moore, he loved to consider animals in his work, though often it was to extol the virtues of dogs and lament the existence of cats; one poem is called "Cat Naps Are Too Good for Cats"!

⇒ Favorite Poems ⇐

"So Does Everybody Else, Only Not So Much"

"Just Keep Quiet and Nobody Will Notice"

"The Boy Who Laughed at Santa Claus"   ∾   "More About People"

"Children's Party"

No Doctors Today, Thank You

They tell me that euphoria is the feeling of feeling wonderful, well,
    today I feel euphorian,
Today I have the agility of a Greek god and the appetite of a Victorian.
Yes, today I may even go forth without my galoshes,
Today I am a swashbuckler, would anybody like me to buckle any
    swashes?
This is my euphorian day,
I will ring welkins and before anybody answers I will run away.
I will tame me a caribou
And bedeck it with marabou.
I will pen me my memoirs.
Ah youth, youth! What euphorian days them was!
I wasn't much of a hand for the boudoirs,
I was generally to be found where the food was.
Does anybody want any flotsam?
I've gotsam.
Does anybody want any jetsam?
I can getsam.
I can play chopsticks on the Wurlitzer,
I can speak Portuguese like a Berlitzer.
I can don or doff my shoes without tying or untying the laces because I
    am wearing moccasins,
And I practically know the difference between serums and
    antitoccasins.
Kind people, don't think me purse-proud, don't set me down as
    vainglorious,
I'm just a little euphorious.

The Carnival of the Animals is an orchestral suite composed by Camille Saint-Saëns in 1886. This composition is beloved around the world and is a particular favorite of mine. I once had the unique pleasure of performing in a New York City Ballet production choreographed to this music, for which I wrote a rhymed narration that became a children's book. Ogden Nash must have loved *Carnival* as much as I do, as he wrote a collection of funny poems to accompany each movement of the suite. I especially love his poem "The Lion," which goes with the first movement:

> *The lion is the king of beasts,*
> *And husband of the lioness.*
> *Gazelles and things on which he feasts*
> *Address him as your highoness.*
> *There are those that admire that roar of his,*
> *In the African jungles and velds,*
> *But, I think that wherever the lion is,*
> *I'd rather be somewhere else.*

This poem has everything I love about Nash—the vividness, the use of ridiculous words, and a giddiness to it all. It is exuberant and, well, euphoric! It's the joy of words, as simple as that. And the pace, classic Nash, urges you along to the point that you can't wait for the next line. There is the wonderfully true sense of what it feels like to be alive on a really great day—you can do anything, rise to any occasion, conquer any fear. You have the "agility of a Greek god" and you can "play chopsticks on the Wurlitzer"—*that* is a terrific day. You feel smart and snappy and like clicking your heels. Just the way this poem makes you feel.

Nash had an edge of antiestablishment to him, but it was balanced by his good nature. He once quipped, "My field—the minor idiocies of mankind." Yes, the idiocies, if you count the ordinary subjects of ordinary life, like work and marriage and families. But they're also the joys, especially as Nash puts his inimitable spin on it.

Dorothy Parker

The Caustic Poet

(1893–1967)

I can't help but think that Dorothy Parker would laugh out loud to find herself included in a collection along with Shakespeare and John Donne or Keats and T. S. Eliot. But included she is, as her poetry reflects a unique sense of perception and cuts like a knife—this is the essence of the one-and-only Dorothy Parker.

Parker was born in West End, New Jersey, and grew up mostly in Manhattan. Her mother died when she was five and her father when she was twenty-one. She never described her family life or childhood with affection; her education ended when she was thirteen and she moved to a boardinghouse in New York at the age of eighteen. To support herself, she played the piano at a dance school, but within just a few years she was submitting poems to magazines and newspapers; her first published poem, "Any Porch," was featured in *Vanity Fair* in 1914.

So began a career of writing poetry and prose for magazines like *Vanity Fair*, *Vogue*, and eventually the *New Yorker* that would span her whole life. Her first volume of poetry, *Enough Rope*, was published in 1926 and was a critical and commercial success. She wrote a total of seven volumes of poetry and short stories, as well as plays, several successful film scripts, and a lot of popular literary criticism.

It's hard to imagine how Dorothy Parker had the time to produce such an impressive body of work—she lived a famously tumultuous life, with unhappy marriages, drinking problems, depression, and a long stint working in the film business that was racked with familiar Hollywood drama. She pronounced herself a Communist in the middle of the McCarthy era and promptly landed on the Hollywood blacklist.

Parker was as acerbic in person as on paper, and though most of her friends stood by her throughout her career, some admitted it could be hard at times to love her. Yet it was just this biting demeanor that made her who she was—her dry, sardonic point of view informed everything she wrote, while her urbane wit gave her work an unmatched elegance and crispness.

Listen to Dorothy Parker read more than two dozen of her favorite poems in *An Informal Hour with Dorothy Parker*, or go to www .dorothyparker.com/dotaudio.htm to listen to individual clips of these poems. Her gravelly voice sounds just the way you'd imagine it.

Afternoon

When I am old, and comforted,
    And done with this desire,
With Memory to share my bed
    And Peace to share my fire,

I'll comb my hair in scalloped bands
    Beneath my laundered cap,
And watch my cool and fragile hands
    Lie light upon my lap.

And I will have a sprigged gown
    With lace to kiss my throat;
I'll draw my curtain to the town,
    And hum a purring note.

And I'll forget the way of tears,
    And rock, and stir my tea.
But oh, I wish those blessed years
    Were further than they be!

"Afternoon" is an elegant piece of poetry paced like a brilliant little joke that sets up with carefully drawn details and works toward a very ironic, caustic punch line. Classic Dorothy Parker. I love this poem for all kinds of reasons. First, what a funny notion, Parker wearing a dowager's cap, tucked into a rocking chair, stirring her tea with "fragile hands." There wasn't a fragile bone in her body, and she had too much spit and fire to ever end up in a rocker, quietly lamenting her old age.

This was a common trick of Parker's, to make herself the main character in her poem, however unlikely the connection. Whether she wrote of unsuccessful love, youth, age, or modern life, she was not afraid to put herself right in the middle of the picture she painted and didn't mind being the object of her own jokes.

Dorothy Parker is pure 1920s and '30s dry, cynical wit. She and her writer friends, a loosely organized lunch bunch known as the Algonquin Round Table, were famous for their clever banter and memorable quips. They made an art form out of traded barbs and structured jokes and became the literary masters of parody and putdown.

One can't just look at Dorothy Parker's poetry without considering her life. The critic Brendan Gill described the titles of her books—*Enough Rope, Sunset Gun, Laments for Living, Death and Taxes, After Such Pleasures,* and *Not So Deep as a Well*—as a "capsule autobiography." Whereas her contemporary Ogden Nash wrote with a kind of happy, upbeat irreverence, Parker had a dark streak that brought an edge of viciousness to her humor. She famously quipped, "The first thing I do in the morning is brush my teeth and sharpen my tongue." Which is a little something else she may have had in common with Shakespeare, besides appearing in this book.

Favorite Poems

"Little Words" ∞ "Men" ∞ "The Gentlest Lady"

"Interior" ∞ "Symptom Recital"

Edgar Allan Poe

The Macabre Poet

(1809–1849)

Edgar Allan Poe was like a character in one of his own poems or short stories—troubled, obsessive, and probably not a little lacking in sleep! He has had his fans, from Charles Dickens to Walt Whitman, Herman Melville, Charles Baudelaire, Oscar Wilde, and William Faulkner. He has also had his critics, from Mark Twain to T. S. Eliot, who sniped that Poe had "the intellect of a highly gifted person before puberty." Not everyone agreed as to the *nature* of his genius—whether it was a keen intelligence or a kind of madness—but his genius was undeniable.

Born the son of two actors in Boston, Poe lost both his parents before he was three. He was taken in by a wealthy tobacco merchant from Richmond, Virginia, named John Allan, who saw to Poe's excellent education and made him a part of the Allan family. Poe and the Allans lived in Scotland and England from 1815 through 1820, before returning to Richmond. Poe attended the University of Virginia in 1826, but had to drop out after just a year, when Mr. Allan refused to help him pay his gambling debts. At the age of eighteen, Poe moved to Boston and anonymously published his first book of poetry, called *Tamerlane and Other Poems*.

With no way to support himself, Poe enlisted in the army in 1827 and served for two years. After reconciling briefly with Mr. Allan, who arranged for his appointment to the United States Military Academy at West Point, he broke off from the quarreling Allan family for good and got himself kicked out of West Point for disobedience. By this time, in 1831, he had published his third book of poetry and was gaining a reputation as a poet and story writer, getting published occasionally in literary magazines and newspapers. Eventually he wrote for and edited several magazines, and circulations rose in the periodicals that published his work. By now he was writing poetry, short stories, literary criticism, and book reviews, and in 1845, when his poem "The Raven" was published, he became an overnight sensation.

Though he wrote steadily and was published regularly, Poe's work life was far from stable. Most of his experiences working for magazines ended badly, either due to personality difficulties or the effects of one of his regular bouts of drinking and depression. He had trouble at first convincing publishers to take on his macabre fiction—ironically, now the work for which he is most famous. He publicly feuded with fellow poet Henry Wadsworth Longfellow, who was the most popular literary figure in America at the time. When Poe's wife died of tuberculosis in 1847, Poe fell more deeply into his "darknesses," and in October 1849 he turned up drunk and gravely ill in Baltimore, incoherent and wearing someone else's clothes. He died a few days later.

It's tempting to account for Poe's dark themes by pointing to his fractured and difficult life, and you might not be wrong. But he wasn't a slave to his themes, rather a master craftsman in their service. And there's no denying his considerable influence on style and structure in American poetry, and as the "architect" of the modern short story. For these contributions, he's considered one of the first important and world-renowned distinctly American writers.

Annabel Lee

It was many and many a year ago,
   In a kingdom by the sea,
That a maiden there lived whom you may know
   By the name of Annabel Lee;
And this maiden she lived with no other thought
   Than to love and be loved by me.

I was a child and *she* was a child,
   In this kingdom by the sea:
But we loved with a love that was more than love—
   I and my Annabel Lee;
With a love that the winged seraphs of heaven
   Coveted her and me.

And this was the reason that, long ago,
   In this kingdom by the sea,
A wind blew out of a cloud, chilling
   My beautiful Annabel Lee;
So that her highborn kinsman came
   And bore her away from me,
To shut her up in a sepulchre
   In this kingdom by the sea.

The angels, not half so happy in heaven,
   Went envying her and me—
Yes!—that was the reason (as all men know,
   In this kingdom by the sea)
That the wind came out of the cloud by night,
   Chilling and killing my Annabel Lee.

But our love it was stronger by far than the love
    Of those who were older than we—
    Of many far wiser than we—
And neither the angels in heaven above,
    Nor the demons down under the sea,
Can ever dissever my soul from the soul
    Of the beautiful Annabel Lee:

For the moon never beams, without bringing me dreams
    Of the beautiful Annabel Lee;
And the stars never rise, but I feel the bright eyes
    Of the beautiful Annabel Lee;
And so, all the night-tide, I lie down by the side
Of my darling—my darling—my life and my bride,
    In her sepulchre there by the sea,
    In her tomb by the sounding sea.

To elevate the soul, poetry is necessary.

—Edgar Allan Poe

This was Poe's last poem, published two days after his death. You don't need to know this to feel the feverish grief he expresses for the loss of his young wife, Virginia, two years before. You can imagine his descent into despair at losing her, as it fairly weeps off the words at every turn. And yet, in all his sadness, what amazing control he shows over this poem. The rhythm and the rhyme are carefully crafted to set up a soothing pace that belies the poet's misery and dangerous obsession with his dead bride.

"Annabel Lee" displays Poe's signature musicality to perfect effect. Repeated phrases and a melodious use of language amp up the drama to tell the story like a ballad. It's interesting that Poe's parents were actors, as his poetry always begs to be performed as much as read. Like the best melodramatists, Poe was famous for his almost morbid affection for lost love. Yet this is also a deeply personal poem. When he says that "the moon never beams, without bringing me dreams" you absolutely believe he is speaking for himself.

Poe once said, "Sleep, those little slices of death, how I loathe them." This was his own world, the world of deep and troubling dreams as well as relentless insomnia, obsessive fixations, and reclusive isolation, all painstakingly, perfectly reflected back in his poetry and stories. He was a master craftsman to the end, right down to his last poem.

⇉ Favorite Poems ⇇

"A Dream" ∞ "The Bells" ∞ "The Oval Portrait"

"The Raven" ∞ "Tamerlane"

Alone

From childhood's hour I have not been
As others were—I have not seen
As others saw—I could not bring
My passions from a common spring—
From the same source I have not taken
My sorrow—I could not awaken
My heart to joy at the same tone—
And all I lov'd—*I* lov'd alone—
Then—in my childhood—in the dawn
Of a most stormy life—was drawn
From ev'ry depth of good and ill
The mystery which binds me still—
From the torrent, or the fountain—
From the red cliff of the mountain—
From the sun that 'round me roll'd
In its autumn tint of gold—
From the lightning in the sky
As it pass'd me flying by—
From the thunder, and the storm—
And the cloud that took the form
(When the rest of Heaven was blue)
Of a demon in my view—

Ezra Pound

The Imagist

(1885–1972)

When the critic Hugh Kenner met Ezra Pound, he said, "I suddenly knew that I was in the presence of the center of modernism." Like Wordsworth before him, Pound made it his life's mission to usher in a new literary era. He succeeded famously, encouraging the work of T. S. Eliot, James Joyce, Robert Frost, William Carlos Williams, H.D., Marianne Moore, and Wyndham Lewis—a chorus of voices of modernism.

Pound was born in Hailey, Idaho, and graduated from Hamilton College in 1905. He left for Europe in 1908 and remained an expatriate for most of his life. Married in 1914, he worked in London as the editor of a literary journal until he moved to Italy in 1924. Later he lived in the Montparnasse quarter of Paris, surrounded by the brilliant artists and writers of the Lost Generation. He frequented Gertrude Stein's salon and the café Le Dôme, where he played chess on the terrace with the writer Ford Madox Ford.

Although continuously writing his own poetry, Pound spent considerable time on essays promoting a poetic movement called imagism. He was passionate about its precepts: to use precise imagery and clear, economical language, and to employ unconventional rhyme and meter. While not every poet raised his hand and joined the imagist club, the influence of this thinking was seen in most writers' work at the time.

Pound was proficient in Spanish, ancient Greek, Latin, Italian, French, Japanese, Hindi, Anglo-Saxon, and ancient Egyptian. He translated works from Provençal and Chinese. A respected and feared critic, he was a great friend and supporter of poets in Europe and America. He got into hot water for supporting Mussolini's Fascist politics while living in Italy; he was arrested and sent back to America in 1945, where he was tried for treason. An insanity plea resulted in twelve years in an institution.

Despite his incarceration, Pound continued to write and was awarded the 1949 Bollingen Prize for his masterwork, *Pisan Cantos*. After his friends successfully campaigned for his release, he returned to Italy, where he died in Venice in 1972. Ezra Pound was a giant of the twentieth century, but he spent his last years a recluse, reliving his "errors and wrecks."

⯈ Favorite Poems ⯇

Canto I ⍟ "The Garden"

"Exile's Letter" ⍟ "Hugh Selwyn Mauberley"

The River-Merchant's Wife: A Letter

While my hair was still cut straight across my forehead
I played about the front gate, pulling flowers.
You came by on bamboo stilts, playing horse,
You walked about my seat, playing with blue plums.
And we went on living in the village of Chokan:
Two small people, without dislike or suspicion.

At fourteen I married My Lord you.
I never laughed, being bashful.
Lowering my head, I looked at the wall.
Called to, a thousand times, I never looked back.

At fifteen I stopped scowling,
I desired my dust to be mingled with yours
Forever and forever and forever.
Why should I climb the look out?

At sixteen you departed,
You went into far Ku-to-Yen, by the river of swirling eddies,
And you have been gone five months.
The monkeys make sorrowful noise overhead.

You dragged your feet when you went out.
By the gate now, the moss is grown, the different mosses,
Too deep to clear them away!
The leaves fall early this autumn, in wind.

The paired butterflies are already yellow with August
Over the grass in the West garden;

They hurt me. I grow older.
If you are coming down through the narrows of the river Kiang,

Please let me know beforehand,
And I will come out to meet you
    As far as Cho-fu-Sa.

Good writers are those who keep the language efficient. That is to say, keep it accurate, keep it clear.

—Ezra Pound

Ezra Pound

In translating this poem by Li T'ai Po (Rihaku in Japanese) from Chinese to English, Ezra Pound made it his own. He believed that Chinese characters were compressed visual metaphors, which he channeled into the gorgeous free-verse English of "The River-Merchant's Wife." What a trick, to make this imaginative leap on three levels—Pound is a Western man translating an Eastern poet's poem in the voice of a woman. There is a tension in these leaps that reminds me of *M. Butterfly*.

And yet the poem is perfectly believable. You are moved by the haunting voice of this young girl who is not yet twenty years old, but has lived a whole lifetime, going through all the stages of childhood, marriage, the discovery of desire, and then loss. "The paired butterflies are already yellow with August"—how sad for someone so young to be so world-weary.

The poem is certainly a westerner's tale of the East, but at the same time entirely universal. It gently points to the unknowability of the East by the West.

Pound was influenced by the leanness of Asian poetry. One of his most famous poems, "In a Station of the Metro," is like a haiku:

The apparition of these faces in the crowd;
Petals on a wet, black bough.

In *Gaudier-Brzeska: A Memoir*, Pound recalls seeing a stream of beautiful faces on the Paris Metro, and then spending the rest of the day trying to put the moment into words. He tried to find words "as worthy, or as lovely as that sudden emotion. And that evening . . . I was still trying and I found, suddenly, the expression. I do not mean that I found words, but there came an equation . . . not in speech, but in little splotches of color." He wrote a thirty-line poem and then pared it down to just these two simple perfect lines.

It's not always easy to read Ezra Pound. He throws in snips of Greek, references to Homer and Dante, and maybe William Gladstone, the nineteenth-century British prime minister. You may feel like you're not in on the joke, that perhaps he's a little too smart and cultured for you. You may not know that "Burne-Jones" refers to sketches for paintings, or that "Paquin" is a Parisian dressmaker. But it's enriching to read the poems of a man who seems to have taken in the whole world, from Babylon to Brooklyn. He described his epic work, the *Cantos*, as "a mosaic of images, ideas, phrases—politics, ethics, economics—anecdotes, insults, denunciations—English, Greek, Italian, Provençal, Chinese."

Christina Rossetti

The Victorian

(1830–1894)

Christina Rossetti was born in London, one of four children of Italian parents. Her boisterous family turned their home into a lively hub for Italian exiles, where politics and culture were thrashed out long into the night. Their house was filled with a love for art and literature; her father was a poet and so was her brother Dante Gabriel, which inspired Christina to write verse from a young age.

Rossetti was caught between her deep religious faith and worldly delights: she was a devout High Anglican, and an equally passionate poet. She turned down two marriage proposals for religious reasons, despite being quite in love with one of the men, and lived a sequestered, spinsterly life. William Michael Rossetti said his sister was "replete with the spirit of self-postponement." A true fan of self-discipline, Christina quit playing chess because she enjoyed winning too much, turned down seeing Wagner's opera *Parsifal* because it celebrated pagan mythology, snubbed nudity in paintings, and glued paper strips over the anti-Christian parts of Algernon Swinburne's poem *Atalanta in Calydon*.

Rossetti's *Goblin Market and Other Poems*, published in 1862, was a critical success and established her as the preeminent female poet and Elizabeth Barrett Browning's successor. She tackled the big topics: love and death, religion and renunciation. In an essay on her, Virginia Woolf said, "Your instinct was so sure, so direct, so intense that it produced poems that sing like music in one's ears—like a melody by Mozart or an air by Gluck."

➤ Favorite Poems ◄

"Song"   ❧   "Remember"   ❧   "In an Artist's Studio"

"Echo"   ❧   "I watched a rosebud"

Up-Hill

Does the road wind up-hill all the way?
    Yes, to the very end.
Will the day's journey take the whole long day?
    From morn to night, my friend.

But is there for the night a resting-place?
    A roof for when the slow dark hours begin.
May not the darkness hide it from my face?
    You cannot miss that inn.

Shall I meet other wayfarers at night?
    Those who have gone before.
Then must I knock, or call when just in sight?
    They will not keep you standing at that door.

Shall I find comfort, travel-sore and weak?
    Of labour you shall find the sum.
Will there be beds for me and all who seek?
    Yea, beds for all who come.

The structure of this poem is so appealing. A dialogue poem, it never identifies either of the parties involved. The simple banter and singsong rhythm in this tale of a weary traveler belie the seriousness of the conversation, so much so that it comes off almost as a kind of a riddle. Is it about a hard, long trek, and the promise of comfort and a warm bed at the end, with Rossetti cheering us on in our voyage? Or is she telling us that life is hard and death awaits, but you must keep walking up and up? Probably a little bit of both, though artists of her time were famous for wallowing in morbid thoughts, carrying on a kind of swoony infatuation with the ideas of lost innocence and lost youth.

I prefer to be reassured by this poem, to be heartened by the experience of those who've gone before. The second voice in this poem offers that reassurance. Yes, life is all uphill, right to the very end, and yes, there's comfort to be found along the way.

Rossetti was trapped between her devotion to the divine and her intense love for the world around her. Woolf says to her, "Your poems are full of gold dust and 'sweet geraniums' varied brightness; your eye noted incessantly how rushes are 'velvet headed,' and lizards have a 'strange metallic mail.' . . . No sooner have you feasted on beauty with your eyes than your mind tells you that beauty is vain and beauty passes." Christina Rossetti may have restrained herself from many things she loved, but she let the world in all its bright glory suffuse her poems.

An Apple Gathering

I plucked pink blossoms from mine apple-tree
    And wore them all that evening in my hair:
Then in due season when I went to see
      I found no apples there.

With dangling basket all along the grass
    As I had come I went the selfsame track:
My neighbours mocked me while they saw me pass
      So empty-handed back.

Lilian and Lilias smiled in trudging by,
    Their heaped-up basket teased me like a jeer;
Sweet-voiced they sang beneath the sunset sky,
      Their mother's home was near.

Plump Gertrude passed me with her basket full,
    A stronger hand than hers helped it along;
A voice talked with her through the shadows cool
      More sweet to me than song.

Ah Willie, Willie, was my love less worth
    Than apples with their green leaves piled above?
I counted rosiest apples on the earth
      Of far less worth than love.

So once it was with me you stooped to talk
    Laughing and listening in this very lane:
To think that by this way we used to walk
      We shall not walk again!

I let my neighbours pass me, ones and twos
    And groups; the latest said the night grew chill,
And hastened: but I loitered, while the dews
    Fell fast I loitered still.

Carl Sandburg

The Patriot

(1878–1967)

When he was nineteen years old, Carl Sandburg left his small hometown of Galesburg, Illinois, due to a bad case of wanderlust. He stowed away inside a railroad car with the intent of seeing what the country had to offer, working his way west through Iowa, Missouri, Kansas, Nebraska, and Colorado, looking for work and adventure. He even spent ten days in the Allegheny County Jail in Pennsylvania in 1902, after he was caught on a train without a ticket. He traveled the country as close to the land as he could get, digging into the valleys and coasting along its hills, and occasionally tasting the various flavors of cities along the way. H. L. Mencken said that Sandburg was "indubitably an American in every pulse-beat"—he absorbed the country right to the core of his heart.

Sandburg loved the stuff of common life: the daily rhythms of laborers, the tides of energy in cities, dirty hands and hard work. He took on a kind of Johnny Appleseed persona, traveling to meet people, trade poems, and swap songs. In a 1907 lecture called "An American Vagabond," Sandburg said, "Books are but empty nothings compared with living, pulsing men and women. Life is stranger and greater than anything ever written about it." His poetry was driven by his passion for these "living, pulsing" things, and reflects the wonderful tangle of hopes and dreams he saw in every corner of the America he loved.

❧ Favorite Poems ❧

"Happiness" ❧ "Onion Days" ❧ "I Am the People, the Mob"

"Manitoba Childe Roland" ❧ "The People, Yes"

Sandburg worked as an advertising copywriter and newspaper reporter in Milwaukee, then moved to Chicago with his wife to write editorials for the *Chicago Daily News*. He began seeing his poems published in a poetry journal, whose editor, Harriet Monroe, encouraged him to keep working in his plainspoken style. In 1916 his *Chicago Poems* firmly established his reputation as a poet of note. Subsequent volumes, *Cornhuskers* and *Smoke and Steel*, published in 1918 and 1920 respectively, made him famous for his celebration of the American landscape, skyscrapers, smokestacks, and all. His collection *Complete Poems* received the Pulitzer Prize in 1950.

Sandburg spent his last years at Connemara, a rolling farm in North Carolina, surrounded by his wife's champion dairy goats and thousands of books. In the preface to *Complete Poems*, Sandburg humbly says, "All my life I have been trying to learn to read, to see and hear, and to write."

Chicago

    Hog Butcher for the World,
    Tool maker, Stacker of Wheat,
    Player with Railroads and the Nation's Freight Handler;
    Stormy, husky, brawling,
    City of the Big Shoulders:

They tell me you are wicked and I believe them, for I have seen your
    painted women under the gas lamps luring the farm boys.
And they tell me you are crooked and I answer: Yes, it is true I have
    seen the gunman kill and go free to kill again.
And they tell me you are brutal and my reply is: On the faces of
    women and children I have seen the marks of wanton hunger.
And having answered so I turn once more to those who sneer at this
    my city, and I give them back the sneer and say to them:
Come and show me another city with lifted head singing so proud to
    be alive and coarse and strong and cunning.
Flinging magnetic curses amid the toil of piling job on job, here is a
    tall bold slugger set vivid against the little soft cities;
Fierce as a dog with tongue lapping for action, cunning as a savage
    pitted against the wilderness,
    Bareheaded,
    Shoveling,
    Wrecking,
    Planning,
    Building, breaking, rebuilding,
Under the smoke, dust all over his mouth, laughing with white teeth,
Under the terrible burden of destiny laughing as a young man laughs,
Laughing even as an ignorant fighter laughs who has never lost a
    battle,

Bragging and laughing that under his wrist is the pulse, and under his ribs the heart of the people,
Laughing!
Laughing the stormy, husky, brawling laughter of Youth, half-naked, sweating, proud to be Hog Butcher, Tool Maker, Stacker of Wheat, Player with Railroads and Freight Handler to the Nation.

Listen to Sandburg read "The People, Yes" at http://archive.salon.com/ audio/poetry/2002/05/06/sandburg/index.html.

Carl Sandburg

This may be the most arrogant poem ever written. Oh, the intimidating, muscle-flexing glory of it! And it's all true, every word of it, even though those days of commercial supremacy are long gone for Chicago. The city's hardy sureness of itself is perfectly expressed in this poem. And what a wonderful image of a city as a "husky, brawling" youth, laughing, with "dust all over his mouth"—I love that.

The people of Chicago do have a unique character that is masterfully captured in this poem. They are so proud of where they come from, and it shows in their passion for their sports, theater, art, and architecture. Great Chicago actors I have known—like John Malkovich, Laurie Metcalfe, and Gary Sinise—believe so much in themselves and have a confidence in their work that is extraordinary. This poem is simply ringing with that same confidence. It makes you wish you were from Chicago, doesn't it?

Sandburg's poems are rough and raring to go. He uses regular words and phrasing that could be heard at the dock just as easily as in a classroom. He told the *New York Times*, "Slang is a language that rolls up its sleeves, spits on its hands and goes to work." His subject is "the people—the mob—the crowd—the mass." He experimented with every practical form of expression—award-winning biographies, ballads, fairy tales, folk songs, and, of course, poetry. It makes sense to me that the man who celebrated the crazy-quilt quality of America would whistle so many different tunes.

Honky Tonk in Cleveland, Ohio

It's a jazz affair, drum crashes and cornet razzes.
The trombone pony neighs and the tuba jackass snorts.
The banjo tickles and titters too awful.
The chippies talk about the funnies in the papers.
 The cartoonists weep in their beer.
 Ship riveters talk with their feet
 To the feet of floozies under the tables.
A quartet of white hopes mourn with interspersed snickers:
 "I got the blues.
 I got the blues.
 I got the blues."
And . . . as we said earlier:
 The cartoonists weep in their beer.

William Shakespeare

The Bard

(1564–1616)

As there is an entire industry devoted to analyzing, summarizing, and scrutinizing the life and works of Shakespeare, it seems a little silly to try to do that here. Suffice it to say that the great and mighty William Shakespeare left a mark that would affect drama, poetry, art, and even music for centuries to come.

He was born in Stratford-on-Avon, England, where he is believed to have received a good primary education and was exposed to Latin, Greek, and the Roman dramatists. He married at the age of eighteen and had two daughters and one son. Shakespeare worked as an actor and budding playwright in his early years, but it was one of his first poems, *Venus and Adonis*, that brought him to the attention of the public.

While he is considered now to be the world's greatest dramatist, Shakespeare may have considered his poetry to be his most important legacy. His sonnets were published in 1609, in a collection called *The Sonnets of Shakespeare*. The 154 sonnets contained in this volume are believed to be addressed to a dear friend and to a lady with whom he was in love, though this is one of many subjects of vigorous Shakespearean debate.

William Shakespeare was well-known in his day, but has become perhaps the most famous and admired literary figure in the world in the four centuries since his death. His plays and his poetry—and in the case of the poem featured below, his poetry *in* his plays—are a legacy on par with the Seven Wonders of the World.

❧ Favorite Poems ❧

"Let me not to the marriage of true minds" (Sonnet 116)

"Blow, blow, thou winter wind" (from *As You Like It*)

"All the world's a stage" (from *As You Like It*)

"When that I was a little tiny boy" (from *Twelfth Night*)

"It was a lover and his lass" (from *As You Like It*)

"The Willow Song" (from *Othello*)

Fear no more the heat o' the sun

Fear no more the heat o' the sun,
    Nor the furious winter's rages;
Though thy worldly task hast done,
    Home art gone, and ta'en thy wages:
Golden lads and girls all must,
As chimney-sweepers, come to dust.

Fear no more the frown o' the great;
    Thou art past the tyrant's stroke:
Care no more to clothe and eat;
    To thee the reed is as the oak:
The scepter, learning, physic, must
All follow this, and come to dust.

Fear no more the lightning-flash,
    Nor the all-dreaded thunder-stone;
Fear not slander, censure rash;
    Thou has finish'd joy and moan:
All lovers young, all lovers must
Consign to thee, and come to dust.

No exerciser harm thee!
    Nor no witchcraft charm thee!
Ghost unlaid forbear thee!
    Nothing will come near thee!
Quiet consummation have;
And renownèd be thy grave!

The brief and lovely "Fear no more" is spoken as a dirge by the brothers Guiderius and Arviragus in *Cymbeline*, one of Shakespeare's last plays. *Cymbeline* is known as a romance, a play in which tragedy looms all around but in the end is kept at bay. Lovers are reconciled, brothers and sisters reunited, and for all but the villains there's a happy ending. Of course! In act 4, scene 2, Guiderius and Arviragus come upon their friend, Fidele, in the forest and suppose him dead. They chant over the body, not realizing that Fidele is actually their sister, Imogen, in disguise, and that she is not really dead but sleeping, having drunk a magic potion.

In the play, the first stanza is spoken by Guiderius, the second by Arviragus. The brothers agree to speak the lines of the song rather than "sing him to the ground" because "notes of sorrow out of tune are worse / Than priests and fanes that lie." Guiderius and Arviragus alternate lines in the third and fourth stanzas, speaking together the couplets at the end of each. While the poem is not religious, its recital in the scene evokes tenderness and a ritualistic feeling. The brothers' performance of the song is comforting, even though the audience is in on the joke that this eulogy is being spoken for naught.

Still, the eulogy *is* beautiful and wrenching. I have spoken it myself at several memorial services, including that of my own father, who loved Shakespeare, and my father-in-law, who was a Montana farmer. I thought this was the perfect poem for a farmer, because the first two lines refer to the weather, which is all a farmer thinks about! And though we all must "come to dust," it is possible still to rest in this deeply comforting poem, even just for a moment.

An actorly aside: I once saw *Cymbeline* performed in a contemporary interpretation that featured the characters in this scene as ranch hands in the American West, and this eulogy performed as a country-and-western song. As I watched the play, I began to dread how they would treat my favorite moment. But it was beautiful and moving and took me happily by surprise.

Shall I compare thee to a summer's day? (Sonnet 18)

Shall I compare thee to a summer's day?
Thou art more lovely and more temperate:
Rough winds do shake the darling buds of May,
And summer's lease hath all too short a date:
Sometime too hot the eye of heaven shines,
And oft' is his gold complexion dimm'd;
And every fair from fair sometime declines,
By chance or nature's changing course untrimm'd:
But thy eternal summer shall not fade
Nor lose possession of that fair thou owest;
Nor shall death brag thou wanderest in his shade,
When in eternal lines to time thou growest:
So long as men can breathe, or eyes can see,
So long lives this, and this gives life to thee.

Percy Bysshe Shelley

The Radical

(1792–1822)

Although Percy Shelley and Lord Byron were great friends and among the most notable poets of their time, Byron enjoyed the status of a literary idol, while Shelley was perceived as a dangerous renegade. It wasn't until long after his death that he came into his rightful reputation as an important Romantic poet. As he cared more about his political passions than his popularity in his lifetime, this probably would have been fine by Shelley.

Born into an aristocratic English family, Shelley was educated at Eton and Oxford and began writing poetry as a teenager. He also wrote gothic novels and pamphlets of verse that reflected his atheism and radical politics, which promptly got him tossed out of Oxford. His refusal to renounce his atheism caused a permanent rift between himself and his father, which left him with no financial resources. This did not deter the nineteen-year-old Shelley from scandalously running off to Scotland to marry a sixteen-year-old girl, after which he settled in the Lake District of England to study and write, with intervals of travel to Ireland to participate in political protests.

In 1813, Shelley's first important poem, *Queen Mab: A Philosophical Poem*, was published by his friend, the editor and poet Leigh Hunt. This was the public's first introduction to Shelley's unique personal philosophy, a freethinking mix of atheism, socialism, and the advocacy of open relationships and vegetarianism. Throughout his life he was fearless about expressing these beliefs in his poetry, his associations, and his behavior. While the public romanticized Byron's persona and lifestyle, Shelley's radical beliefs only caused people to spurn him.

Shelley ran off to Europe with Mary Godwin in 1814, abandoning his young wife back in England. They eventually settled in Italy, where he enjoyed the most productive and creative years of his short life, creating masterworks including "Mont Blanc," "Hymn to Intellectual Beauty," "Ode to the West Wind," "To a Skylark," and *Adonais*, which he wrote to memorialize his late friend and fellow poet John Keats.

Shelley spent time in Italy with Byron and Leigh Hunt, discussing poetry and politics and making plans to launch a journal called the *Liberal*. Shortly after the first edition of the magazine was published, Percy Shelley drowned when his sailboat ran into an unexpected storm; his body was discovered several days later with a volume of Keats's poetry in his pocket.

Shelley, Keats, and Byron were the eternally youthful poster boys of the Romantic movement in poetry. They explored many of the same themes in their work, such as beauty, nature, creativity, and the imagination. It was Shelley, though, who believed that beauty, as expressed in art and poetry, could actually improve society. This was Shelley the passionate idealist—he believed that beauty was as necessary a component of human happiness as justice. This is the point where his radical politics and his poetry met.

⇨ Favorite Poems ⇦

Adonais ∝ "Ode to the West Wind"

"Hymn to Intellectual Beauty" ∝ "Ozymandias"

"When the Lamp Is Shattered"

To a Skylark

Hail to thee, blithe Spirit!
  Bird thou never wert,
That from Heaven, or near it,
  Pourest thy full heart
In profuse strains of unpremeditated art.

Higher still and higher
  From the earth thou springest
Like a cloud of fire;
  The blue deep thou wingest,
And singing still dost soar, and soaring ever singest.

In the golden lightning
  Of the sunken sun
O'er which clouds are bright'ning,
  Thou dost float and run;
Like an unbodied joy whose race is just begun.

The pale purple even
  Melts around thy flight;
Like a star of Heaven,
  In the broad daylight
Thou art unseen, but yet I hear thy shrill delight,

Keen as are the arrows
  Of that silver sphere,
Whose intense lamp narrows
  In the white dawn clear
Until we hardly see—we feel that it is there.

All the earth and air
    With thy voice is loud,
As, when night is bare,
    From one lonely cloud
The moon rains out her beams, and Heaven is overflowed.

What thou art we know not;
    What is most like thee?
From rainbow clouds there flow not
    Drops so bright to see
As from thy presence showers a rain of melody.

Like a Poet hidden
    In the light of thought,
Singing hymns unbidden,
    Till the world is wrought
To sympathy with hopes and fears it heeded not:

Like a high-born maiden
    In a palace tower,
Soothing her love-laden
    Soul in secret hour
With music sweet as love, which overflows her bower:

Like a glow-worm golden
    In a dell of dew,
Scattering unbeholden
    Its aerial hue
Among the flowers and grass, which screen it from the view!

Like a rose embowered
    In its own green leaves,
By warm winds deflowered,

Till the scent it gives
Makes faint with too much sweet these heavy-wingéd thieves;

Sound of vernal showers
On the twinkling grass,
Rain-awakened flowers,
All that ever was
Joyous, and clear, and fresh, thy music doth surpass:

Teach us, Sprite or Bird,
What sweet thoughts are thine:
I have never heard
Praise of love or wine
That panted forth a flood of rapture so divine.

Chorus Hymeneal,
Or triumphal chant,
Matched with thine would be all
But an empty vaunt,
A thing wherein we feel there is some hidden want.

What objects are the fountains
Of thy happy strain?
What fields, or waves, or mountains?
What shapes of sky or plain?
What love of thine own kind? what ignorance of pain?

With thy clear keen joyance
Languor cannot be:
Shadow of annoyance
Never came near thee:
Thou lovest—but ne'er knew love's sad satiety.

Waking or asleep,
    Thou of death must deem
Things more true and deep
    Than we mortals dream,
Or how could thy notes flow in such a crystal stream?

We look before and after,
    And pine for what is not:
Our sincerest laughter
    With some pain is fraught;
Our sweetest songs are those that tell of saddest thought.

Yet if we could scorn
    Hate, and pride, and fear;
If we were things born
    Not to shed a tear,
I know not how thy joy we ever should come near.

Better than all measures
    Of delightful sound,
Better than all treasures
    That in books are found,
Thy skill to poet were, thou scorner of the ground!

Teach me half the gladness
    That thy brain must know,
Such harmonious madness
    From my lips would flow
The world should listen then—as I am listening now.

This poem may be Shelley's—or any Romantic poet's—finest, pure poetic expression. The song of the skylark is not just a metaphor—it *is* that pure poetic expression, that "harmonious madness," of this world but heavenly too, and unspoiled by human encumbrances. The poem is a challenge to any artist to cast aside rational thought and earthly concerns and soar and swoop and sing in a voice as perfect and true as the skylark's. This is a wonderful notion, but it's not easy to do. All art, even great art, is fraught with some self-consciousness and weighed down by its context in the world.

One of Shelley's most gorgeous lyric poems, its words are vivid and evocative of birdsong, a simple tune that is almost maddeningly repetitive. The structure of the poem is a bit like the skylark itself, darting out of sight, coming back into view, rising, darting, and rising again. The many stanzas with the same verse structure are aspiring to the skylark's purity of sound, its "shrill delight." By the end of the poem, we share the poet's urgent, delirious inspiration and the momentary freedom he shares with the skylark.

Shelley does not neglect his deeply held belief that poetry—his "song"—can improve our lot. The bird is "like the poet hidden / In the light of thought / Singing hymns unbidden / Till the world is wrought / To sympathy with hopes and fears it heeded not." If only his song is pure, he can offer hope.

For all his rabble-rousing and unconventional ways, Percy Bysshe Shelley was an endearingly hopeful, morally optimistic man, more so than many of his contemporaries. He genuinely believed in the possibility of human happiness and used his imagination and his poetry to inspire himself and others to attain it.

>
> ✦·✦
>
> *Poetry lifts the veil from the hidden beauty of the world, and makes familiar objects be as if they were not familiar.*
>
> —Percy Bysshe Shelley

Mutability

I.

The flower that smiles to-day
   To-morrow dies;
All that we wish to stay
   Tempts and then flies
What is this world's delight?
Lightning that mocks the night
   Brief even as bright.

I I.

Virtue, how frail it is!
   Friendship how rare!
Love, how it sells poor bliss
   For proud despair!
But we, though soon they fall,
Survive their joy, and all
   Which ours we call.

I I I.

Whilst skies are blue and bright,
   Whilst flowers are gay,
Whilst eyes that change ere night
   Make glad the day;
Whilst yet the calm hours creep,
Dream thou—and from thy sleep
   Then wake to weep.

Edmund Spenser

The Faerie Poet

(1552–1599)

A monument erected to Edmund Spenser in Westminster Abbey is inscribed, "The Prince of Poets in His Tyme." Spenser would have relished this honor, as he was entranced by princes and legends, and King Arthur was his lifelong hero.

Edmund Spenser was born in London and went to Cambridge as a "poore scholler," where he studied rhetoric, logic, astronomy, Greek, mathematics, and philosophy. A fiercely ambitious man, both as a poet and a politician, he was appointed secretary to the lord deputy of Ireland, where he lived for most of his life.

Edmund Spenser was an influential poet whose style defined an entire period of English poetry. His epic poem *The Faerie Queene* was devoured by readers, both for its literary prowess and its political riddles. He showed it to Queen Elizabeth, who liked it and granted him a pension of fifty pounds (almost a hundred dollars). *The Faerie Queene*, an epic rife with heroes and villains, derring-do and wickedness, showed the Tudor dynasty as the continuation of King Arthur's line. Spenser slipped his own friends and enemies into the poem as faintly disguised characters.

The Faerie Queene has held up for hundreds of years, especially influencing the Romantic movement with Spenser's magic and melody. Milton described him as "our sage and serious Spenser, a better teacher than Scotus or Aquinas." Edmund Spenser was buried near Chaucer in Westminster Abbey and poets tossed elegies into his grave.

➤ Favorite Poems ◀

The Faerie Queen ❧ *The Shepheardes Calendar*

Epithalamion ❧ *Colin Clouts Come Home Againe* ❧

Muipotmos: Or, The Fate of the Butterflie

Sonnet LXXV
(One day I wrote her name upon the strand)

One day I wrote her name upon the strand,
But came the waves and washed it away:
Again I wrote it with a second hand,
But came the tide, and made my pains his prey.
Vain man, said she, that dost in vain assay
A mortal thing so to immortalize,
For I myself shall like to this decay,
And eek my name be wiped out likewise.
Not so (quoth I), let baser things devise
To die in dust, but you shall live by fame:
My verse your virtues rare shall eternize,
And in the heavens write your glorious name.
Where when as Death shall all the world subdue,
Our love shall live, and later life renew.

Edmund Spenser

This sonnet was published in a collection titled *Amoretti*, or "little cupids." They were all dedicated to Elizabeth Boyle, and describe the pair's courtship and marriage. The poem tells of a time when Spenser and his young bride visited the seaside and is evocative of Shakespearean sonnets, touching on a familiar theme lamenting our short time on earth. It doesn't deny that our lives are but a microscopic speck on the time line of the universe, and our love—so important to us when we're in its grip—even less lasting. But in a rhyme that is effortless, and language that is unhurried and clean, Spenser cleverly offers a way to think about it that is consoling.

The poets' scrolls will outlive the monuments of stone. Genius survives; all else is claimed by death.

—Edmund Spenser

This is a smart dialogue poem that is simple but profound. His love's name written in the sand represents all the passion and pain that goes into such a relationship, only to be washed away again and again, as if it never happened. But Spenser has a sturdier medium than sand—his "verse." By memorializing his love in this poem, he ensures that it will last forever. We are, after all, reading it now, more than four hundred years after it was written, and it's as fresh and as resonant as ever.

Sonnet VIII
(from *Amoretti*)

More then most faire, full of the liuing fire,
Kindled aboue vnto the maker neere:
no eies buy ioyes, in which al powers conspire,
that to the world naught else be counted deare.
Thrugh your bright beams doth not ye blinded guest,
shoot out his darts to base affections wound:
but Angels come to lead fraile mindes to rest
in chast desires on heauenly beauty bound.
You frame my thoughts and fashion me within,
you stop my toung, and teach my hart to speake,
you calme the storme that passion did begin,
stro[n]g thrugh your cause, but by your vertue weak.
Dark is the world, where your light shined neuer;
well is he borne, that may behold you euer.

Gertrude Stein

The Salon Poet

(1874–1946)

Gertrude Stein was a force to be reckoned with. In her *Geographical History of America* in 1935, she declared that she was doing the most important literary thinking of the era. Indeed, her intelligence, confidence, and imperious demeanor demanded attention—and fans and critics alike obliged. She bewildered readers with her experiments with form and language, but she was no one-trick shock artist. People may not have understood what she was saying, but they were stunned by the new and unexpected ways she was saying it.

In 1936, she said, "America is my country and Paris is my home town." She was born in Allegheny, Pennsylvania, lived for a time with her family in Europe, and eventually settled in Oakland, California, for the rest of her childhood. She attended Radcliffe College and then went to medical school at Johns Hopkins for a time. In 1903 Stein moved with her brother to Paris, where she made her home for the rest of her life.

Stein's house at 27 Rue de Fleurus became a salon where all the best and brightest artists, writers, and intellectuals gathered. The walls were crowded with paintings by some of her closest friends—Pablo Picasso, Henri Matisse, and André Derain. Stein was a sort of godmother to a generation of modern artists and writers. She pushed them to do better, supported their experiments, and always provided a warm room, a soothing beverage, and stimulating conversation. Her writer friends included Ernest Hemingway (Stein was his son's godmother), Ezra Pound, Thornton Wilder, Sherwood Anderson, and Guillaume Apollinaire. She wrote constantly, from essays to plays to poems. Her most popular work is the deliciously difficult *Tender Buttons*, a volume of poetry published in 1914 that is enigmatically organized by "Objects," "Food," and "Rooms."

Gertrude Stein is impossible to categorize. She was a fierce intellect, a puzzling writer, and a firm believer in simple common sense. And she was fearless. On one beautiful spring day during final exams at Radcliffe, she wrote at the top of her paper, "Dear Professor James [the famous psychologist William James], I am sorry but really I do not feel a bit like an examination paper in philosophy today." The next day, the professor sent her a postcard reading, "I understand perfectly how you feel I often feel like that myself." She received the highest grade in his course. Her recklessness extended to everything. A friend said of her driving, "She regarded a corner as something to cut, and another car as something to pass, and she could scare the daylights out of all concerned."

Stein famously called her writer friends in Paris a "lost generation." The term stuck, and it still conjures up an era of disillusioned but brilliant women and men, caught between hope and two devastating world wars. Stein was in France for both wars. During World War I, she and her lifelong companion, Alice B. Toklas, drove supplies to French hospitals, and during World War II she and Toklas hid in the French countryside. One night after the Germans had left France, Stein heard a man whistling on the street: "What a sense of freedom to hear someone at midnight go down the street whistling." The times were terrifying, but Stein faced them resolutely. After the war, she welcomed dozens of GIs into her home, saying she felt like "everybody's grandmother." She died in Paris, an icon of an era.

In 1905, Picasso painted a portrait of Stein. It is stark and almost gloomy, but she liked it. She said—in a way only she could say it—"I was and still am satisfied with my portrait, for me it is I, and it is the only reproduction of me which is always I, for me." In return, some twenty years later, she wrote a poem portrait of Picasso. Just as he tried to capture her essence on canvas, she tried to express his genius in words—*her* kind of words.

Listen to Gertrude Stein read "If I Told Him" at Salon.com (http://www
.salon.com/audio/2000/10/05/stein/index.html). It will change the way
you think of her. In fact, it will change the way you think!
Also look at the portrait of Stein by Pablo Picasso at
http://www.artchive.com/artchive/P/picasso/stein.jpg.html.

If I Told Him:
A Completed Portrait of Picasso

If I told him would he like it. Would he like it if I told him.

Would he like it would Napoleon would Napoleon would would he like it

If Napoleon if I told him if I told him if Napoleon. Would he like it if I told him if I told him if Napoleon. Would he like it if Napoleon if Napoleon if I told him. If I told him if Napoleon if Napoleon if I told him. If I told him would he like it would he like it if I told him.

Now.

Not now.

And now.

Now.

Exactly as as kings.

Feeling full for it.

Exactitude as kings.

So to beseech you as full as for it.

Exactly or as kings.

Shutters shut and open so do queens. Shutters shut and shutters and so shutters shut and shutters and so and so shutters and so shutters shut and so shutters shut and shutters and so. And so shutters shut and so and also. And also and so and so and also.

Exact resemblance to exact resemblance the exact resemblance as exact as a resemblance, exactly as resembling, exactly resembling, exactly in resemblance exactly a resemblance, exactly and resemblance. For this is so. Because.

Now actively repeat at all, now actively repeat at all, now actively repeat at all.

Have hold and hear, actively repeat at all.

I judge judge.

As a resemblance to him.

Who comes first. Napoleon the first.

Who comes too coming coming too, who goes there, as they go they
share, who shares all, all is as all as as yet or as yet.

Now to date now to date. Now and now and date and the date.

Who came first. Napoleon at first. Who came first Napoleon the first.
Who came first, Napoleon first.

Presently.

Exactly do they do.

First exactly.

Exactly do they do too.

First exactly.

And first exactly.

Exactly do they do.

And first exactly and exactly.

And do they do.

At first exactly and first exactly and do they do.

The first exactly.

And do they do.

The first exactly.

At first exactly.

First as exactly.

At first as exactly.

Presently.

As presently.

As as presently.

He he he he and he and he and and he and he and he and and as and
as he and as he and he. He is and as he is, and as he is and he is, he is
and as he and he and as he is and he and he and and he and he.

Can curls rob can curls quote, quotable.

As presently.

As exactitude.

As trains.

Has trains.
Has trains.
As trains.
As trains.
Presently.
Proportions.
Presently.
As proportions as presently.
Father and farther.
Was the king or room.
Farther and whether.
Was there was there was there what was there was there what was there was there there was there.
Whether and in there.
As even say so.
One.
I land.
Two.
I land.
Three.
The land.
Three
The land.
Three
The land.
Two
I land.
Two
I land.
One
I land.
Two
I land.

As a so.
They cannot.
A note
They cannot.
A float.
They cannot.
They dote.
They cannot.
They as denote.
Miracles play
Play fairly.
Play fairly well.
A well.
As well.
As or as presently.
Let me recite what history teaches. History teaches.

This poem is maddening and infuriating but utterly compelling to recite. It reminds me of some of Philip Glass's serial music that also has a hypnotic relentlessness. Still, it's fascinating, how the words sound crazy, in all their repetitiveness and mysterious relation to each other. One word or phrase is worked and worked and spun and riffed on to the point of exhaustion, and then on to another. Reading this poem aloud cannot help but force you to regard language and the way words can relate to each other in a whole new way.

⇥ Favorite Poems ⇤

"Red Faces" ∞ "In Between" ∞ "A Light in the Moon"

"A Long Dress" ∞ "A Mounted Umbrella"

I am also, of course, reminded of the work of Stein's friend, Picasso, about whom this poem is written. His paintings broke down shapes and forms, removing rationality, removing familiar connections of forms, and then reassembling to force an original interpretation. In this regard, this poem is a perfectly apt poetic portrait of Picasso, an original poetic likeness in the cubist manner.

Gertrude Stein used words in loops and circles, as in her famous phrase, "Rose is a rose is a rose is a rose." Her experiments with words were meant to recall "the excitingness of pure being," without any regard for the traditional forms and structures of poetry. She wanted to convey the living moment and challenged the reader to rise to the occasion and tackle her work head-on. I admire her intent, and even her accomplishment, but I have to admit, she really gets my goat.

Wallace Stevens

The Businessman

(1879–1955)

Surely no one who encountered the austere, dignified Wallace Stevens in his office at the insurance company where he worked all his life would have pegged him as a poet. But not only was he a poet, he also invented a completely original style of poetry, filled with imaginative flights of language, a sense of the absurd, puns and symbols that he insisted were merely the thing itself, not symbols at all.

Stevens went to Harvard, studied law, and eventually joined the Hartford Accident and Indemnity Company in Connecticut, rising to vice president. He appeared to be a typical middle-class executive leading a calm, orderly existence. But while he walked back and forth to his office, he was composing some of the most exciting poems of the twentieth century. As early as 1919, Hart Crane wrote of Stevens, "There is a man whose work makes most of the rest of us quail."

Although he lived in a town many might call provincial, Stevens enjoyed the trappings of a more cosmopolitan lifestyle. On frequent trips to New York City, he visited art galleries and museums, saw concerts and plays, went antiquing, and dined well. He was a sensual man whose appreciation of the finer things, from Stravinksy and Garbo to cinnamon buns and ice cream, found their way into his poems in offbeat ways.

❧ Favorite Poems ❦

"The Snow Man" ❧ "Anecdote of the Jar"

"A High-Toned Old Christian Woman"

"Sunday Morning" ❧ "Tattoo"

The Emperor of Ice-Cream

Call the roller of big cigars,
The muscular one, and bid him whip
In kitchen cups concupiscent curds.
Let the wenches dawdle in such dress
As they are used to wear, and let the boys
Bring flowers in last month's newspapers.
Let be be finale of seem.
The only emperor is the emperor of ice-cream.

Take from the dresser of deal,
Lacking the three glass knobs, that sheet
On which she embroidered fantails once
And spread it so as to cover her face.
If her horny feet protrude, they come
To show how cold she is, and dumb.
Let the lamp affix its beam.
The only emperor is the emperor of ice-cream.

I love Wallace Stevens even though I am often perplexed by him. He said this was his favorite poem, and although it's often included in anthologies, it's not easy to fully appreciate after just one or two readings. The precision of its language and the discipline of its form are rewarding on their own—and Stevens would be the first to discourage any "interpretation" of a poem. But I like to think about what's happening in it.

There is a plot—the first part takes place in the kitchen where ice cream is being made, and the second in the bedroom where a corpse waits to be tended. An unnamed person is giving orders: "Call the roller of big cigars" to make the ice cream. "Take from the dresser" a sheet to cover the corpse. The roller of big cigars is muscular, but so is the kitchen stanza itself, and sensuous too, with reference to "concupiscent curds," dawdling wenches, and boys bearing flowers. The second stanza is practical, addressing directly what needs to be done to the corpse. Where the first stanza is alive with people going about the business of life, the second is an unsentimental acknowledgment of age and death. The notion of a woman who embroidered fantails on the sheet that would cover her own corpse is sad, though. And her "horny feet" protruding from beneath the sheet— nothing looks more dead than a pair of dead feet.

The arc of the poem is what's compelling. Both the kitchen stanza and the bedroom stanza end with the same line: "The only emperor is the emperor of ice-cream." Even faced with death, we will still turn to our coarse appetites for food and beauty and physical desire. There's no inherent judgment to that, just a simple matter-of-factness.

Everything is complicated; if that were not so, life and poetry and everything else would be a bore.

—Wallace Stevens

Dylan Thomas

The Modern Romantic

(1914–1953)

Dylan Thomas was born in Wales and introduced to literature by his father, who was a university professor. He preferred his own course of study to school; this amounted to reading every word of D. H. Lawrence's poetry, and anything by William Blake, Thomas Hardy, and James Joyce, to name a few. He dropped out of school at the age of sixteen and worked as a reporter for a short time. His first poems were published in literary journals, and he was just twenty when his first book, *18 Poems*, was published in 1934 to immediate acclaim.

Shunning Auden's and Eliot's trend toward intellectualism, Thomas was a romantic soul who wrote nostalgic poems about life, death, and lost innocence. He once said, "My poetry is the record of my individual struggle from darkness toward some measure of light." But the boy wonder lived a more complicated life than the one depicted in his idyllic works; by the time Thomas came to America for a speaking tour in 1950, he was a celebrity known as much for his heavy drinking, carousing, and misbehaving at dinner parties as for his wildly popular poetry.

Critics didn't agree as to his brilliance; some found his work to be narrow in scope and redundant in style, likely the influence of the Romantic poets whose work he tried to contemporize. But readers and audiences loved his vivid imagery and his soulful yet modern use of language. Even with all the swagger and swill, Thomas did much to popularize poetry readings. Known for his dramatic delivery and mellifluous voice, he also performed numerous programs for the BBC throughout his career. For Thomas, poetry was always more than words on a page—it was musical and alive.

Too much poetry to-day is flat on the page, a black and white thing of words created by intelligences that no longer think it necessary for a poem to be read and understood by anything but eyes.

—Dylan Thomas

Do not go gentle into that good night

Do not go gentle into that good night,
Old age should burn and rave at close of day;
Rage, rage against the dying of the light.

Though wise men at their end know dark is right,
Because their words had forked no lightning they
Do not go gentle into that good night.

Good men, the last wave by, crying how bright
Their frail deeds might have danced in a green bay,
Rage, rage against the dying of the light.

Wild men who caught and sang the sun in flight,
And learn, too late, they grieved it on its way,
Do not go gentle into that good night.

Grave men, near death, who see with blinding sight
Blind eyes could blaze like meteors and be gay,
Rage, rage against the dying of the light.

And you, my father, there on the sad height,
Curse, bless, me now with your fierce tears, I pray.
Do not go gentle into that good night.
Rage, rage against the dying of the light.

This poem, about the death of a father, is quite poignant to me because when I lost my father, a great lover of poetry, he actually *did* go gently. But unlike my father, giving himself over to a peaceful death, the poem is about the fight to stay alive, the rage against time and deeds undone, and the loss of what has not yet been experienced.

The poem is a villanelle, which is a rhyming scheme that alternates between the last word of the first line (night) and the second line (day) throughout the entire poem. This is an odd form to use in a poem that's about rage and fight; it is traditionally used in sweet, light verse. You understand the poet's purpose, though, when you read this poem aloud. It lulls you even as it works you up to a fist-shaking fury. The tension between the subject and the form forces you to carefully consider what the poet is suggesting.

⇒ Favorite Poems ⇐

"Poem in October" ∞ "I see the boys of summer"

"In my craft or sullen art" ∞ "And death shall have no dominion"

"The Conversation of Prayer"

This poem is often read at funerals and memorial services, usually for fathers. This is understandable but also ironic, because a funeral would indicate that the fight has ended, while the poem tells us to keep on fighting. Perhaps that's because the poem is for *us*, not our fathers. In lamenting loss and anticipating grief, we can be inspired to make the most of our time. Good men, wild men, grave men—that's all of us. And thinking hard about what might have been while there's still something to do about it can be an uplifting exercise.

Walt Whitman

The Voice

(1819–1892)

Walt Whitman used to carry a little green notebook, bound with leather rings, in which he made notes about his everyday business transactions. But in the same notebook he wrote the four seminal words that would shape and define the rest of his life and work: "observing the summer grass."

Whitman was born in West Hills, on New York's Long Island. Like William Blake, he was trained at a young age to be a printer, a trade that turned him into a voracious reader and lover of words. He worked as a shopkeeper, a teacher, and a journalist before he turned to poetry; Whitman was thirty-five years old when he started to write the poems he would self-publish anonymously in 1855 as *Leaves of Grass*.

After reading the poems, the author and philosopher Ralph Waldo Emerson wrote a private note to Whitman saying he found the work to be the "most extraordinary piece of wit and wisdom that America has yet contributed." Whitman shamelessly used the Emerson letter to promote *Leaves of Grass*, causing Emerson to shy away from his initial praise. Whitman's audaciousness—both poetical and political—would cost him the unqualified recognition he deserved in his lifetime. Undaunted by criticism and lack of financial success, he continued to revise and rework *Leaves of Grass*, publishing eight different editions over forty years. It was pronounced complete by the author in the "Death-bed Edition" published in 1892.

In an essay published in 1844, Emerson had called for a poet to emerge and sing the virtues of our new country: "Our logrolling, our stumps and their politics, our fisheries, our Negroes, and Indians, our boasts, and our repudiations, the wrath of rogues, and the pusillanimity of honest men, the northern trade, the southern planting, the western clearing, Oregon, and Texas, are yet unsung." Walt Whitman read Emerson's essay and consciously set out to sing America's song and to become our national poet.

❧ Favorite Poems ❧

"Song of Myself" ❧ "I Hear America Singing"

"O Captain! My Captain!" ❧ "Song at Sunset"

"The Wound Dresser"

There Was a Child Went Forth

There was a child went forth every day;
And the first object he look'd upon, that object he became,
And that object became part of him for the day or a certain part
    of the day,
Or for many years or stretching cycles of years.

The early lilacs became part of this child,
And grass and white and red morning-glories, and white and red
    clover, and the song of the phoebe-bird,
And the Third-month lambs and the sow's pink-faint litter, and
    the mare's foal and the cow's calf,
And the noisy brood of the barnyard, or by the mire of the pond-
    side,
And the fish suspending themselves so curiously below there, and
    the beautiful curious liquid,
And the water-plants with their graceful flat heads, all became part
    of him.

The field-sprouts of Fourth-month and Fifth-month became part
    of him,
Winter-grain sprouts and those of the light-yellow corn, and the
    esculent roots of the garden,
And the apple-trees cover'd with blossoms and the fruit afterward,
    and wood-berries, and the commonest weeds by the road,
And the old drunkard staggering home from the outhouse of the
    tavern whence he had lately risen,
And the schoolmistress that pass'd on her way to the school,
And the friendly boys that pass'd, and the quarrelsome boys,

And the tidy and fresh-cheek'd girls, and the barefoot negro boy
   and girl,
And all the changes of city and country wherever he went.

His own parents, he that had father'd him, and she that had con-
   ceiv'd him in her womb and birth'd him,
They gave this child more of themselves than that,
They gave him afterward every day, they became part of him.

The mother at home quietly placing the dishes on the supper-
   table,
The mother with mild words, clean her cap and gown, a whole-
   some odor falling off her person and clothes as she walks by,
The father, strong, self-sufficient, manly, mean, anger'd, unjust,
The blow, the quick loud word, the tight bargain, the crafty lure,
The family usages, the language, the company, the furniture, the
   yearning and swelling heart,
Affection that will not be gainsay'd, the sense of what is real, the
   thought if after all it should prove unreal,
The doubts of day-time and the doubts of night-time, the curious
   whether and how,
Whether that which appears so is so, or is it all flashes and specks?
Men and women crowding fast in the streets, if they are not flashes
   and specks, what are they?
The streets themselves and the façades of houses, and goods in
   the windows,
Vehicles, teams, the heavy-plank'd wharves, the huge crossing at
   the ferries,
The village on the highland seen from afar at sunset, the river
   between,
Shadows, aureola and mist, the light falling on roofs and gables of
   white or brown two miles off,

The schooner near by sleepily dropping down the tide, the little
    boat slack-tow'd astern,
The hurrying tumbling waves, quick-broken crests, slapping,
The strata of color'd clouds, the long bar of maroon-tint, away
    solitary by itself—the spread of purity it lies motionless in,
The horizon's edge, the flying sea-crow, the fragrance of salt
    marsh and shore mud,
These became part of that child who went forth every day, and
    who now goes, and will always go forth every day.

Walt Whitman is surely the most glorious poet to read aloud, and this poem proves it. You read and become a part of the exuberance of the poem, an active participant without whom it would not be so fully alive. Not all poetry—even some great poetry—accomplishes that.

Whitman once said that the "proof of a poet is that his country absorbs him as affectionately as he has absorbed it." This poem is a near-perfect reflection of the absorbing of life, which was an idea Whitman came back to again and again. The child in the poem absorbs and becomes everything he looks upon in a day and in a lifetime. The universe is full of life ("the song of the phoebe-bird") and meaning ("the curious whether and how"). Whitman offers this sparklingly brilliant composite of impressions—the "flashes and specks"—so that we might open ourselves to experience.

This is typical of Whitman's spectacularly ambitious verse. He fearlessly creates a construct that encompasses all of life. You could pick out any single chunk from this poem and be reminded of a moment in your own existence. "The early lilacs," the "grass, and white and red morning-glories" or "the streets themselves, and the façades of houses, and goods in the windows"—all these objects, these memories, "became part of that child who went forth every day, and who now goes, and will / always go / forth / every day." To Whitman, this is how we become ourselves, by truly connecting with our own experience, by realizing, I *am* that child that went forth.

Whitman was a singer of words, a divine one-man chorus who celebrated his country and the human experience. He is considered the inventor of contemporary American literature, the first to forge a style that broke from traditional European forms and expressed the uniqueness of the American spirit. Underappreciated in his own time, elevated to a literary godlike status in ours, Walt Whitman is the voice of America.

from "Song of Myself"

I celebrate myself, and sing myself,
And what I assume you shall assume,
For every atom belonging to me as good belongs to you.

I loafe and invite my soul,
I lean and loafe at my ease observing a spear of summer grass.

And your very flesh shall be a great poem.

—Walt Whitman

William Carlos Williams

The Doctor Poet

(1883–1963)

William Carlos Williams may have had one of the most unexpected day jobs of any poet included in this book. When he wasn't swanning around Europe with Ezra Pound, or roaming the streets of New York with Wallace Stevens and Man Ray, or mentoring Allen Ginsberg and the other Beat poets, he was conscientiously tending to his busy practice as a pediatrician in Rutherford, New Jersey.

Born in Rutherford, he returned after traveling in Europe following medical school and settled there with his wife and two sons. Williams used his experience in medicine as material for his poetry. In 1938, he told Ezra Pound, "I've met a hell of a lot more of all kinds of people than you'll ever get your eyes on and I've known them inside and out in ways you'll never know." He listened carefully to his patients, who mostly came from modest means and mixed ethnic backgrounds. Their stories, hopes, and dreams were reflected back in tiny fragments and momentary glimpses in his poetry. Oddly, most of his patients were unaware of his career as a poet. To them, he was the small-town doctor who delivered and tended their children. To the literary world, he was to become one of the most original poetic voices of the twentieth century.

➤ **Favorite Poems** ⬳

"Spring and All" ∝ "At the Ballgame" ∝ "To Asphodel"

"These" ∝ "The Young Housewife"

Like Walt Whitman, Williams consciously sought to make a new poetry that was reflective of the tone and rhythms of American speech and everyday life. He wanted to redefine what it meant to be a poem, not for the sake of experiment but in the interest of authenticity. He was one of the leaders, with Ezra Pound, of the imagist movement, which sought to pare poetry down to its essence, to things, not ideas. He had a deeply felt understanding of what being an American meant, and focused on the details and objects of ordinary daily life to show his readers how poetic their own lives were. He had a hardy optimism that ran counter to the grim perspectives of T. S. Eliot and some of the other modernists. He didn't want readers to see how bad things were; he wanted them to see how beautifully real they could be.

The Red Wheelbarrow

so much depends
upon

a red wheel
barrow

glazed with rain
water

beside the white
chickens.

William Carlos Williams

According to his friend Kenneth Burke, Williams was "the master of the glimpse. What Williams sees, he sees in a flash." In "The Red Wheelbarrow," Williams turns one glimpse of a scene into a still life. He finds a single image and removes all of the clutter around it. The poem makes use of the page—the white space is refreshing, the words like drops of rain. He breaks up the words and gives them mystery; he doesn't let you skip over them too quickly. With only two colors in this sixteen-word poem, the scene is bright and clear. He gives us room and space to consider what, exactly, depends on the red wheelbarrow. By stripping this down to its most basic elements, he takes away the clues we might seek to figure out what it "means." Which is fine by Williams, who believed in "no ideas but in things."

Every corner of his daily life was fodder for Williams's work. He wrote about dancing naked around his house, "the salt ocean," the ice-man, plums, fire trucks, and "white summer days." He compares a young housewife to a fallen leaf and he speaks of "the tall grass of your ankles" and "flamegreen throats." His poems have collage effect; there is a sense of him seeing the whole world, plucking at the most real and most interesting bits to assemble into a tight little picture.

And what of the plums in "This Is Just to Say" and "To a Poor Old Woman"?

A poem is a small (or large) machine made out of words.

—William Carlos Williams

This Is Just to Say

I have eaten
the plums
that were in
the icebox

and which
you were probably
saving
for breakfast

Forgive me
they were delicious
so sweet
and so cold

To a Poor Old Woman

munching a plum on
the street a paper bag
of them in her hand

They taste good to her
They taste good
to her. They taste
good to her

You can see it by
the way she gives herself
to the one half
sucked out in her hand

Comforted
a solace of ripe plums
seeming to fill the air
They taste good to her

These two poems are the very definition of poetry, the captured moments that connect us through our senses and memory. The plums are "so sweet / and so cold," you can understand the indulgence for which the narrator apologizes. And your heart goes out to the poor old woman, sucking at a plum. Perhaps we can't know her hunger or the pains of her age or her poverty, but we share with her the "solace of ripe plums."

I am entranced by the phrase "They taste good to her," which is repeated four times in this short poem. In the second stanza, look at how it is broken at different junctures from line to line. By doing this, Williams is forcing us to consider very carefully that phrase, "They taste good to her." It also reminds me a little of how older people sometimes begin to repeat themselves.

Williams is the master of glinting, painterly little impressions that stick with you long after you've read the last word and put the book back on the shelf.

William Wordsworth

The Lake Poet

(1770–1850)

The defining moment of William Wordsworth's career as a poet was the day he met Samuel Coleridge in 1795. The creative combustion that occurred between them would turn the two men into the founders of the Romantic movement of English literature.

Wordsworth was born in the scenic Lake District of northwest England. Orphaned at the age of thirteen, he and his four siblings were raised by uncles. Wordsworth parlayed his excellent primary education into an appointment to Cambridge, where he studied without distinction and with little apparent motivation. In the summer of 1790, before his final year at the university, he took a walking tour of Europe, which seemed to awaken his poetic sensibility. He returned to France for a year after graduating and came back to England enamored of the idea of the French Revolution. He dallied for a while with political radicals like Thomas Paine and Mary Wollstonecraft, but it was meeting Coleridge in 1795 that marked the birth of Wordsworth the poet.

In July 1797, Wordsworth and his sister moved from London to a house in the Lake District not far from where Coleridge lived. They began a period of extraordinary collaboration, meeting daily to write and discuss poetry and critique each other's work. The result of this intense year was the publication of *Lyrical Ballads*, a collection of verse by both of them published anonymously, without attribution of the work to either poet. This volume amounted to a revolution against the literary establishment of the time, and featured some of the best work of both men, including Wordsworth's "Tintern Abbey" and Coleridge's "Rime of the Ancient Mariner." A subsequent edition of the work included a preface by Wordsworth that described a new type of poetry and gave a vocabulary to the Romantic vision. With this pronouncement, Wordsworth laid claim to the birth of a movement.

❧ Favorite Poems ❧

"Lines Composed a Few Miles Above Tintern Abbey"

"Ode: Intimations of Immortality" ❧ "The Solitary Reaper"

"The Daffodils" ❧ "The world is too much with us; late and soon"

Lyrical Ballads was indeed groundbreaking, but it also revealed an imbalance in the relationship between Wordsworth and Coleridge. Wordsworth was very conscious of his purpose by this point; he intended to be a standard-bearer for his burgeoning literary philosophy, while Coleridge only wanted to keep writing poetry. Wordsworth was not as generous with credit as he might have been; the newly prefaced edition of *Lyrical Ballads* featured his name alone on the cover. Coleridge was developing an addiction to opium, of which Wordsworth sternly disapproved, and by 1804 their brilliant friendship and creative collaboration was all but finished.

Wordsworth, Coleridge, and fellow poet Robert Southey became known as the Lake Poets. Wordsworth stayed in the area for most of his life, and as his reputation grew to grand proportions, the Lake District became a kind of mecca for adoring fans and literary wannabes. Wordsworth

William Wordsworth

continued to work, but it was clear he had his heyday in the years writing with Coleridge and just after. He took as a matter of fact his role as the dean of the Romantic movement, which kept him busy for the remainder of his life. His autobiographical poem *The Prelude*, which was written and revised several times early in his career and was dedicated to his friend, Coleridge, was published after his death in 1850. This work was later acknowledged to be his undisputed masterpiece.

Wordsworth was an intensely serious person who had an almost religious belief in his own purpose. His best poetry reflects a sympathy for the common man that is poignant in its simplicity: "We have all of us one human heart."

I wandered lonely as a cloud

I wandered lonely as a cloud
That floats on high o'er vales and hills,
When all at once I saw a crowd,
A host, of golden daffodils;
Beside the lake, beneath the trees,
Fluttering and dancing in the breeze.

Continuous as the stars that shine
And twinkle on the milky way,
They stretched in never-ending line
Along the margin of a bay:
Ten thousand saw I at a glance,
Tossing their heads in sprightly dance.

The waves beside them danced; but they
Out-did the sparkling waves in glee:
A poet could not but be gay,
In such a jocund company:
I gazed—and gazed—but little thought
What wealth the show to me had brought:

For oft, when on my couch I lie
In vacant or in pensive mood,
They flash upon that inward eye
Which is the bliss of solitude;
And then my heart with pleasure fills,
And dances with the daffodils.

William Wordsworth

What a splendid description of an accidental but perfectly believable phenomenon, happening upon a field of thousands of daffodils, at just the moment in spring when they lift their heads at once. And how Wordsworth savors this experience, coming once upon the thrilling beauty of nature, and recalling it later in a "bliss of solitude." I have visited the Lake District in England—it is the most verdant landscape and really does evoke an ecstatic response to nature. It wells up in you, almost beyond your control.

The poem has an almost childlike wonder, with the image of wandering "lonely as a cloud," dancing and spinning in a sea of daffodils. No child I know could resist this notion. This is an almost perfect example of a Romantic poem—adoring of nature, elevated almost to a state of rapture, and in a language that rings true.

Wordsworth defined poetry as the "spontaneous overflow of powerful feelings recollected in tranquility." When you measure this poem against that definition, you can imagine the process by which he wrote, his personal evolution as a poet sparking a revolution in English literature.

Come forth into the light of things, Let Nature be your teacher.

—William Wordsworth

Surprised by joy

Surprised by joy—impatient as the Wind
I turned to share the transport—Oh! with whom
But Thee, deep buried in the silent tomb,
That spot which no vicissitude can find?
Love, faithful love, recalled thee to my mind—
But how could I forget thee? Through what power,
Even for the least division of an hour,
Have I been so beguiled as to be blind
To my most grievous loss?—That thought's return
Was the worst pang that sorrow ever bore,
Save one, one only, when I stood forlorn,
Knowing my heart's best treasure was no more;
That neither present time, nor years unborn
Could to my sight that heavenly face restore.

William Butler Yeats

The Nationalist

(1865–1939)

William Butler Yeats loved County Sligo, his childhood home in western Ireland. He also loved mythology and folklore. He was passionate about art, politics, and theater, but by far his greatest loves were Ireland—which, he wrote, "must be the subject-matter of my poetry"—and the beautiful actress and Irish revolutionary Maud Gonne. Yeats would later say of his first meeting with Gonne, that's when "all of the trouble of my life began."

Yeats's unrequited love for Maud Gonne was truly a love story for the ages. She helped him found the National Literary Society in Dublin but also repeatedly refused his marriage proposals. His involvement with Irish nationalism was inspired in part by Gonne, and she was a muse and a central figure in much of his poetry. A cultural leader as well as a major playwright (he was a founder of the Irish Literary Theatre and its director to the end of his life), he received the Nobel Prize for Literature for his dramatic works in 1923. Today he is more widely known as one of the greatest poets of the twentieth century, having written many of his major works after receiving the Nobel Prize.

There are two periods of Yeats's work: his early romantic period, which was much inspired by Percy Bysshe Shelley; and his modern period, where his poetry became leaner and more focused, influenced by Ezra Pound. Actively involved in Irish politics and reform, Yeats was a passionate, political, action-oriented man. Though this was sometimes at odds with the contemplative life of a poet, these two sides of himself came together in poems such as "September 1913" and "Easter 1916." Yeats is buried in his beloved County Sligo, Ireland. Unable as he was to resist one last rallying cry, the epitaph at his gravesite is the last line from one of his final poems, "Under Ben Bulben": "Cast a cold eye on life, on death; horseman, pass by!"

Listen to Yeats read "The Lake Isle of Innisfree" at www.poets.org/viewmedia.php/prmMID/15529. It will go right to your bones.

The Lake Isle of Innisfree

I will arise and go now, and go to Innisfree,
And a small cabin build there, of clay and wattles made;
Nine bean-rows will I have there, a hive for the honey-bee,
And live alone in the bee-loud glade.

And I shall have some peace there, for peace comes dropping slow,
Dropping from the veils of the morning to where the cricket sings;
There midnight's all a glimmer, and noon a purple glow,
And evening full of the linnet's wings.

I will arise and go now, for always night and day
I hear lake water lapping with low sounds by the shore;
While I stand on the roadway, or on the pavements gray,
I hear it in the deep heart's core.

In his autobiography, Yeats wrote about the creation of "The Lake Isle of Innisfree": "I had still the ambition, formed in Sligo in my teens, of living in imitation of Thoreau on Innisfree, a little island in Lough Gill, and when walking through Fleet Street very homesick I heard a little tinkle of water and saw a fountain in a shop-window which balanced a little ball upon its jet, and began to remember lake water."

What a longing poem. This is not just a bit of nostalgia; it's a country boy's lament—a deep, almost painful yearning to return to the simplicity and beauty of a life in his memory that is far away from the gray pavement of the life he leads now. It's often a sound that triggers this kind of memory and longing in us, from a far-off train whistle to the call of a whip-poor-will to the "tinkle of water." These sounds and the places they take us back to are comforting, but they also let loose that longing for what's lost.

I picture a man sitting at his desk in a high-rise office building, thinking of the place he loves most. I see him thinking of standing up, walking out the door, and going to this place and never coming back. "I will arise and go now"—it won't really happen, but the man will imagine it again and again, as both a comfort and an ache he can't get rid of.

This poem was one of Yeats's first great works and is perhaps one of the most personally resonant. He invokes the place called Innisfree for himself and for all of us, reminding us that the heart and imagination are always able to return to a place where the cricket sings.

❧ Favorite Poems ❧

"Leda and the Swan" ❧ "A Prayer for My Daughter"

"Among School Children" ❧ "The Circus Animals' Desertion"

"September 1913"

Sailing to Byzantium

That is no country for old men. The young
In one another's arms, birds in the trees
—Those dying generations—at their song,
The salmon-falls, the mackerel-crowded seas,
Fish, flesh, or fowl, commend all summer long
Whatever is begotten, born, and dies.
Caught in that sensual music all neglect
Monuments of unageing intellect.

An aged man is but a paltry thing,
A tattered coat upon a stick, unless
Soul clap its hands and sing, and louder sing
For every tatter in its mortal dress,
Nor is there singing school but studying
Monuments of its own magnificence;
And therefore I have sailed the seas and come
To the holy city of Byzantium.

O sages standing in God's holy fire
As in the gold mosaic of a wall,
Come from the holy fire, perne in a gyre,
And be the singing-masters of my soul.
Consume my heart away; sick with desire
And fastened to a dying animal
It knows not what it is; and gather me
Into the artifice of eternity.

Once out of nature I shall never take
My bodily form from any natural thing,
But such a form as Grecian goldsmiths make

Of hammered gold and gold enamelling
To keep a drowsy Emperor awake;
Or set upon a golden bough to sing
To lords and ladies of Byzantium
Of what is past, or passing, or to come.

Permissions

Permissions

THE
CRIMSON
CAP

Ellen Howard

Holiday House / New York

Map by Leonard Everett Fisher

Library of Congress Cataloging-in-Publication Data
Howard, Ellen.
The crimson cap / by Ellen Howard.—1st ed.
p. cm.
Summary: In 1684, wearing his father's faded cap, eleven-year-old Pierre Talon joins
explorer Rene-Robert Cavelier on an ill-fated expedition to seek the Mississippi River,
but after the expedition falls apart Pierre, deathly ill, is taken in
by Hasinai Indians. Includes historical facts.
ISBN 978-0-8234-2152-7 [hardcover]
[1. Explorers—Fiction. 2. Hasinai Indians—Fiction. 3. Indians of North America—Texas—Fiction.
4. La Salle, Robert Cavelier, sieur de, 1643-1687—Fiction. 5. Texas—History—To 1846—Fiction.
6. America—Discovery and exploration—Fiction.] I. Title.
PZ7.H83274Cri 2009
[Fic]—dc22
2009025551

For Chuck
We go forward together.

ACKNOWLEDGMENTS

The author is deeply indebted to Robert S. Weddle, whose many fine books and articles on La Salle's last expedition formed the basis for this story. Particularly helpful were *Wilderness Manhunt: The Spanish Search for La Salle*; *La Salle, the Mississippi, and the Gulf*; and *The Wreck of the Belle, the Ruin of La Salle*. In addition, Mr. Weddle kindly agreed to read the manuscript and make suggestions. Without him, this book could not have been written.

A book like *The Crimson Cap* cannot come into being without the kindness of many people. Cecile Elkins Carter, cultural liaison for the Caddo Tribe of Oklahoma, also read the manuscript. Her help, and her book *Caddo Indians: Where We Come From*, contributed materially to my understanding of the Hasinai people of the seventeenth century.

Three writers' groups have listened to and commented on portions of this manuscript over a period of ten years, in Michigan, Colorado, and Oregon. I imagine that many of my writer friends are thoroughly sick of it, and yet they never ceased encouraging me.

Two skillful and perceptive editors helped to shape this story. My gratitude to Regina Griffin and Julie Amper.

Finally, my husband, Charles Howard, Jr., has always believed in Pierre's story, and in my ability to write it.

For all of this, there are no thank-yous sufficient.

Characters in This Story

The Talon Family

Pierre Talon

Maman—Isabelle Planteau Talon, Pierre's mother

Magda—Marie-Magdelaine Talon, Pierre's sister

Jean-Baptiste—Jean-Baptiste Talon, Pierre's brother

"Petit" Lucien and Robert—Lucien and Robert Talon, Pierre's baby
    brothers

Papa and Lisette—Lucien Talon, Pierre's father, and Marie-Élisabeth
    Talon, Pierre's eldest sister; disappeared or died before the
    story begins

La Salle's Household

Monsieur de La Salle—René-Robert Cavelier, Sieur de La Salle, explorer

Abbé Jean—Jean Cavelier, La Salle's brother, a Sulpician priest

Colin—Colin Cavelier, younger nephew of La Salle and Abbé Jean

Nika—Shawnee servant, given to La Salle by the Iroquois in New France

Another servant

An older nephew

Those Who Remained at the Settlement

Maman, Magda, Jean-Baptiste, "Petit" Lucien, and Robert

Eustache Bréman—orphaned son of the expedition's paymaster

About a dozen others

Members of the Rescue Party

Pierre Talon, Monsieur de La Salle, the Abbé Jean, Colin, Nika and . . .
Monsieur Liotot—Étienne Liotot, a surgeon
Meunier—Pierre Meunier, Sieur de Preville
Père Anastase—Anastase Douay, a Franciscan
Joutel—Henri Joutel, a retired soldier, La Salle's next in command
English Jem—Hiems, a German who had been a gunner with
    English pirates
Duhaut—Pierre Duhaut, a merchant
L'Archevêque—Jean L'Archevêque, Duhaut's servant
Five others, including La Salle's older nephew

Deserters Who Went to Live with the Natives

Grollet—Jacques Grollet, a sailor
Rutre—a sailor
The Provençal—an unnamed Frenchman from Provençe

The Hasinai

The Caddi—hereditary tribal leader
Na'-ta-ty—wife of the Caddi
The Caddi's father and mother
Bah'din, the Tamma—overseer and expediter of tribal activities,
    Meunier's foster father
The daughter of Bah'din—Meunier's sweetheart
The Hasinai townspeople of Nabedache town

The Spaniards

General Alonso de León—Leader of two expeditions [1689 and 1690] to
search for La Salle and his survivors

Fray Damián Massanet—Missionary priest on the 1690 expedition

Captain Francisco Martínez—Translator who was fluent in French

Padre Miquel—Miguel de Fontcubreta, one of three Franciscan priests
who founded the mission of San Francisco de los Tejas in the
Hasinai town of Nabedache

About one hundred soldiers

Pronunciation Guide

Pierre Talon	Pee-EHR Tah-LOHN
Maman	Mah-MAHN
Magda	MAHG-dah
Jean-Baptiste	Zhahn-Bap-TEESTUH
"Petit" Lucien	Puh-TEE Loo-SYAHN
Robert	Roh-BEHR
Papa	Pah-PAH
Lisette	Lee-ZETUH
Monsieur de La Salle	Muh-SYUH duh Lah SAHL
Abbé Jean	Ah-BAY ZHAHN
Colin	Koh-LEEN
Nika	Nee-KAH
Eustache Brémen	You-STAHSHUH Bray-MEHN
Monsieur Liotot	Muh-SYUH Lee-oh-TOH
Meunier	Muhn-YAY
Père Anastase	PEHR Ah-nah-STAHZUH
Joutel	Zhoo-TEHL
Duhaut	Dyu-OH
L'Archevêque	LAHRSH-eh-VEHK
Grollet	Groh-YAY
Rutre	ROOTruh
The Provençal	The Proh-vehn-SAHL
The Caddi	The CAH-dee
Na'-ta-ty	NAH-tah-tee
Bah'din, the Tamma	Bah-DEEN, the Tah-MAH
Hasinai	HAS-in-nay
Nabedache	Nah-beh-DAH-chay

PRONUNCIATION GUIDE, 2

Alonso de León	Ah-LOHN-soh day Lay-OHN
Fray Damián Massanet	Fry Dah-mee-AHN Mahs-sah-NAY
Francisco Martínez	Frahn-SEES-koh Mar-TEEN-ez
Padre Miguel	PAH-dray Mee-GELL

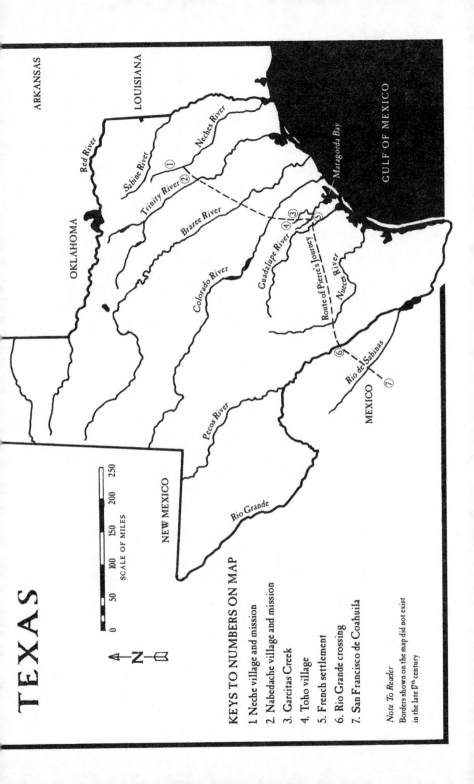

TEXAS

KEYS TO NUMBERS ON MAP

1. Neche village and mission
2. Nabedache village and mission
3. Garcitas Creek
4. Toho village
5. French settlement
6. Rio Grande crossing
7. San Francisco de Coahuila

Note To Reader

Borders shown on the map did not exist
in the late 17th century

SCALE OF MILES

0   50   100   150   200   250

N

ARKANSAS

LOUISIANA

Red River

Sabine River

Neches River

Trinity River

Brazos River

Guadalupe River

Colorado River

Pecos River

Rio Grande

OKLAHOMA

NEW MEXICO

GULF OF MEXICO

Matagorda Bay

Route of Pierre's Journey

Nueces River

Rio de Sabinas

MEXICO

Before

On a blustery winter day in 1685, a small boy clung to the rail of a sailing ship off the coast of what is now Texas, trying to see land. Sometimes, when the ship climbed to the top of a wave, he caught a glimpse of low-lying sandy marshes, crisscrossed by streams that glinted dully in the gray light. This was to be his new home.

The boy was named Pierre Talon. He was only eight years old, but already in his short life he had become accustomed to long sea voyages and new places.

Pierre had been born in Canada, in what French explorers of that time referred to as New France, which is now the province of Québec. He was the son of Lucien Talon, a soldier who, when his enlistment was up, had stayed in New France to take possession of land awarded to French soldiers willing to settle there. Pierre's mother was Isabelle Planteau, a destitute young woman recruited from the streets of Paris and shipped to New France to marry a settler. Pierre was their oldest son, though they had five other children. Robert, the youngest, was born on the ship on which Pierre now stood.

When Lucien Talon, unsuited to a farmer's life, gambled away their land, the family had sailed back to France. There, Lucien claimed to be a carpenter, though he had no such skill, and enlisted with an expedition to the New World led by the renowned explorer, René-Robert Cavelier, Sieur de La Salle. The sponsor of the expedition was no less than the king of France, Louis XIV, who had been convinced by La Salle to establish a colony inland from the mouth of the Mississippi River from which France might harrass the Spanish settlements and silver mines of northern Mexico. Lucien could take his growing family with him, and once again in the New World, he and his wife hoped to be rewarded with land and riches.

The La Salle expedition arrived on the Gulf coast in three ships but could not find the mouth of the Mississippi. A few years earlier, La Salle had led a land expedition from Canada to the Gulf of Mexico, following lakes and rivers across the continent to the Mississippi and down the Mississippi to its mouth. But the mouth of the Mississippi, which is a wide, low-lying delta with many tributaries flowing through it, looked quite different from the sea than from the land. La Salle could not identify the delta by sight, and his maps were faulty, so he miscalculated, and instead of landing the ships at the Mississippi delta, he went ashore at what is now known as Matagorda Bay in southern Texas, four hundred miles west of their goal. La Salle took ashore about two hundred soldiers, sailors, and would-be colonists, including Pierre's family. The largest ship returned to France, but two smaller ships remained with the expedition.

The fortunes of the settlers went from bad to worse. Both of their ships sank, taking with them most of the expedition's supplies and making a return to France impossible. For two years the settlers suffered extreme hardships. Many died of starvation, disease, or attacks by the area's natives. Some of the men, including Pierre's father, simply disappeared, either killed while hunting or exploring, or deserting to the natives.

During these two years, La Salle searched desperately for the Mississippi, knowing that if he could find it, he could journey to Canada to bring back help. But at last only forty or so settlers still survived in the barren settlement on Garcitas Creek. Many were too sick to travel. Some were women and children, including Pierre and his mother and four remaining siblings.

In January 1687, La Salle chose sixteen of the healthiest men and boys to join him in one last attempt to find the Mississippi River. Ten-year-old Pierre Talon was one of them.

PART I

PIERRE

CHAPTER I

January 12, 1687
The French Settlement on the Gulf of Mexico

Slowly, quietly, Pierre lifted the lid of Maman's sea chest. He glanced over his shoulder to see if she was watching, but her eyes were closed. She slumped against the wall of the hut while the little brothers crawled about her in the dirt. She did not stir.

The little brothers were smeared with filth. He could smell them from the other side of the hut, and he wondered where his sister, Magda, had got to. She should take care of them, if Maman would not. She should help Pierre get ready to go. Maman should help him . . .

He turned back to the chest and began to take out the things that Maman had hoarded. He would not take much, he told himself, only what was necessary for the journey.

Here was Papa's winter coat. Pierre's own coat was long ago outgrown and handed down to his brother, Jean-Baptiste. But Pierre would need something warm, and if what Maman said was true, Papa would not be needing it. He set it aside, smoothing its worn, thick wool.

He lifted out Maman's wedding sheets, which, after all this time, all that had happened, she would not allow to be used. He lifted out a few frayed and patched baby dresses, a saltwater-stained hat with a broken feather, Maman's other gown, and a linen shirt. He might need another shirt. No telling how long he would be gone. He put it on top of the coat.

Near the bottom of the chest, Pierre found Maman's stash of sea biscuits, weevily and black with age, but still, Maman had said they would offer nourishment if none else were at hand. He counted out a few of them, considered, glancing once again at Maman's sagging face, then took a few more and tied them into the shirt.

Baby Robert was whining now, tugging at Maman's bodice, but Maman did not move. Was she truly so deeply asleep? Perhaps she would have given Pierre what he needed, if she had wakened. But perhaps she did not want to wake, to see him go.

Pierre felt about in the dim corners of the almost empty chest, and his fingers brushed something soft and scratchy. He lifted it into the dim light from the doorway. It was Papa's crimson cap, the one Maman had knitted for him just before they set out from France. What was it she had said as she set it on his head?

"This cap will bring you good fortune, *mon mari* . . . and courage."

It had brought neither to Papa.

Pierre stroked the yarn stitches, tight and felted now by seawater and sweat. The cap's crimson had faded to a lifeless red.

Maman moaned, and Pierre, starting, saw her push Robert away. The baby set up a howl, and his brother joined his cries.

Pierre stuffed the cap back into the sea chest. He piled in the other things, save the coat and shirt and biscuits, and closed the lid. Then he backed from the hut, his finds clutched to his chest. As he straightened, he bumped into Jean-Baptiste, who was stirring a puddle beside the doorway with a broken staff.

"Go find Magda," Pierre ordered. "The babies are crying."

"Go find her yourself," said his brother.

Pierre looked through the drizzle at the muddy open space between the settlement's ramshackle buildings. The men chosen for the new expedition hurried between the huts and the plank building that was Monsieur de La Salle's headquarters. The five horses remaining to the colony were being loaded with supplies and trade goods. A few priests and women carried things from the storage sheds and helped to pack bundles. Magda was nowhere in sight.

"I must get my things together," Pierre said, struggling into the ample coat. He stuffed the biscuits and shirt into his pack.

Jean-Baptiste did not cease stirring the puddle.

"I want to go, too," he whined. Then he stamped his foot, like the baby he was.

"Monsieur de La Salle will not take infants like you on so important a mission," Pierre snapped. He would be glad, glad when he no longer had to put up with these children! But his heart lurched at the thought.

Was it not his duty to stay here at the settlement, now that Papa had disappeared? Now that his older sister, Lisette, was dead? Did not Maman, overwhelmed by these losses, need him? Did not his remaining sister and brothers need him?

"Family," Maman always said. "Family is all we can rely on." But Maman was not taking care of the family now!

"I'll wager those Indians you're going to will have food, plenty of food . . ." Jean-Baptiste's voice was quivering, and Pierre suddenly saw how thin his face was, how his chapped elbows and knees poked through his rags. Jean-Baptiste was only seven, Pierre reminded himself, and he was hungry and cold and exhausted, as they all were.

The sudden emptiness in Pierre's middle was not only hunger, he knew. He should take care of his family. He was not a child, like Jean-Baptiste. He was almost eleven, the oldest son, the heir to his father's duty . . .

. . . And yet, Monsieur de La Salle had requested him most particularly for this journey, because of his ease in picking up Indian languages. They would need Indian help to find the great river, the Mississippi, which was the only known route toward New France. And if they found the river, some of them would need to set out for New France immediately to bring back aid to the settlers. Others could enlist the Indians as allies, perhaps convince them to bring badly needed food and supplies to the settlement. Though the coastal Indians had proven to be their enemies, there was a friendly tribe, the Cenis, that La Salle had encountered on his search for the Mississippi last autumn . . .

Surely, going with Monsieur de La Salle was an even better way to save his family. It was up to those who were still strong to seek help for the others, Monsieur de La Salle said. And Pierre was still strong. He was young, but not too young. He was *almost* a man . . .

Pierre stood a little straighter. He tried to gentle his voice.

"Jean-Baptiste," he said, putting an arm around his brother's shoulder. "I cannot stay, and you cannot go. You must be the man of the family now. They need you." Pierre hated the way his voice trembled.

But Jean-Baptiste only shrugged away. "Magda is older than me," he said. "She can take care of them."

"Magda is only a girl—"

"Pierre. Pierre Talon!" It was the young gentleman, the one the men called Meunier. He was gesturing to Pierre to join the ragged line of men forming at the edge of the settlement.

Pierre cast a despairing glance at Jean-Baptiste. Jean-Baptiste should know that girls were weak, that girls could die, even as Lisette had died—Yet, so many *men* had died, too! Even Papa, Maman said.

Pierre saw the younger of La Salle's nephews, Colin Cavelier, splash across the yard to take his place near the head of the column. Colin had no divided loyalties. All *his* family, two uncles and a cousin, would be going on the expedition.

Pierre grabbed his pack. Was Maman truly not going to wake, truly not going to bid Pierre adieu?

"Tell Maman I depart," he yelled to Jean-Baptiste as he started across the yard.

But Jean-Baptiste only kicked at the mud to make it splash on the back of Pierre's breeches, and followed him toward the departing company.

Then, Monsieur de La Salle was there, emerging from the buffalo-hide-covered doorway of his headquarters. He strode to the center of the field.

People were crawling from the huts. Even the sick dragged themselves out.

"*Allons-y*!" Monsieur de La Salle cried to the men of the expedition. There was something fevered in his thin, hawklike face, something fevered and fierce in his voice.

He was their leader, a famous explorer, a favorite of the king. He was the father of the colony, the only father Pierre had now, so when he cried, "To our destiny!" something in Pierre's chest swelled, filling the emptiness.

Pierre heard sobs, cries of farewell, then Magda's voice calling out to him. His sister darted from behind a hut. "Oh, Pierre! Have a care for yourself!" She grabbed him, kissed him until Pierre felt himself go hot and red. When he pushed her away, he saw that she was weeping.

"What is wrong with you?" he cried. "We will return. We will bring help."

He saw the hurt in her eyes, but he could not make his voice less gruff. He could not soften now.

Pierre grabbed Jean-Baptiste and roughly kissed his grubby cheeks. "We will not be gone long," he said. He hoped it was not a lie.

Pierre shoved Jean-Baptiste toward Magda. He turned away, his eyesight blurring. Then he glimpsed movement in the doorway of their hut, the bright blue flash of Maman's neckerchief. She was emerging, his baby brothers dragging at her skirts. She straightened up and beckoned. Perhaps she would refuse to let him go!

What would the men, what would Monsieur de La Salle think of him if he ran back to his mother? He glanced at the column of men, already moving out, their leader at its head. Someone called, "Do you come with us, or not, Talon? What? Are you afraid?" Pierre's face went hot, and his throat tightened. Then he saw Meunier motion for him to hurry. What would Meunier think of him?

But Pierre dropped his pack and bolted toward Maman. She was gazing at him with dark, tearless eyes. He felt her arms clasp him, her cheek press against his. How could he leave her?

She pulled something from her bosom—Papa's crimson cap—and set it on his head. She pulled it down snugly over his ears, and though she said nothing, Pierre heard an echo in his mind—*It will bring you good fortune and courage.*

The baby brothers were wailing, sitting in the cold mud at their feet. Magda was sobbing, and Jean-Baptiste stomped away. But Maman heeded none of them. Her eyes were on Pierre.

"Go with God, my son," she said. Then she turned him, released him, gave him a push.

Pierre stumbled away. Tears mingled with the rain on his cheeks, and he gave his face a swipe of his sleeve. Behind him, he heard Maman. "You are not only your father's son, but mine," she called. "You can bring honor to our name."

Pierre did not look back as he ran to grab his pack. He sprinted behind the line of marching men and horses, the crimson cap on his head, Papa's long coat flapping about his legs. He was *not* like Papa! He was her son, too, and no one had been stronger, braver than Maman.

As he took his place at the end of the column, he could hear her voice still.

"Remember," she called. "Remember your family!"

CHAPTER II

Over the mutters and curses of the men, over the dripping of the rain, Pierre heard behind him the voice of the young gentleman, Meunier.

"We should not have abandoned the dugouts so soon," he called. "They would be useful now."

"Shut your trap," someone snarled, and someone else groaned aloud, but Pierre knew that the gentleman had made a joke. He was like that, this young aristocrat. He seemed to find something funny, or hopeful, in almost any situation.

But it was not much of a joke. They had marched in mud and water, sometimes up to their knees, for most of this day. The ground of this swamp *could* float a canoe! It was worse today than it had been any day since they left the settlement—was it only a week ago?

Pierre pulled his foot from the sucking mud and staggered forward, grabbing for the tail of the brown pack horse in front of him. The twisted trees and bushes pressed close about him, and the fog was so thick he could not see the man who led the horse.

"Eh, Pierre," the young gentleman called again. "Would you not like a canoe?"

Pierre turned his head and, at the same moment, stumbled and went down. The brown horse started forward, kicking mud in his face.

Pierre raised his face from the mud. Someone was lifting him, and he heard a laugh. "Leave me be," he mumbled, pulling away and lurching to his feet.

"I am sorry, *mon brave*," the young gentleman said, the grin on his face disappearing. "You remind me of my brother, who is a clumsy lout, if it must be told—I mean . . ." Pierre glared at him, and the gentleman seemed distressed. "I mean . . . Oh, it is I who is the clumsy lout. I should not have laughed . . ." He was offering a handkerchief, ragged and gray, but clean, it appeared. "Please, please, accept my apologies."

The men who marched behind them were shouldering past.

"Out of the way!" the man called English Jem snarled. "This march is hell enough without children hindering us."

The young gentleman drew himself up, and a haughty look, what Pierre might expect of an aristocrat, came over his sparsely bearded face.

"*Children* do not do the harm that errant *rogues* may do," he said, his voice clear and loud.

English Jem did not turn back to answer.

Pierre took the handkerchief and began to walk again, now at the gentleman's side. Pierre wiped his face, and when he handed back the muddy handkerchief, he saw that the gentleman was grinning again. Pierre felt a smile tugging at his own lips.

"Errant rogue," he dared to say, beginning, in spite of himself, to chuckle. "I wonder who you mean, monsieur?"

"Call me Meunier," said the young gentleman. "We are comrades on this journey, and I miss my clumsy brother, left behind in France. You can take his place."

Pierre's lip twitched. Again the young gentleman jested, for how could Pierre, a commoner, be comrade to a gentleman? How could he, a boy of ten, be comrade to one so much older than himself—sixteen or seventeen at least? And how could he take the place of a noble brother?

"I am clumsy enough," he admitted, "but not worthy, monsieur."

"Meunier," said the gentleman firmly. "Meunier. I insist."

The rain still drizzled down the neck of Pierre's coat. The mud still dragged at his boots. And the brown horse, with its handy tail, was far ahead. But now Meunier marched beside him. When a bird exploded from the bushes, or he heard rustling in the undergrowth—alligators or snakes?—he was not quite so afraid.

Pierre could not feel his feet. The aching cold had long since turned them to wooden blocks. He glanced sideways at Meunier and opened his mouth to complain, but he saw that Meunier also dragged his feet through the mud, his face white and pinched.

All along the line, Pierre could hear the men cursing. But Meunier said nothing, only marched. From time to time, his grim face lighted with an encouraging smile as he glanced at Pierre.

Pierre clamped his mouth shut. He shouldered his pack to a less painful place on his back. He drew his foot from the mud and set it down again.

Meunier was like Maman. She had always done what must be done without murmur. Indeed, even when Papa did not return from hunting, she had not complained. Even when Lisette died, and she slid down the wall of the hut insensible, she had not cried out her anguish . . .

Suddenly, Pierre's wooden feet were scrabbling up a slope where the mud was less deep. He was walking on solid, grassy ground. The horses whinnied and lowered their heads to crop the grass. Pierre pushed past the flank of the brown horse. His breath sobbed in his throat.

"We will camp here!" Monsieur Joutel, second in command, shouted the long-awaited order. A ragged cheer went up, and Pierre and Meunier joined in.

Peering ahead through the gathering darkness and fog, Pierre could just make out that they were on a high riverbank. The Mississippi? The river they sought? But no, it was too soon, and someone would have said so if it were. Pierre gazed across a misty, turf-covered field, surrounded by trees and undergrowth.

"Rest at last, Pierre," Meunier said, and Pierre could hear the tiredness in his voice.

But before they could sink down, Monsieur Liotot, the surgeon, laid a hand on Pierre's shoulder. "Firewood, boys," he reminded them.

Monsieur Liotot was Maman's friend. He had helped her to birth baby Robert on the ship, and he had done what he could for Lisette. It was he who had told Maman the night Lisette died, "Madame, it is no use. She is gone." It was he who had carried Pierre's sister's body away to be buried. Pierre remembered his kindness. Now it seemed to Pierre that the surgeon watched over him, too.

Obediently, he drew his hatchet from his pack and followed Meunier and Liotot into the woods. Perhaps he had two friends now.

Dry wood was impossible to find. Pierre and the others brought wet branches and damp logs, and after a while a smoky fire was smoldering. The men gathered around it, shivering.

Pierre wondered if Meunier might be tiring of him by now. Perhaps he should find a place near the servants, as he had on other nights. But before he could decide, Monsieur de La Salle himself began to pace among the reclining men, kicking their legs and shouting.

"A barricade, you louts!" he yelled. "This night is no different from any other. We could be murdered in our sleep."

Pierre saw the surgeon pull himself to his feet. "How could the savages find us?" he murmured. "The smoke of our fire is lost in this fog."

He was right, but Pierre noticed that Meunier only turned silently away to find brush for the barricade. Pierre followed him.

Monsieur Duhaut, the merchant, was muttering. "I'd as soon be murdered," he said. "At least then I could lie down."

English Jem hacked at a small tree and snarled, "La Salle is a coward, afraid of his shadow."

Pierre glanced back at Monsieur de La Salle. He stood at the edge of the clearing, his hands on his hips. It was not true. They were still in the territory of unfriendly Indians, and Monsieur de La Salle wished to keep them safe. He was as brave as a lion! Perhaps it was English Jem who was the coward. Pierre moved closer to Meunier.

Finally, when saplings and brush had been dragged into a rough wall around the camp, Pierre saw Monsieur de La Salle turn to speak with Monsieur Joutel, and the surly men tramped back to the fire.

It threw shadows across the campsite, making the men look

like demons from hell. Nika, Monsieur de La Salle's Shawnee servant, seemed like the demon chief in his scarlet coat, but he was spearing chunks of meat on green sticks to suspend above the flames. Meat! Today's hunt must have been successful. Pierre's mouth watered as the smell of roasting meat pierced him like a knife.

"C'est ça, mon brave," Meunier said in his ear, putting an arm around him. "You have done enough."

Pierre let himself lean against Meunier as the older boy shouldered their way between the others to find a place near the fire. As they settled on the ground, Pierre pulled off his soaked cap and squeezed the water from it.

"Take off your boots before they dry and stiffen," Meunier warned. He was indeed acting like an older brother. It was the kind of instruction Pierre would have given Jean-Baptiste.

But Pierre was not sure he had the strength to take off his boots. His feet would begin to pain once they warmed. So he lay, unmoving, while the cold wet of the ground seeped through his coat and breeches. Though the fire thawed his face and hands, he could not stop the chattering of his teeth.

Meunier finished with his own boots. He grimaced as he extended his feet toward the fire, and Pierre saw they were as raw and bleeding as the butchered meat Nika cooked. Then Meunier reached over and began to struggle with the thong that held Pierre's untanned footgear in place.

"I can do it," Pierre muttered, pulling himself up and tugging at the thong. He did not look at his own feet.

Meunier chuckled and slapped his shoulder.

"I told you you were like my brother," he said. "Clumsy *and* stubborn."

The servants were handing around portions of the half-cooked meat. Pierre forgot his painful feet and tore at it with fingers and teeth.

"Slowly, boy. Slowly," the surgeon called to him, but Pierre was so hungry he could scarcely take time to chew.

The men, though, found time to grouse as they ate.

"Look at the size of *their* portions," Monsieur Duhaut said, with a jerk of his head toward Monsieur de La Salle's family. "The gentlefolk do not carry their own gear, so I cannot fathom why they deserve more food than us."

Meunier shrugged. "I carry my own burdens," he said, "and some, no doubt, of yours." All of them carried goods brought from France by Duhaut for trade with the Indians.

"Those goods are mine no longer," Monsieur Duhaut said. "*He*"—He looked again toward La Salle. "He has stolen them from me."

Pierre looked across the fire at Monsieur de La Salle and his kinsmen. They were settled in the bower Nika had built for their comfort. La Salle's brother, the abbé, and the two nephews wrapped themselves in their blankets for sleep.

Their packs *had* been on the horses, unlike his own, unlike Duhaut's, unlike even Meunier's and those of the other gentlemen. So why were they fatigued? But Pierre put away the thought. Meunier was not resentful. As for the trade goods, what use were they to Monsieur Duhaut if all perished for want of aid from the Indians? Monsieur de La Salle had every right to confiscate them for the good of the company.

Pierre's belly was full, but his jaws, his tongue, and teeth still longed for the comfort of food. He sucked on a bone and put the other bones into his pocket to gnaw during the march tomorrow.

Around him, one by one, the men curled up and slumped down, asleep. The priest, Père Anastase, snored where he sat, propped against his pack.

Of La Salle's family, only Monsieur de La Salle remained awake. Pierre saw him wipe his greasy fingers on a linen handkerchief and carefully refold it into his pouch. He took out a small notebook, a quill, and a pot of ink.

Beside Pierre, Meunier turned on his side and stretched out a hand to touch Pierre's arm.

"Morning will come soon, *mon brave*," he murmured.

Pierre lay down and closed his eyes. On his eyelids was burned the image of Monsieur de La Salle, hunched over his notebook. He did not carry his own pack, it was true. But Monsieur de La Salle's burden was heavy. The whole colony depended on him to find a way out of the wilderness before they all died. It was Pierre's last thought before he fell asleep.

CHAPTER III

From then on, Pierre usually marched with Meunier, and the young gentleman seemed glad of his company, though Pierre did not know why.

Much of the time it took all their energy just to put one foot in front of the other, but sometimes, when the ground was less rough, the trees and bushes thinner, Meunier spoke, and Pierre found himself answering.

"It must be hard to leave one's mother behind," Meunier said one day. "My own mother is with the angels, but I did not like to leave my father in France."

"Then, why did you?" The question was impertinent, Pierre knew, but it slipped out before he thought. He would not have left Maman were it not for the chance to save her, he told himself.

"Why did I?" Meunier mused. "I am a younger son, you see. Our lands will go to my elder brother, and I must make my own way in life. Monsieur de La Salle's father was a compatriot of my father. When he offered me a place with his expedition to the New World, it seemed a way to make my fortune . . . and go adventuring." He laughed ruefully and bent to adjust his boot, which chafed him,

Pierre knew. "I must admit it," Meunier added. "I have had more adventure than I bargained for."

Pierre nodded. "I also," he said. "When Papa . . ." How could he say Papa had gambled away the farm? "When Papa . . . lost our farm in New France, Maman thought our kin in Paris might help us, but after sailing all that way . . . Well, I was only a child when we came to France, but I remember how their doors shut in our faces." Was he sounding as though he asked for pity? He hastened on. "Maman was not discouraged. She heard of Monsieur de La Salle. 'We will be rich with Spanish silver when La Salle claims that land in the New World,' she said."

"Oh, yes," Meunier said. "I thought some of that silver would line my pocket, too. Who would not think so, knowing the fame of La Salle? Knowing the king had warranted the expedition, financed it, given him ships."

The lost ships . . .

One had been captured by pirates early in the passage from France. "I should have gone with those pirates," English Jem sometimes lamented. He had been a pirate himself, it was said. On an English ship. Which, though he was German, explained his name.

"Perhaps we should have gone back to France with the warship," Duhaut would mourn. "But how were we to know that our leader had lost his way?"

The surgeon would speak quietly. "Nor could we know that both our remaining ships would founder in the bay," he would say, putting an end to it. "It is no use thinking what we should have done."

That was the sort of thing Maman said. She did not lose heart, but set about helping to salvage what could be saved from the wrecks. Then she had set her whole family, even griping Papa, to building the settlement on the creek, inland from the bay. When Papa railed against Monsieur de La Salle, she said no one knew better the way to the Mississippi River.

And Monsieur de La Salle had never ceased searching for it. For the last two years he had led exploratory expeditions in all directions. Only last autumn he had discovered the Cenis village, far to the east, where the Indians said they knew the way to a great river. But he had had to turn back then. Winter was upon him, and he had not men nor supplies enough for a journey to New France.

By the beginning of this year, 1687, there were only forty or so left in the settlement. They sickened and starved, like Lisette. They were murdered by hostile Indians, as Maman insisted Papa must have been when he did not return from a hunt. But Pierre had heard the men jest about Papa. "Lucien Talon has found solace in the arms of an Indian maid," they said. "Not only does the lazy coward avoid his share of the work, but he's deserted his family."

However Papa had disappeared, the fact was he was gone, and Maman and the children waited back at the settlement for the rescue that only this straggling band could bring. No longer did they seek riches or adventure, but only survival.

Pierre sighed. "You cannot eat silver," he said.

Meunier looked down at him, a startled expression on his face. Then he barked a laugh.

"That you cannot, *mon brave,*" he said. "That you surely cannot."

Pierre had lost sight of the men in front of them, but now, as he and Meunier rounded a curve in the buffalo track they followed, he saw the men gathered beneath the spreading branches of a great tree. They seemed to have stopped to rest, though this was not usual. It was one of the things the men complained about—Monsieur de La Salle never rested.

"Here are the straggling pantywaists," English Jem cried as they approached.

Monsieur de La Salle did not glance up. He inclined his head toward his brother, Abbé Cavelier, and called out, "*Mon abbé!* Duhaut! Barthélemy!"

"Nika reports a village up ahead," Monsieur Liotot whispered to the boys as they came up beside him. "La Salle is choosing those who will go first, to see that it is safe."

"Meunier!" La Salle called.

He had chosen Meunier. Pierre wanted to go, too. He had not yet had contact with the Indians, but he should be learning to speak with them. Monsieur de La Salle had wanted him to come because he had learned to speak with some of the Indians near the settlement.

Choose me, Pierre wanted to cry.

"Mon père!" The priest, Père Anastase, was chosen.

"Nika!" The Shawnee made a sound of assent.

Monsieur de La Salle paused, his eyes sweeping their faces.

Me, me! Pierre pushed himself in front of Monsieur Liotot. He felt Monsieur de La Salle's eyes measuring him.

"Pierre Talon," Monsieur de La Salle said. "It would be well for you to come also. These are not the people we seek, but still you can learn from them. Pay close mind to their customs. Attempt, if you can, the meaning of their speech. It will stand you in good stead."

Pierre stepped forward. The other chosen ones were adding more trade goods to their bundles, from the packs on the horses. Monsieur Joutel handed Pierre a musket and a pouch of knives and beads. As Pierre stuffed them into his pack, he grinned at Meunier.

At last, something was happening. In a village, too, there would be food. Perhaps even horses, which they sorely needed. And he would see Monsieur de La Salle do what he was famous for, negotiate with the Indians.

They marched half a league, then came to a well-beaten road, running east. They followed it, and finally Shawnee Nika pointed ahead and halted.

Pierre stretched to see over the heads and shoulders of the others. They were clasping hands and slapping backs, jubilant. What did they see? There, in a meadow beside the road, were horses! Perhaps the men would cease their grumbling if Monsieur de La Salle could procure more horses. So much depended on it. Their own were exhausted and rubbed raw by their packs.

Monsieur de La Salle was conferring with Nika.

"Watch this," said Meunier, coming to stand beside Pierre. "They will don their fancy dress now."

Even as Meunier spoke, Nika pulled from his bundle a fine scarlet hat and placed it atop his long black hair. Monsieur de La Salle shook out a ragged purple cloak and threw it about his shoulders. He looked back at the men.

"Look smart," he ordered. "We must make an impression." Monsieur de La Salle unwrapped his calumet, the Indian peace pipe. He straightened his shoulders, motioned them forward toward some beehive-shaped buildings ahead. Then he led the way, bearing the calumet as though it were a communion chalice, instead of a heathen pipe.

Pierre cocked his crimson cap. It was all he could think to do to "look smart." He held his head high, his heart stuttering, and tried to look dignified as he marched after the others.

CHAPTER IV

A commotion rose from the village. Dogs barked. Someone shouted. Voices babbled as people streamed from the dwellings to stand staring at the approaching Frenchmen. From the corner of his eye, Pierre noticed three young Indians sprint past them toward the horse meadow.

"Look," he whispered to Meunier, pointing. The Indians were rounding up the horses and driving them away. Meunier tapped the shoulder of the man in front of him, and Pierre saw the message pass silently to La Salle. Monsieur de La Salle paused, turned, frowned.

Now a party of old men, splendid in feathers and painted buffalo hides, approached. Monsieur de La Salle held out the calumet. The old men examined it gravely and nodded.

Pierre, halted with the others, stood soldier straight, trying to keep his eyes forward. He did not want to gawk like a child. The children of the village were naked. Pierre nudged Meunier, standing at attention beside him. A boy, easily as old as Pierre, stood nearby wearing not a stitch. Didn't he feel the cold? His black hair was drawn back with shell ornaments, and a piece of bone pierced his nose.

The old men were stroking the faces of Monsieur de La Salle and the abbé and Nika. Monsieur de La Salle and the others returned the gesture. Then other Indians stepped forward, and Pierre realized the boy had come up to him. The boy rubbed his cheeks, once, twice, three times, four. Pierre did not know where to look. At the boy? Over his head? Suddenly he realized his cap was gone. The boy was turning it over in his hands, grinning.

Pierre snatched it back. The boy yelped as though it had been Pierre who stole it. Pierre jammed the cap back on his head and held on to it with one hand. He glared.

Then a man elbowed the boy aside and began stroking Pierre's face. It was hard to stand without flinching.

"I think it is like the way we kiss one another's cheeks in greeting," Meunier muttered from the side of his mouth.

But it did not feel like a greeting to Pierre. It felt peculiar and threatening. He didn't know what to do.

The elders gestured for Monsieur de La Salle's party to come into the largest of the beehive dwellings. It was bigger than the headquarters at the settlement. These cane-mat buildings were as large and sturdily built as the cabins Pierre remembered from his childhood in New France, not at all like the flimsy camps of the coastal Indians near the settlement.

The women, who had hung back while the face-stroking greetings were made, now hurried away. Pierre hoped they went to their cooking fires, for he was hungry.

Ahead of him, Monsieur de La Salle stooped through the doorway, followed by his men. Children gathered, jostling for a glimpse within. The pierced-nosed boy who had snatched Pierre's cap glared at him as Pierre passed through the low opening. The men of the village followed inside until there was scarcely room for all.

Pierre kept his eye on Meunier and squatted as he did on buffalo hides spread on the floor. He resisted an impulse to pull off his cap, and he waited for his eyes to adjust to the dimness.

A burly Indian crouched beside him, and Pierre tried not to stare at him. He could feel knees pressed against his back, shoulders touching his. The greasy, sweat-stained coat of Meunier was in front of him. The air was thick with smells and heat and an uncanny silence.

Then a voice rumbled. It came from the oldest-looking Indian in the dwelling. He was seated a bit above them on a cane-mat bench. Pierre peered around Meunier. Was this the Indian chief? The man's small black eyes shone from a cobweb of wrinkles, and his mouth was sunken into a cavern from which only two snaggled teeth gleamed.

Meunier reached back to poke him, and Pierre followed his gaze to a place above the old man's head where he made out a dozen or more scalps dangling, trailing beads and feathers. He had seen scalps before, brandished by his countrymen after skirmishes with the Indians. But the hair of one of these was light brown, about the shade of Maman's hair—a white man's scalp—and Pierre caught his breath and felt his stomach turn. He squeezed shut his eyes.

But he could not shut his nose. Pierre did not mind the stink of his companions, the honest smell of sweat and dirt, but the Indians' smell was foreign. He tried to breathe through his mouth.

Then he caught a whiff of tobacco. The calumet was being smoked. Would it be handed to him? Pierre concentrated on its passage from hand to hand. He tried not to gape when, as the house grew warmer, the Indians threw back their robes. He wished he could shed Papa's coat, but none of the Frenchmen took off theirs, so he sweated until two young Indians began to remove the lowest mats that formed the walls. A breeze wafted through the openings. Pierre saw that some children squatted outside, peering under the mats.

Once again Meunier turned and nudged him, grinning this time, and Pierre took the long calumet. So he, too, was expected to smoke. He must put it to his lips, and he must not shame himself. Pierre drew in the fragrant smoke as he had often done when he sneaked Maman's clay pipe. He fought down an urge to cough and slowly exhaled. His head felt light, and his throat and lungs burned.

Pierre handed the pipe to the Indian beside him. He had done it! They had included him as a man, and he had behaved as a man. His hands were shaking.

Then he saw the Indian lift the pipe to the four directions, before he put it to his mouth. All the men had done that, Pierre realized. *He* should have done it! He felt himself go hot. Monsieur de La Salle's face was expressionless, but Pierre knew he must have shamed him. Pierre lowered his eyes.

The others would have one more thing with which to mock him. It was what he deserved. Monsieur de La Salle had told him to pay attention, and he had let him down.

When the pipe was lain aside at last, and the talk began, Pierre sat up, his back rigid, his eyes following every movement. Whenever the old man spoke, a younger Indian beside him moved his hands in sign language.

"All peoples, same sign, north to south, east to west," Nika had told Pierre when, some nights beside the campfire, he taught him a few of them. But now Pierre was able to catch only the sign of welcome. The brown hands moved fast!

Monsieur de La Salle's words and manner were grand. Even Nika, in his scarlet hat and coat, seemed to move his hands majestically as he put La Salle's words into signs.

The Frenchmen came in peace, La Salle told the Indians, from the Great Captain of the World, King Louis XIV of France. Much good the king's favor has done us, Pierre found himself thinking. But perhaps it *would* do them some good. The Indians seemed impressed, and even more impressed when Monsieur de La Salle presented them with gifts "from the king," though Duhaut would have said they were from *him*. They exclaimed over the crude trade knives as though they were damascened steel. They turned the strings of gaudy trade beads to catch their colors in the light.

Then two young Indians carried forward a stack of well-dressed hides and presented them to La Salle. It would be good to have boots cobbled from tanned skins!

But here, Pierre realized, the true task of the council began. For, useful as they were, it was not hides that Monsieur de La Salle desired from these Indians.

Monsieur de La Salle expressed his exceeding gratitude for so magnificent a gift, but . . . He shook his head. He regretted he had no means to carry the hides. His men and few horses were overburdened. He paused, and seemed to think. "Perchance," he said. "Perchance this noble tribe has horses to trade?"

Pierre felt the change in the room. The faces of the Indians grew unreadable. No one moved.

Silence.

When the old man spoke again, Pierre strained to understand him, but his words seemed meaningless. He lifted his hands and shook his head as though in regret.

Monsieur de La Salle's face reddened, but his voice stayed steady. "Surely," he said, "those were *horses* we saw grazing in your meadow?"

The old chief looked offended. He shook his head. He shrugged.

Then he brightened and began talking at a great rate. Pierre suspected he was changing the subject.

Monsieur de La Salle leaned forward, and Pierre craned to watch him. "Where might they be found?" La Salle asked.

Where might what be found? Horses?

The old man answered.

"Do you know their names? Are they Frenchmen or Spaniards? How long have they dwelt there?"

Pierre rose to his knees and leaned forward. The chief was not speaking of horses, but of men!

The abbé looked at his brother La Salle, a question in his eyes. Père Anastase murmured to Monsieur Duhaut, and Meunier was looking back at Pierre, his face alive with interest.

Monsieur de La Salle turned to his men.

"He says three Frenchmen dwell with the Cenis, in the village we seek," he said.

Pierre's breath caught in his throat. His hands trembled. His heart beat fast.

Maman said that Papa was dead, in battle with the Indians, that otherwise he would have returned to them . . . But Pierre did not think so. He had shamed them so many times with his fecklessness, his cowardice. It was hard to imagine him dying bravely in battle. More likely he had done as the other men said—run away. If so, could Papa have found his way to the Cenis, the very tribe Monsieur de La Salle now sought for help?

Three Frenchmen among the Cenis . . . Could one of them be Papa?

Chapter V

More than two weeks passed after they left the Indian village, and still they did not reach the land of the Cenis, the place where—was it possible?—Papa might be. One dull afternoon, Pierre stood on a riverbank, waiting his turn to cross. Below him, at the edge of the water, English Jem and Monsieur Duhaut settled a buffalo boat into the stream.

It was Monsieur de La Salle—and Nika, of course—who knew how to build the lightweight boats from the whips of willows and the hides of the buffalo Nika and others hunted. English Jem and Duhaut should be grateful they did not have to swim across the river, but Pierre saw that, as usual, their heads were together, complaints on their lips, sullen anger in their eyes. What an unlikely pair they were! Duhaut had been a respectable, middle-class merchant in France, while English Jem was but a baseborn ruffian. But their discontent seemed to draw them together. Duhaut nursed his grudge about the confiscation of his goods, and English Jem once again declared that their leader led the company astray.

"Who does he think he is?" Pierre heard Jem's voice rise above the muttering of the river.

Monsieur Duhaut's servant, L'Archevêque, staggered down the

bank, his arms full of provisions to load into the boat. Indians were swimming the five horses across. The old chief had refused them more horses, but he had offered some of his men to help carry their goods.

It seemed Monsieur Duhaut and English Jem were not going in this boatload after all. Monsieur de La Salle's brother, the abbé, and the priest, Père Anastase, shouldered them aside and were settling themselves into the boat—something more the malcontents would have to complain about. The abbé held so tightly to the boat's sides that Pierre imagined his knuckles would turn white. Two more Indians slipped into the water to guide the boat. Pierre wished *he* knew how to swim.

Another Indian, with a scar from his eye to where his ear should be, lowered his huge basket to the ground and gestured to Pierre to help unload it.

The basket was half as tall as Pierre, tightly woven of marsh reeds and caulked with pitch. Why not put it into the boat loaded? Pierre motioned, trying some of the signs he was learning. But the Indian grinned and shook his head, his bone earring swinging in the distended lobe of his single ear.

Pierre shrugged and got to his feet. Monsieur de La Salle had ordered them not to antagonize the Indians. "They are easily offended, these savages," he had said. "We cannot afford their ill will."

Pierre reached into the basket and began lifting out bundles. When the basket was empty, the Indian gestured for Pierre to follow him down the bank. He set the basket upon the water, where it floated, and turned, pointing to Colin Cavelier, Monsieur de La Salle's young nephew, who sat some distance from the other men. Colin was not much older than Pierre, though he was accorded all the respect due kin of a nobleman. Usually silent and haughty, he shadowed his uncles or his ill-tempered cousin.

"What do you want with *him?*" Pierre said, in what he thought might be a language the Indian understood. Colin could not be called on to carry bundles or unload baskets, as a commoner might.

The Indian made a sound of disgust and grabbed Pierre's arm, placing it on the basket rim, so the basket would not float away. Then he leaped up the bank to where Colin sat. On his way, he shouted to Monsieur de La Salle, who looked up for a moment, listened as the Indian repeated himself, then nodded.

"Petit Colin," he called to his nephew, "go with that man. He will take you across the river."

The Indian gestured. Colin shrank back, but then struggled to his feet and followed the Indian back to where Pierre stood, still holding on to the basket, his feet in the water.

"How will he take me across?" Colin murmured. "The boat is on the other side, and I cannot swim."

Pierre shrugged. "I know not," he said, and suddenly felt himself lifted off his feet.

"Unhand me!" he yelled. He was thrust into the basket. He crouched and clutched at its sides. It lurched, and he thought he would be dumped into the river when, *thump*! Colin landed, shouting, in the basket beside him. He felt Colin's arms clamp around his neck as the basket righted itself, balanced by his weight. Now Pierre was struggling, not to remain upright, but to escape Colin's choking grasp.

The basket was bobbing, low in the water, scraping along the river bottom. It was not sinking, even under their weight, but floated, the Indian's steadying hand upon it as he shoved it into deeper water.

"Let go," Pierre muttered to Colin, who had fallen silent but still clung. Pierre realized the men on the bank were laughing and pointing. He spotted Meunier. His friend would think him a coward, like Papa! "Let go, you milksop," he said through his teeth. "If you cease thrashing, we may not drown."

They were being thrust through the water, propelled by the strong kicks of the swimming Indian. Colin's arms loosened, and he grabbed the basket rim. Pierre could hear his gasps of fear, or was that Pierre's own breathing so loud in his ears? The water sloshed over the top, shocking him and wetting him through, but still the basket did not sink. The laughing men on the bank grew farther away. Pierre took a deep breath. If he drowned, he would not drown like a coward. If Maman could not be proud of Papa, she could be proud of him.

Crammed beside him, crouching, Colin trembled. His teeth chattered.

"Do not be afraid, Maître Colin," he said.

He saw Colin's eyes open and glance toward the approaching shore.

"I am not afraid," Colin said, but his voice shook.

And then the basket tipped, taking in a rush of water.

Pierre threw up his arms. He heard Colin scream. They were no longer floating. The basket sank beneath them. Once more, Colin was clutching him, and he, too, was clutching for some handhold. The water rushed up his nose, over his eyes. He had taken a gulp. He kicked, and his foot struck something. His feet scrabbled beneath him and found purchase. He stretched upward. His head broke water. He gasped in a lungful of air and choked. Then he felt pain in his scalp and heard a chortling laugh. The Indian was between him and Colin, grasping them both by the hair. Pierre realized he could stand. The water came only to his shoulders. He coughed and sputtered. The Indian let go, throwing him off balance. Pierre nearly went under again. But he recovered himself and shook the wet from his eyes.

From across the river, he could hear the Indian's laughter echoed by the watching men. He jerked away, his teeth chattering, and slogged up the bank where the two priests stood. The abbé was laughing, too—now that he himself was safely across! But Père Anastase was grave. Only his eyes twinkled.

"Are you unhurt, my sons?" he said.

Pierre did not answer.

"*Mon oncle*," he heard Colin cry as he rushed into the arms of the abbé.

Pierre stomped toward the tall grass, where, without warning, his legs gave way, and he sat down hard.

Chapter VI

It was the first and the last time Pierre crossed a river in a basket, and Pierre was glad of that. But it was not the last time they crossed a river, wading or by buffalo boat or crawling over makeshift bridges of felled trees. Pierre lost count, as the days went by, of the rivers and swamps and plains. But despite the mutterings of the men, Monsieur de La Salle must know where they were going. Had not he come this way before? Had not the Cenis Indians told him they could lead him to the Mississippi?

In the evenings, Shawnee Nika instructed Pierre in sign language and taught him a few words of the Cenis tongue. Pierre tried them out on the Indians they met along the way. Though the words did not seem to have meaning for most of them, the signs were understood. When Pierre signed for food, the Indians shared the cornmeal and dried meat they carried, but it was not much. Indians seemed accustomed to going without food, but Pierre and his countrymen were always hungry.

That was why, several days ago, when at last a few horses had been obtained by trading with an Indian hunting party, some of the strongest among them had been sent ahead with Nika to find food. Meunier had gone with them. Gone, and not returned. Now

Monsieur de La Salle and Père Anastase had gone after them. They would all be back soon.

They would be back soon. They *would* be back.

Pierre forced the tip of his knife through a scrap of goatskin, muttering the words like an incantation as he sat, cross-legged, near the dying breakfast fire. He was trying to mend his latest pair of foot coverings.

Meunier was much better at this boot-mending business than Pierre. Perhaps I should wait for him to do it, Pierre told himself. He will be back, perhaps today. Monsieur de La Salle will find him and bring him back.

Pierre had a sudden thought. *"Mon abbé,"* he said. Behind him in a rough shelter of brush, the abbé and his nephew Colin were repacking a bundle of silver communion vessels—a heavy bundle, which could be neither worn nor eaten nor drunk, yet took up space on the horses. It seemed a waste, but that was not Pierre's affair . . .

"Mon abbé," he said. "Has the twentieth day of March yet passed?"

The abbé looked up, pursed his lips.

"Yesterday was the Feast of St. Joseph," he said, frowning in thought. "Do you not remember? We said Mass, and again today for the Sabbath. That makes today the twentieth exactly. For more than two months we have walked."

Pierre put down his knife. "Today is the anniversary of my birth," he said. Was Maman thinking of him today? "I am eleven years old."

The abbé's frown cleared. "You will soon be a man," he said.

"*I* am almost thirteen," said Colin.

Did he think that made *him* a man? Pierre glowered. Pierre felt he was already grown. He had sailed the oceans from New France to

France, from France to this New World. He had worked in the settlement's garden plot, helped build his family's shelter. He helped Maman care for the family, even before Papa disappeared. He *was* grown.

But here, on this expedition, he was still young, younger even than that cockerel, Colin. He pressed together his lips and punched the knife through the goatskin.

"Hark!" the abbé cried. "Someone approaches."

Pierre leaped to his feet. "They are back!" he yelled, his heart blossoming in his chest. "Now we shall eat!" Meunier was back! Monsieur de La Salle was back!

Now Colin leaped up, too. The boys raced toward the rise, where they would be able to see the nearby river. Pierre exulted as his bare feet thudded on the ground. Colin might be older, but he, Pierre, was faster. He waved his arms. He would be the first Monsieur de La Salle saw when he looked toward camp.

But it was not Monsieur de La Salle. Pierre stopped on the rise, scanning the men fording the river. There were some Indians, leading horses. There was Père Anastase, his bedraggled cassock wet to the knees. There were many of the foraging party—Pierre made them out, one by one, as they splashed through the shallows of the ford. Surgeon Liotot was there. And there, there was Meunier! But where was the tall, gaunt figure of La Salle? Where was the scarlet coat of Nika?

"Is not my cousin among them?" asked Colin, panting. He leaned over, his hands on his knees, to catch his breath. "Where is my uncle?"

Where *was* Colin's cousin? Pierre had forgotten to look for him. None of La Salle's absent household was returning, it seemed.

Monsieur Duhaut and English Jem were in the lead. There was something strange in their faces. Something . . . furtive?

"Where is Monsieur de La Salle?" others were demanding as they joined the boys on the rise. "Did he not find our men?"

"He must have," Pierre muttered. "Père Anastase went with him, and he is coming back."

It did not make sense. All were there, save La Salle and his nephew and servants. Why did Père Anastase walk so heavily, his shoulders bowed, his face hidden in his cowl? Why did Meunier and Monsieur Liotot look so grim?

"Hail!" Pierre greeted them.

But no one, not even Meunier, answered.

"Where is my uncle?" cried Colin. "Where is my cousin?"

English Jem pushed past, knocking Colin aside. Pierre was shocked by such rudeness to a kinsman of their leader.

"We would speak to the abbé," said Monsieur Duhaut, his voice too loud and shrill. He brushed past, following hard on the heels of English Jem.

One by one, the others tramped past without greeting. Pierre looked into the face of Père Anastase. Tear tracks stained his cheeks. His eyes were bloodshot and swollen.

Pierre's throat tightened. He caught at Meunier's sleeve, falling in beside him. Meunier would tell him what was wrong. But Meunier would not meet his eyes. He jerked his arm away and hastened his step.

"Meunier . . ." Pierre said.

Colin's face was pale. His eyes were wide and scared. Pierre slapped him on the back, as Meunier should have slapped *him* in reassurance.

"Come along," he said. "We will not learn anything standing here, staring at their backs."

By the time Pierre reached the campsite, most of the returning men had sunk to the ground around the dead fire. Monsieur Duhaut and English Jem had hurried over to the abbé. Père Anastase had followed. The four men huddled together out of earshot of the others. Colin went hurrying toward them, calling out, *"Mon oncle!"*

But the abbé did not answer. Monsieur Duhaut's lips were moving, and the abbé cried out and sank to his knees, his hands held out as though in supplication. Père Anastase knelt down beside him and put an arm around his shoulders. Colin faltered and stared.

"Where is Monsieur Joutel?" Duhaut's servant, L'Archevêque, murmured in Pierre's ear.

Pierre pointed in the direction of the meadow, where Joutel had gone to care for the horses. L'Archevêque nodded and slipped away. Pierre looked after him. Monsieur Joutel had saved the young man more than once from his master's unreasonable wrath. Was he going to warn Joutel of some danger?

Pierre hurried to Meunier and squatted down beside him.

"What is it?" he demanded. "What has happened?"

Meunier only shook his head.

But Liotot beckoned. Pierre moved closer to him, keeping an eye on the tableau in the shelter. Monsieur Duhaut was still talking, gesturing in agitation. The abbé looked appalled.

"This is none of your affair," the surgeon whispered. "Pretend you know nothing."

"But I *do* know nothing," Pierre protested. "Tell me. What has happened?"

Liotot's gaze lowered. A muscle in his jaw jerked, then he spoke. "Monsieur de La Salle is dead."

CHAPTER VII

Other men died. Pierre had seen them die. But Monsieur de La Salle? Dead? All that day, all that night, Pierre lay awake with a sick, hollow place where his belly should be.

Dead? Dead? Not only dead, but *murdered*?

"It was my master Duhaut," L'Archevêque told them. "Duhaut shot him."

Pierre could not believe it.

"But where was Nika?" he asked. "Nika watched over Monsieur de La Salle like a mastiff."

L'Archevêque sighed. "Nika was already dead . . . and the nephew and poor Saget, who served him. They killed them the night before. As they slept. With axes."

Pierre closed his eyes against the image.

"Who?" he demanded. "Who killed Nika? Who dared to kill the kinsman of Monsieur de La Salle?"

No one would say. Not even Meunier.

"You do not want to know," he said. "It is better you not know."

Pierre searched his eyes for the merry companion of only days ago, but found only shock.

"It was all the fault of Duhaut and that pirate, English Jem, and their endless complaining," said Meunier with bitterness in his voice.

The earth seemed to tilt beneath Pierre's feet.

Then he heard Monsieur Duhaut himself admit it, almost boast of it. "La Salle was leading us to our deaths," he said. "We are better without him."

Better without him? Who would lead them now? Duhaut, who swaggered and gave himself airs, strutting about in La Salle's best coat? That brute, English Jem? The terrified priests, or the stunned Joutel? Perhaps Surgeon Liotot? But he, with the others, faltered.

For some days they dithered in camp. The Indians melted away, taking some of the horses with them. Without Nika, the hunters brought back little game. And Nika had also been their guide and interpreter. Now they were blind and deaf and dumb. Now there was no one to serve the gentlemen, except for L'Archevêque, and he had developed a reluctance to serve any but Monsieur Joutel.

One evening as they sat around the dead fire, Duhaut and English Jem began arguing. Duhaut thought they could not be far from the Cenis village, and so they should keep on. Jem wanted to return to the settlement.

"We know the way back," he snarled, "and we do not know with certainty the way forward. It is stupid to keep on following La Salle's plans."

"Stupid!" Duhaut's laugh was ugly. "La Salle is dead, and still you dispute with him."

But no one laughed with Duhaut. The other men sat, heads sunk into their shoulders, and stared at the ground. He glared around at them.

"Where is that worthless boy, L'Archevêque?" he demanded. "He should build up the fire and heat some water at least, to warm our bellies."

Pierre was gnawing on his last sea biscuit. If the others saw it, they might wrest it from him, so he had drawn into the shadow of the shelter.

"You sent the boy to check on the horses," observed Monsieur Joutel.

"We could eat one of the horses—" English Jem turned his head, suddenly alert.

Pierre stuffed the last crumbs of the biscuit into his mouth and peered out.

"Messieurs!" L'Archevêque stumbled out of the thicket. "Messieurs, we have guests."

Behind him, two stocky Indians emerged. They were laden with packs, as were the women who came after them. All four had faces darkened by tattoos.

"Pierre!" L'Archevêque called. "Can you understand the signs of these savages? I cannot make them out."

The eyes of all the party turned toward Pierre. He wondered if there were crumbs about his mouth, to give him away. But they did not seem to notice.

"Yes, Pierre," said Monsieur Liotot. "It was you Nika was teaching. Ask them if they know where the Cenis village lies."

Pierre ducked out of the shelter and straightened his back.

Père Anastase reached out to pull him forward. "Go on, my son. Give it a try."

Pierre swallowed. His eyes darted about, looking for escape. He could not remember a single sign or word that Nika had taught him! Then his eyes were drawn to the hands of the taller of the Indians. He was moving them in a sign. The sign for peace. The sign for friend.

Oh, yes!

Pierre stepped forward. Awkwardly, his hands copied the

Indian's signs. Peace. Friend. Suddenly he remembered what Nika had shown him. Welcome. He pointed to himself, to his companions. "Frenchmen," he signed.

The Indian responded. His arm gestured proudly to himself and the other Indian. His hands moved.

"Cenis," he signed.

The Cenis men and their wives would lead them to their village. When Pierre told this to the others, they slapped his back and capered about like madmen.

"You are our savior, *mon brave*," Meunier said, his eyes alight for the first time in days.

Even English Jem grudgingly conceded. "We need food and horses," he said.

"We will go to the Cenis village," Duhaut ordered, taking command.

Pierre saw Monsieur Joutel nod. "There we can find guides to the Mississippi," he said quietly, but the other two paid him no heed. They did not speak of finding the way to New France. They did not speak of bringing aid to the settlement where Maman and the children waited. They seemed only to think of themselves. Abbé Jean seemed so terrified of meeting his brother's fate that he had already sworn fealty to the murderers. Even Monsieur Liotot and Meunier said nothing of their mission. Could they also have forgotten the rescue of the colony, duty to La Salle, or the king, or God? . . . Had they forgotten all that Monsieur de La Salle had done for them?

But Pierre did not speak either. How could a boy speak his mind among men?

The march—and the rain—resumed the next day. The men strode behind their Indian guides, and Pierre marched with them.

Perhaps when they reached the Cenis, when they were once more fed and rested, they would remember their mission, Pierre told himself.

But he found it harder and harder to put one foot in front of the other. He hunched his shoulders against the rain. His hair was plastered to his forehead and neck, and his crimson cap was sodden. He could feel the wetness seep inside his clothes. His teeth chattered. His head felt hot. His nose ran. Pierre stumbled, and Meunier reached out a steadying hand.

"Are you unwell, *mon brave*?" he asked.

Pierre shook his head and managed a weak smile. Once again, the old Meunier marched beside him.

"Think of a bed beside the fire in a Cenis hut," Meunier said. "We will give you a place of honor, since you are our interpreter now."

A warm bed beside a fire . . . Pierre's thoughts came at last to this. A warm bed . . . a fire . . . His head was heavy. He staggered forward, his eyes closed against the rain—

He woke, jarred as he landed in the mud, the breath knocked out of him.

"Pierre!" he heard Meunier cry. Then the surgeon and Meunier were kneeling beside him.

"Pierre?" Monsieur Liotot was saying. "Can you speak, boy?"

Pierre could not speak. He felt himself lifted and knew he was in Monsieur Liotot's arms.

"You are feverish," the surgeon said. His voice sounded accusing to Pierre. "You are ill!"

Ill? Yes, that was it. That was why his head whirled and he felt himself shaking. If he were ill, he no longer need put one foot in front of the other.

Pierre closed his eyes.

CHAPTER VIII

Coolness moved across Pierre's skin. He was naked. Where were his clothes? He tried to open his eyes, to lift his head, but someone pressed him back into softness . . .

. . . *"Mon Dieu,* save my child," Maman was crying. She was crying for Lisette, and her brow was furrowed, her eyes tight shut. Lisette was dying . . . No, it was Pierre who was dying. Maman's mouth stretched open. *"Mon Dieu, mon Dieu!"* The cry became a scream, the scream a shriek. Her mouth was like a cave, and he was being pulled into it . . .

. . . He was dead. His arms and legs were stiff and cold. He could not turn his head, open his eyes. He could not cry out. He was a coward, like Papa, and he was dead . . .

. . . Very far away, someone was singing. It was a strange, haunting song. He had never heard anything like it, and yet it comforted him. Who was singing? Maman . . . ?

His mouth was full of something pleasant. He swallowed and felt it pass into his belly. It strengthened him. He wanted more. He opened his mouth . . .

. . . Maman would not speak to him. He stretched out his arms to her, but she turned away. Her back was rigid, and he cried to it. I am sorry I left you, he cried. *Je regret, je regret!*

Pierre opened his eyes, but still he saw darkness. He smelled wood smoke and cooking food and something else . . . What was it? He turned his head. There was a light, a fire burning low. A shadow moved between him and the fire. He lifted his head, felt the pain that sliced through it like a rapier . . . Darkness.

Pierre could hear voices. He strained to find meaning in them, but there was none. He felt someone lean over him and he opened his eyes.

"Who is it?" he said, and was surprised at the croaking he made. "Maman?"

The voice spoke again. This time he could hear it clearly. A woman's voice. But still there was no meaning.

"Maman?" he repeated. He realized he was looking up into two gleaming eyes, a face over his.

The face spoke. When the head turned, Pierre saw coils of plaited hair, black and shining in the firelight. Maman's hair was brown. Her face was not so round and dark. It was not Maman. He wanted to weep.

Another voice spoke far above him. He heard the swish of cloth. Then it was Père Anastase who bent over him.

"You return to life, my son," the priest said.

"Where . . . ?" Pierre said.

"In the village of the Cenis. You have been ill. We thought you near death many times, despite the surgeon's ministrations. But the nursing of this good woman brought you back to life."

Pierre shook his head feebly. The priest's face swam in the dimness, before he turned away and nodded at someone behind him.

"She has a healing drink for you," the priest said. "Let me help you to sit up."

Pierre *was* thirsty. With the aid of the priest, he struggled up and put his head in his hands.

The woman's voice spoke again, through the whirling in his head. It was the voice he remembered from his dreams. It sang, he remembered, sang a lullaby. Like Maman . . .

The woman held a gourd to Pierre's lips. Black tattooed streaks ran from the parting in her hair to her chin, and there were shells in her ears. She was young.

"Drink," he thought he heard her say, though, of course, she did not say the French word. She was an Indian woman.

"Dee-dah-yahk'cah," she said.

As Père Anastase supported him, the strengthening liquid flowed into Pierre's mouth. It was good, and he grasped the gourd with his own hands and swallowed again and again, greedily, until he choked.

The young woman held up her hand, palm forward, and said something. "Slowly," he imagined she was saying, as Monsieur Liotot used to say to him. "Drink slowly."

Then she rose and was gone.

Père Anastase lowered him back onto his bed. It was a narrow bed, Pierre realized, built against the wall of an Indian dwelling. He lay, wrapped in soft hides, the furred sides next to his skin. He was naked, and he blushed to realize it. His skin felt strange and smelled sweet when he held up an arm and sniffed it.

"I rejoice you have wakened, my son," Père Anastase was saying, "before we must depart."

Pierre blinked. Were they going somewhere? Somewhere away from this comfort, this safety?

"Depart?"

Père Anastase nodded. Pierre saw how thin and creased his face had become.

"Yes," he said. "Much has happened while you tarried in the valley of the shadow. There have been quarrels, and Monsieur Duhaut is dead—"

"Dead?" Pierre whispered. "Monsieur Duhaut was also ill?"

"*Non*. . . not ill." The priest hesitated. "There is much to be told, my son. Are you strong enough to hear it?"

Pierre nodded, his heart a stone within him.

"Duhaut was shot. . . in a quarrel with English Jem." But Monsieur Duhaut and English Jem had been cronies! Pierre frowned, trying to remember. . .

"They contested who should lead us, and where." Pierre did remember. The angry voices that had shouted in his dreams . . .

"After we came here, English Jem ordered us to join a Cenis raiding party to do battle with the enemies of the Cenis. But some of us followed the advice of Monsieur Joutel and refused to go. We stayed here in the village."

Pierre nodded again. Monsieur Joutel had been La Salle's second in command. *He* should be their leader, not that pirate English Jem.

The priest still talked. ". . . tell us that Jem and his followers are on their way back with the victorious warriors. Our firearms routed their enemies, so Jem is their hero . . ."

Pierre sighed, suddenly deeply tired. He did not care about any of this. There was something else . . .

"My father," he managed to say. "Is my father here?"

The priest shook his head. "*Non,* my son. Do you not remember? It was not your father, but three other deserters from the settlement whom we found here. Of Lucien Talon, there is no sign."

Maman was right. Papa must be dead. Pierre should grieve, as he grieved for Lisette, but he was too tired. He put his hand over his eyes and saw painful flashes of light in the darkness. His head ached. What did it matter? What did anything matter?

"I have tired you," the priest said. "Henri Joutel will give our comrades one more chance to come with us, but then he is determined to depart for New France at the first opportunity."

New France! Then Joutel was still intent on Monsieur de La Salle's plan of rescue.

"We have guides now," Père Anastase said, "and we do not wish to be caught by the northern winter."

Winter? Pierre was startled. They had left the settlement in winter. Surely another winter could not be upon them already!

"How long have I been ill?" he asked.

Père Anastase stirred and touched Pierre's arm.

"You have been ill for a long time. More than a month. It is now early May by the abbé's calculations, and it will take many months to reach help."

May. They had left the settlement in January, and now they must depart to find help for the settlement, as Monsieur de La Salle had planned.

Pierre thought of the home of his childhood, of its rich riverfront fields and cozy cabins, of its town of steep streets and houses he had thought magnificent until he saw Paris. An image of Maman bending over their cabin hearth flashed into his mind, but he shook his head. Maman was not in New France, he reminded himself. She waited with the children at the settlement, waited for the rescue promised by La Salle.

"Who . . . ?" he whispered.

"Who goes to Canada?"

Pierre nodded.

"Monsieur Joutel, as I have said, and the abbé and Colin Cavalier and . . . I and whichever others may choose to follow Monsieur Joutel," said Père Anastase. "Meunier has decided to go no farther, though he will not follow English Jem either, he says. He also has been ill, and he says he has journeyed far enough . . ."

Meunier! Why had Pierre not thought of Meunier before? Pierre tried to lift his head—was Meunier near?—but his neck felt boneless.

"Will he go back to the settlement, then?" he asked.

The priest shook his head. "That would be foolish, my son. What? Go back to add another mouth to feed to their worries? *Non*, no one speaks of returning. Those who do not go with Monsieur Joutel will stay here with the Cenis. Monsieur Liotot will stay—" Pierre remembered the surgeon's arms around him, lifting him from the mud when he fell. He had not thought of Monsieur Liotot either. What was wrong with him?

"—and Rutre."

"Rutre?" It was a name unfamiliar to Pierre.

"Rutre is one of our sailors, one of the deserters who has been living here with the Cenis—Rutre and Grollet and a man from Provençe. They came out to greet us when we neared this village."

A memory flashed into Pierre's mind. Three Indians on horseback, who whirled into the camp and leaped from their mounts to greet them with shouts and kisses. One of them had hair that curled. Another had no tattoos. The third was blond. Pierre remembered realizing that they were not Indians at all . . . and that Papa was not one of them.

"I . . . I remember," he said. "I do remember."

The priest nodded.

Pierre drew a trembling breath of wood smoke and the strange, mild smell of the Indians. The fire glowed and murmured. Beneath him the bed was soft and warm.

For a moment, he squeezed his eyes shut. What should *he* do?

"Will English Jem go with Monsieur Joutel, do you think?" Pierre asked. He wanted nothing to do with English Jem.

Père Anastase shrugged. "He is like a weathercock, turning in the wind. Who knows what he will do?"

If Pierre stayed, perhaps he could convince Meunier and Monsieur Liotot to go back to the settlement with him. When he was stronger. They could work and hunt for the colony, protect them . . .

Pierre was so tired. He wanted only to sleep. How could he walk all the way to New France now? What good did he do his family, dead on the trail somewhere?

He opened his eyes and looked into the face of Père Anastase, who waited silently beside him.

"*Moi aussi*," Pierre whispered. "I, too, shall stay with the Cenis."

Père Anastase looked relieved.

"I think it is wise, my son," he said.

CHAPTER IX

Pierre sat bolt upright. He was alone in the Cenis dwelling house, but outside, people were shouting, and someone screamed. There was a pounding of feet on the ground and the pounding of a drum somewhere in the distance, growing nearer.

Pierre's heart was pounding, too. What was it? Trembling, he swung his legs over the side of the bed platform, and the buffalo robes slid to the floor. He tried to stand, but his legs gave way, and he found himself sitting on the packed dirt floor beside the buffalo robes.

"Père Anastase!" he called.

No one answered.

Pierre began to crawl toward the leather-hinged door. Outside, the noise increased. He could make out a rhythmic chant, sung in women's voices and punctuated by anguished screams. He heard someone laugh. He dragged himself across the floor, past the low-burning fire.

Every few feet he had to stop to rest. His arms and legs quivered, and his breath came in labored gasps. He realized once again that he was naked and glanced about for something to cover him. A man's coat hung over the edge of a bed, but it was a distance away, an eternity away.

He would just look out the door. No one would see him. He began to crawl again.

His head was throbbing, but he caught his breath, then pushed on the door with all his might. It seemed as heavy as a gate of oak, though he saw it was only thatched grass on a framework of slender poles. It moved a hand's span. He put his face to the opening and looked out into the torchlit night.

At first he saw only feet and legs. Moccasined feet and brown, muscular legs and the long black skirts of women. He faced an open courtyard, and across it was a building as large as a good-sized Canadian barn, set above a courtyard on a platform of packed earth. It was lit by torches and a great fire burning before it. Was it their holy building? Their . . . temple? Or perhaps the dwelling house of their priests or chief?

The women were crowded around something, while the men stood back, watching. Pierre saw that many of the women brandished pointed sticks and jabbed them toward the center of their circle. They were screaming and chanting. There was a shriek, and the women laughed and surged together.

Pierre pulled himself up on the door frame and tottered there, his eye to the opening. He craned his neck. The women wore skins and feathers, and in the firelight their sweating faces were ghoulish with paint and tattoos.

Then, for an instant, they moved apart. Something crouched in their midst. An animal? But human hands covered its head, running with blood.

A woman with a flint knife leaped forward, grabbed one of the hands and hacked off a finger. A ghastly scream. A spurt of blood. The knife woman waved her trophy in triumph, and the crowd surged inward again, obscuring the bloody, broken, moaning *thing*.

But Pierre was already turning his head away, the gorge rising in his throat. He spewed bile onto the earthen floor.

They were barbarians, these Indians!

Pierre's legs failed him again, and he crumpled to the ground. He buried his face in his arms.

Savages!

It was the young Indian woman who found him there, the woman Père Anastase had called "good."

"*Ay'shah!*" she cried.

Then her hands were on him, her arms around him. She was scolding, just as Maman would have scolded, sharply and gently both. The woman half carried him back to the bed, and he smelled her sweat and dust and smoke in her hair.

He could not stop shivering. His teeth chattered, and his skin shrank from her touch. She pulled the warm buffalo robe over him, tucking it under his chin. She brought coals from the fire to place under his bed, and he felt the heat rise beneath him, but still he shivered. He clamped his teeth together.

"*Laissez-moi tranquille,*" he hissed. "Leave me be!"

But, of course, she did not understand. She bent over the fire, placing something in the coals, and then she came back to him. She put her hand on his forehead and smoothed his hair. She murmured low in her throat.

Pierre did not want to be comforted, not by her. He could still see in his mind's eye the bloody, moaning *thing* in the courtyard, the bloodthirsty faces of the women. Had this young woman been among them? Her face was smudged, her hair disheveled. Of course she had!

In a moment she brought him a warm drink.

Pierre did not want a drink from *her* hand! But his throat was parched, and he could feel the emptiness of his belly, its quivering emptiness.

She helped him to lift his head and held the gourd to his lips. It was the drink he had had before. He felt it flow down his throat, warm his belly.

The woman still murmured, a crooning sound. As she lowered his head to the bed, he could not help but look into her eyes, and all he saw there was compassion.

But she had been with the women in the courtyard! Doing unspeakable things. Surely she had been there . . .

Once again the young woman smoothed his hair, and her hand felt like the hand of Maman.

Pierre turned his head away.

It was near dawn when the others staggered into the dwelling. Pierre had tossed between waking and sleep, unable to clear his head of what he had seen. Now his eyes felt filled with sand, his head throbbed so he could not order his thoughts, save one. He had made a mistake! He could not dwell with these savages for another day.

But would his own people take him with them? He had seen the look of relief in Père Anastase's eyes when he said that he would stay. A boy as sick and weak as he was only a burden. And, if they agreed to take him, could he rise from this bed?

It was Meunier who came to sit beside him. The others, Père Anastase, Monsieur Joutel, the abbé, and Colin, fell upon their beds, which were ranged, as Pierre's was, around the walls of the dwelling house.

"They said you had wakened, *mon brave*," Meunier whispered. "Forgive me for not coming sooner. We were required at the feasting in honor of the Cenis victory. The Indians are well satisfied with the effect of our guns on their enemies, and English Jem's boastfulness knows no bounds."

Pierre stared at the dark silhouette of his friend. He could see only the gleam of Meunier's eyes, but he felt the familiar reassuring hand on his shoulder.

"Did you. . . Did you fight?"

"Alongside English Jem? Not likely, even were I well enough!"

Ah, yes. Meunier had been ill. Père Anastase had said. Where was he, then, when the women . . . ?

"Meunier, they were torturing someone . . . outside this house . . . I saw . . ."

He put his hand over his eyes.

"I am sorry you saw that. It was a woman of the enemy, unable to keep up when they fled. She had a newborn child. The Cenis captured her and turned her over to their women."

"But . . . But, Meunier, it was inhuman!" Pierre was aghast at Meunier's matter-of-fact tone.

Meunier nodded. The low fire hissed. Père Anastase began to snore.

"I must sleep, Pierre," Meunier said, stirring. "I perish with fatigue. Only I wanted to tell you I am glad you will stay here with me. It will be good to have a comrade."

Pierre could not catch his breath.

"You will stay—" He choked. "You will stay with these savages after . . ."

"After?" Meunier said. "You mean after we have seen their savagery? But, *mon brave,* we stayed with Duhaut and his cronies after they butchered our leader."

Pierre shuddered. "I . . . I was ill," he stammered.

"The Cenis are no more savage than we are, I think," Meunier said. "Indeed, it was one of us, I am told, who killed that woman's infant before her eyes. The Cenis will do *us* no harm, I wager. They seem to think it an honor to host us, I know not why. Perhaps because of our guns. I will take advantage of their hospitality, *mon brave*. I want to live, and I do not believe those who set out for New France will ever arrive there."

"But they must," Pierre croaked.

"Well, perhaps . . . But I am sick of the trail, and you, Pierre, are too weak to travel, I think."

Pierre could not deny it. He turned his head back and forth, trying to think of some other way . . .

"If I do not go to New France, I must go back to the settlement, to my family. I can help them—"

"Sleep, *mon brave*," Meunier whispered. "We will talk again tomorrow."

His soft footsteps retreated across the earthen floor. The willow-branch frame of his bed sighed. Then there was no sound, save the fire's soft crackle and the priest's snore.

PART II

TAY'SHA

CHAPTER I
Early summer 1687
Nabedache Town

Pierre leaned on Meunier's arm and watched the last horse disappear from view. Naked boys had run alongside the mounted men, crying out for them to stay, and in his heart Pierre ran with them. But now the boys, too, were out of sight. The farewell delegation of Cenis elders was turning away, shedding their ceremonial robes. One or two cast glances at Pierre and the remaining Frenchmen, gathered in the temple courtyard to bid their comrades adieu.

They were gone. Monsieur Joutel was gone. The priests were gone. Colin Cavelier was gone. Pierre was surprised to realize he would miss Colin.

"Come, *mon brave*," Meunier said. "Come rest."

Pierre was not alone. His friends had stayed—Meunier and Monsieur Liotot. Duhaut's servant, L'Archevêque, released from his servitude by Duhaut's death, had stayed. So had the deserters, Rutre, Grollet, and the Provençal. So had English Jem.

Pierre shook his head. "I will sit here awhile," he said, lowering himself to a bench against the temple wall.

English Jem was at that moment ducking into the house the Cenis had given over to the Frenchmen. It was where Pierre slept, now that he was feeling better, but he did not relish sharing it with

English Jem and the deserters, Rutre, and Grollet. Perhaps, when he felt stronger, he would do as Monsieur Liotot did and sleep outside in a buffalo robe.

"The sun will put color back into your cheeks," Meunier agreed now with a smile, turning away.

But Pierre thought the smile was unconvincing. Behind it, Meunier looked as downhearted as Pierre felt. Would they see their comrades again? Would they find their way back to the settlement? Or would they become like the Provençal? He was not downcast. Pierre saw him now striding toward the dwelling where he lived with his Cenis wife. Of them all, only the Provençal never slept in the Frenchmen's house.

"This town *is* my home," he had declared last evening when, gathered together about the fire, the others had talked of home.

"Ah, but I would dance again with a golden-haired wench," English Jem said. "I would quaff some good German beer and eat food fit for men."

"You should have gone with Joutel," said Meunier.

"Someone must captain those who stay behind," English Jem had replied.

But Pierre thought he stayed because he was afraid of hanging if he went back to New France. He *was* a murderer.

The Cenis community was more town than village. A wide roadway linked the dwellings, which were scattered among fields and woods, not crowded together as in European towns. The temple stood in the open upon a mound, commanding a view of the whole spacious town. There were no fortifications, and Pierre wondered if the Cenis were so powerful they did not fear attack.

The temple courtyard was swept clean of all evidence of the torture Pierre had witnessed the night of the warriors' return. A man gathered sticks from a pile of wood. Nearby some women and girls ground corn beneath a shelter of thatch. Their tattooed faces shone with sweat, and the muscles of their arms strained as they leaned over the mortar, pounding their pestles in rhythm. They chattered as they worked, and Pierre saw they were ignoring Rutre, who crouched behind a plump little woman English Jem was also courting. Another woman flung handfuls of beans into an earthen pot of boiling water. The smell of the cooking beans drifted to Pierre, and his stomach growled.

"Come," he heard a voice say in his ear, and he turned to see the young Indian woman who cared for him. "*Dah-yah'ay-hoot*," she repeated, and Pierre was surprised to realize that the word she spoke was not French, and yet he knew its meaning. She was urging him to rise, with a hand under his forearm. "You must rest," she said, and Pierre understood her words.

Monsieur de La Salle would have been pleased with him.

He resisted the woman's guiding hands and shook his head. "I do not wish to rest," he said, struggling to find the Cenis words.

The pestles of the corn grinders thumped. Three small children ran giggling by. The good, rich smell of the beans tickled Pierre's nose. He would not become like the Provençal, but he must learn to live with these people until he was strong enough to set out for the settlement. He searched his mind.

"*Huk-koo-na'nooh-sah*," he stammered. "I am hungry."

Her name was Na'-ta-ty, which meant little woman, Pierre came to know, but soon he was calling her T'ahay-ti-ti, which was to say elder sister. She tended him with more care than ever his own sister Lisette had done. Day by day, under her care, Pierre grew strong.

Na'-ta-ty called him Tay'sha, which Pierre knew meant friend, but Pierre corrected her.

"I am Pierre," he said. "Pierre Talon."

"Tay'sha," she insisted, smiling.

Pierre finally surrendered. He *was* her friend, made so by her care. He seldom thought now of the torture he had witnessed, and when he did, he decided that Na'-ta-ty could not have been one of the torturers.

One morning—he could not have told how much time had passed since Joutel and his party had left—Pierre woke to the sound of Na'-ta-ty's voice. "Tay'sha!" she was saying, but what followed was spoken through such giggling that he could not make it out.

He sat up and swung his breeched legs over the side of his bed. It was too hot these nights for buffalo robes, but Pierre would not sleep naked as the others did, and now he was glad, since Na'-ta-ty stood beside his bed.

"What is it?" he asked. "What do you want?"

Na'-ta-ty was pinching her nose with her fingers, making a comic face of disgust.

"I think she says you stink, *mon brave*." Meunier was standing behind her, laughing. "You should come with us to the river to bathe."

"But she washed me when first I came here," said Pierre. "I might fall ill again were I to bathe so soon."

Was that where Meunier went the mornings Pierre awoke to find him already gone from the house? Was he *bathing* in the river? Pierre looked more closely at his friend. Meunier was astonishingly clean. Pierre had not thought of it before, but Meunier's body gleamed white in the dim light from the smoke hole. His face was unsmudged. His smell had become much like the smell of the Indians, much like Na'-ta-ty's smell. Was that what accounted for it? They bathed?

Pierre pulled his feet back onto the bed and shook his head.

"I am just beginning to feel well," he said.

But Na'-ta-ty was pulling at his arm and scolding. She was saying that he would have no food until he bathed.

"They bathe even in winter," Meunier said. "At birth, I am told, the first thing a Cenis mother does is to plunge her child into the river, even if she must break ice to do it. They say it makes them strong."

"If it does not kill them!" Pierre cried. "I have bathed no more than twice or thrice in all my life. Maman said it was not wise."

"These people bathe every day—even the old and feeble. Even the girls! It keeps down the lice and fleas wonderfully. Have you not seen how little I scratch myself these days?"

Pierre looked toward English Jem's bed. His hairy chest rose and fell with his snores.

"*He* does not bathe," Pierre said, "nor does the surgeon, nor—"

"No," Meunier conceded. "The pirate does not bathe, if you will make a model of *him*, but Monsieur Liotot has tried it half a dozen times. He says it is invigorating. He talks of starting the fashion in France for health's sake, if ever he finds himself there again. By my trow, Pierre, I begin to agree with the woman. You do stink! Come along. What do you fear?"

"Nothing!" Pierre cried, stung. "Simply, I do not wish to bathe."

But Meunier laughed and grabbed Pierre's crimson cap from its peg on the wall. He danced about, holding it high.

"Come along, and I'll return your precious cap," he said, tossing it to L'Archevêque, who had risen from his bed.

Pierre jumped up and lunged for it, but L'Archevêque was too quick for him. The cap sailed through the air to Meunier and back again, while Pierre leaped after it.

Na'-ta-ty backed away, her hand over her smiling mouth. She cried encouragement.

Suddenly Meunier dashed for the door, pausing at the thresh-hold to dangle Pierre's cap, before he disappeared from view. L'Archevêque raced after him.

Pierre threw a despairing glance at the giggling Na'-ta-ty and followed.

Chapter II

The river danced and sparkled in the morning light. Boys and men splashed in the shallows, and one naked warrior dove from a rock into the deep center of the stream as Pierre ran up. Downstream, around a bend, Pierre could hear the voices of women and the shrieks and splashings of children. The whole village seemed to be in the sun-misted river. A boy scrubbed himself with a handful of sand, and another floated on his back like an otter.

"Pierre, you have come to bathe!" It was Monsieur Liotot, his hair and beard sleek with water.

Meunier, with Pierre's cap on his head, had jumped into the water. L'Archevêque followed.

"But I cannot swim," Pierre cried.

"It is not deep." Meunier stood up. The water came only to his waist. "Come along, *mon brave*. Come rid yourself of your stink."

"Yes, come, my boy," the surgeon called.

Pierre hesitated at the edge of the river. His bare toes squished in the mud. He wanted his cap! He turned away and pulled off his breeches. Then, holding a hand over his privates, he advanced toward the water and dipped in a foot. The water was cool. Pierre pulled back his foot.

The men in the river shouted, and the closest of them slapped the water, sending a plume of cool spray to spatter on Pierre's sweaty skin.

Then Meunier waded toward him, out of the water, and grabbed his arm. Pierre saw that his cap was now on L'Archevêque's head. Pierre felt other hands grab him, slippery with wet. The water rose about his ankles, about his shins, as he was dragged into it. He felt it on his thighs, then up to his waist, up to his chest; someone pushed on his head, and his face went under.

Beneath the water, the hands let go. Pierre rose, sputtering, to the laughter of the others. He blinked the wet from his eyes and flung back the dank weight of his hair, seething. Even Monsieur Liotot was laughing! He turned to splash out of the water. The air rang with shouts, and he relived the humiliation of the day he and Colin had overturned the floating basket.

Then the breeze struck his wet skin. Around his waist and thighs the water was warm, warmer than the air, and without thinking, he sank into it up to his neck. A cheer went up. Meunier, Liotot, L'Archevêque, and the Cenis men and boys were all grinning.

"Bravo!" cried Monsieur Liotot.

"*Ha'-ah-hut!*" the Cenis were yelling. "Good, good!"

"Ah, *mon brave*, I knew you were no coward!" Meunier laughed and tossed Pierre's cap to him.

The sun had barely risen the next day when the house of the Frenchmen was astir. Once again Pierre could hear Na'-ta-ty's voice, but this time it was Rutre who protested.

"All must help clear the Caddi's field," Na'-ta-ty said. The Caddi was the mayor of this Cenis town, and Na'-ta-ty lived in his house. But he was more than a civic leader. He was also, somehow, the head priest. "Quickly, quickly," Na'-ta-ty urged. "This is the day appointed. You must arise, or the Tammas will thrash you."

"Leave me be, woman," snarled Rutre in French.

"Tay'sha! Mun! Yah-cooh!" Na'-ta-ty cried, calling their Cenis names. "Get out of bed."

"Come along, Rutre," Grollet said. "You don't want to bring their policemen down upon us. The work will not be hard."

"Do it, then. I am not stopping you. But I will sleep, and to hell with them." Rutre turned to the wall.

The surgeon was donning the breechclout he had taken to wearing. "Boys," he said. "The woman brought food. Let us eat it and we will go. Leave Rutre to the Tammas."

Pierre squatted beside the banked fire with Meunier and L'Archevêque. He dipped his hand into the basket of dried berries Na'-ta-ty had set there. Grollet dipped some cooked cornmeal, and the surgeon gulped water from a gourd.

This was something new, this call to labor. Up to now, the Frenchmen had been treated as guests, observers only when the fields had been broken earlier in the spring. But last evening three Cenis elders had visited, smoking with them on the wooden benches outside the house. They talked of a hunt, planned for the near future, and of a fishing expedition. Finally, one of them spoke of the field clearing the next day.

"It is time to put in a second crop," he said, "but first the fields must be cleared and readied. We will be pleased when you join us. All men will help, and while we work, the women will prepare a feast."

English Jem had accepted the invitation for all of them, and at the time, Monsieur Liotot, Rutre, and Grollet had nodded in agreement. But now English Jem's bed was empty, and Rutre would not rise.

"Where is the pirate?" the surgeon asked. "Did he not sleep here last night?"

Rutre groaned and turned over, opening one eye.

Grollet shrugged. "Perhaps he rose early," he said.

"Or never came to bed." L'Archevêque sniggered. "I saw him last evening sweet-talking that little pigeon of a woman, the one he and Rutre have been mooning over like lovesick calves."

There was a snarl from Rutre's bed, and he swung himself up with a sudden movement.

"What? What's that you say?" he yelled, lunging for L'Archevêque.

L'Archevêque cringed backward and fell over. Pierre laughed with the others.

"Leave him be," Grollet said. "He only speaks what we all know. You have lost her to the pirate, Rutre. Forget her. There are others willing enough."

But Rutre was awake now. He stood, one foot in the ashes at the edge of the fire, swinging his head like an enraged bull.

"He shall not have her!" he cried.

Things were moving too fast for Pierre. He was still grinning as Rutre turned toward the heap of goods beneath his bed and scrabbled among them for his flintlock.

"Rutre, don't be a fool!" cried Meunier.

"Have some sense, man!" yelled Grollet.

But Rutre was already leaping across the room, his loaded gun in his hand. He flung open the door.

Pierre jumped to his feet. He stood gaping with the others.

Na'-ta-ty righted the water jug, overturned in Rutre's flight. "What does he do?" she cried. "Where does he go?"

The surgeon turned to his own things, ranged neatly on a shelf.

He poured powder into the muzzle of his gun and rammed a patched ball in after it. Then he, too, ran out the door.

Pierre crowded forward with the others, pushed through the door after him. Several houses away, he could hear Rutre's enraged cries. From every house, people were emerging. Pierre began to run, glimpsing the surgeon ahead of him. He felt the cool smoothness of the beaten earth beneath his bare feet. Their impact on the ground sent shudders through him. His heart thumped.

Then an explosion echoed over the shouts of the Cenis. A child screamed. Dogs barked.

Pierre saw the surgeon break through the crowd, and then, beyond him, he saw Rutre standing over someone fallen in a doorway. English Jem's red scarf was about the fallen man's throat. Blood was soaking into it, dripping on the ground. From inside the house came the high-pitched keening of a woman.

"That is the last man you shall shoot, Rutre," the surgeon cried.

Rutre looked up, his eyes dazed. Another explosion. Rutre crumpled to the ground, sprawling across the body of English Jem.

Monsieur Liotot's back was toward Pierre. His shoulders were heaving. Then he straightened and turned, the smoking flintlock in his hand.

"Monsieur Liotot!" Pierre cried. "What have you done?"

Pierre had stopped running. He stood, his chest heaving, and stared at the surgeon. The morning coolness touched his sweaty face.

The Cenis had fallen silent. The women were hushing their children and slipping away. The men looked at one another.

Meunier came up beside Pierre and put a hand on his arm. L'Archevêque and Grollet were there also, all silent, all staring at the surgeon.

Monsieur Liotot lifted his chin and glared at them.

"It is justice," he croaked, his face gray. "We are better without him."

We are better without him? It was what Duhaut had said after the murder of La Salle. Justice? It seemed that one killing only led to another.

"Monsieur Liotot!" Pierre cried in despair.

Liotot turned on his heel and stalked away.

CHAPTER III

Pierre sat cross-legged on his bed, staring toward the closed door of the house. Nearby hunched Meunier, his head in his hands. They had retreated here after the shooting, fearful of what would come next. Were they still welcome in the Cenis town?

The house was stifling. Pierre longed to open the door, but he was afraid. The town was eerily silent for midday. Where were the children, whose cries and laughter usually rang down its paths? Where were the thumps of the corn grinders' pestles, the chatter of the women? Where were the men?

"Why does not Monsieur Liotot come?" Pierre cried. "Have the Cenis taken him prisoner? Are *we* prisoners? Where are L'Archevêque and Grollet?"

Meunier did not answer.

Pierre groaned and closed his eyes. But behind his closed eyelids, he saw the bloody scarf of English Jem, saw Rutre crumple to the ground.

"Why did he do it?" he cried. "I see that Rutre's jealousy made him shoot English Jem, but why did Monsieur Liotot shoot Rutre? By then the damage was done and Rutre's weapon spent."

"It is not the first time," said Meunier, raising his head. "The surgeon is quick to anger, quick to kill."

"Not the first time?" How could Meunier say such a thing? But the mutterings Pierre had heard after Monsieur de La Salle's murder came back to him uncomfortably now. He had not listened then. Monsieur Liotot was Maman's friend.

"You know it," said Meunier. "You know it was your protector, Liotot, who butchered La Salle's household with an ax as they slept. I'm not saying that he had not provocation. La Salle's nephew treated us all abominably, and English Jem and Duhaut were always at him to join their plots. I think they had all agreed to it, but in the end it was Liotot who, once started, completed the massacre . . ." Meunier shook his head as though to dislodge the memory. "You are old enough to face reality, Pierre. Some men are capable of anything. Men like Liotot."

But Monsieur Liotot was a healer. Look how he had helped Maman, tried to save Lisette. Look how he had watched over Pierre, how he had doctored them all . . . Still, Pierre could not deny what his own eyes had seen.

"I do not understand," he whispered.

There was a noise at the door, and Pierre started up. Na'-ta-ty slipped inside and closed the door behind her.

"Where are our countrymen?" Meunier demanded, rising.

Na'-ta-ty frowned. Even in the dim light, Pierre could see the sweat gleaming on her tattooed upper lip. She was breathing hard. "Why do your people kill one another?" she asked.

Pierre felt Meunier shrug. "Where are our countrymen?" he repeated.

"Wee-hit speaks with the Caddi and with the Cahahas, his advisors," Na'-ta-ty said. Wee-hit was her name for Monsieur Liotot. "I have listened beside the council house, though if the Tammas discovered me, I would be thrashed."

Pierre nodded for her to go on. "What do they say?"

"They ask why your people kill one another, but Wee-hit does not answer. He says only that the dead men were bad."

Meunier spoke up. "Do not the Cenis sometimes quarrel?"

Na'-ta-ty looked shocked. "It is forbidden to kill one of the People," she said. "What would happen in the world if the Hasinai killed their own? Our god, Ayo-Caddi-Aymay, would be angry. All manner of ill-fortune would befall us."

Pierre noticed, as if for the first time, that Na'-ta-ty pronounced the name of her tribe oddly.

"Hasinai?" he said. "You mean Cenis."

"I mean Hasinai, the nine tribes," Na'-ta-ty said. "I know not why you Frenchmen call us Cenis. Our name is Hasinai, and this town and its people are called Nabedache."

"But you war with other tribes," said Meunier.

"You torture people," said Pierre, his stomach clenching at the memory.

"They are our enemies. They are not of the People, the Hasinai," said Na'-ta-ty. "Never would the People war with one another as you Frenchmen do."

Pierre looked down at his feet.

But Meunier said, "English Jem was not a Frenchman. He was German, I think."

Na'-ta-ty cocked her head. "These are different peoples? Enemies?

"In a way," said Pierre, but then he was speaking to Meunier. "But all the rest were Frenchmen."

Meunier nodded, staring at the ground. Then he looked up.

"Na'-ta-ty? Are Grollet and L'Archevêque—the one you call Yah-cooh—also in council?"

She shook her head. "I thought they were here with you, Mun."

"Where can they have gone? What will happen now?" said Meunier.

It made Pierre's heart tremble to hear the uncertainty in his voice.

Na'-ta-ty only shook her head.

Pierre dozed restlessly. As the house grew darker with the waning light, he woke to hear a stirring outside. The women were preparing the evening meal. Food smells rose in the damp, hot dusk. He was hungry.

But Na'-ta-ty did not return, and he and Meunier did not go seeking food.

It was Meunier's silence that was hardest to bear. He hunched on his bed, not speaking. And well he should be silent, after what he had said about Monsieur Liotot! Monsieur Liotot would explain. Perhaps Meunier was mistaken about the ax murders. Perhaps there was some good reason why he had killed Rutre, something Pierre and Meunier did not know . . .

If Monsieur de La Salle were still alive. . . Pierre sighed. Without him, they had become as savage as the Indians. Pierre felt himself blush. Perhaps more savage . . .

"Mes amis!" A whisper hissed suddenly from outside the house.

Pierre was off his bed in an instant, racing to the door. "We are here," he whispered.

The door opened just wide enough to allow the surgeon to enter. Outside, night had fallen. Pierre glimpsed the glow of a fire before the door closed. Then Liotot was beside them.

"Grollet?" the surgeon whispered.

"Non," Pierre said. "It is I, Talon."

"And Meunier," said Meunier. "We do not know where Grollet and L'Archevêque are. We thought you might."

"Not since. . . this morning. I have been all the day in council, listening to the Cenis harangues."

"But they have released you," said Meunier.

"For the moment," the surgeon said. "They cannot agree. The Provençal argued for me. They seem to trust him. Even his woman had a word to say in my defense. But others spoke against me. For now, I am safe."

"It is a puzzle to them, this killing of comrades," said Meunier, and Pierre could hear the accusation in his voice.

He felt the surgeon's sudden movement in the darkness.

"That sneaking deserter was no comrade of mine," he growled. *"I* did not kill English Jem."

That was true. Meunier was silent.

After a moment, the surgeon moved restively. "We must escape before they decide to punish us."

"Us?" Meunier murmured.

Pierre felt a sudden clutching in his gut. "Where?" he said.

"To another tribe."

Pierre could hear the surgeon feeling his way across the packed dirt floor, could see the dark bulk of his body move from bed to bed.

"Come with me," he said. "We have all the firearms and ammunition now—Rutre's and Jem's and Grollet's and L'Archevêque's—as well as our own. Any tribe will welcome our weapons and us to wield them, since these ignorant savages fear to do so themselves. Do you have a flint? We must gather them and be gone."

"Grollet and L'Archevêque may need their weapons," Meunier said.

Monsieur Liotot ignored him, and continued rummaging under the beds. Pierre heard him curse.

"They have taken their guns with them!" he said. "They must have returned here before you got back."

Pierre's mind was racing. "But Na'-ta-ty said there are nine tribes of Cenis—Hasinai, she called them," he said. "She said they are one people. It will profit us nothing to flee to another Hasinai town."

"They are to the east," said the surgeon, rifling through goods stacked against the wall.

Pierre heard the scratch of Meunier's flint. A tiny flame flared and lit Meunier's face, bent over the pile of dry moss and twigs laid ready beside the fire pit. What was Meunier thinking?

The flame caught, crackling softly as Meunier fed larger sticks into it. The flames played against the walls of the closed-up house, throwing shadows.

"Bien!" said Monsieur Liotot. "We will travel toward the west, away from these villages."

"Toward the settlement?" Pierre said. Yes! It was time to go back to Maman. He was stronger now.

Meunier was quiet. He did not move to make a bundle. "I will not go," he said.

"But Meunier! We could be of use to the people at the settlement. We could take them news that Joutel is on his way for help," Pierre said. He could hear the begging in his voice.

The surgeon lifted his head. "It is your choice," he said.

Pierre took a deep breath. He wanted to stay with Meunier, but he needed to get back to Maman and . . .

There was something else.

"What if the Hasinai are angry with all of us, Meunier?"

"I have done nothing to make them angry," said Meunier.

Monsieur Liotot stopped sorting supplies. He looked at Meunier. "You are a young fool," he said.

Pierre was between them, clenching and unclenching his fists. Meunier could be wrong about Monsieur Liotot. He could be wrong about the danger . . .

Pierre turned to Meunier, but Meunier did not look at him. Why did he not ask him to stay?

"If you are coming with me, Pierre, you must hurry," said Monsieur Liotot. The surgeon wanted him.

Pierre went abruptly to his own things and pulled down his crimson cap from its peg. He jammed it onto his head and began to search for his powder horn and flintlock.

CHAPTER IV

"We are in luck," the surgeon grunted when he opened the door. The moon had set. Clouds obscured the stars. The cooking fires had died.

Pierre crept out of the house behind Monsieur Liotot. His bundle made him clumsy, and his heart beat in his ears. He knew that Meunier still hunched over the low fire, but Pierre did not look back, and Meunier did not call out to him, did not beg him to stay.

Pierre hesitated just outside, waiting for his eyes to adjust to the darkness. There was no one in sight. Perhaps the Hasinai meant them no harm after all. Perhaps Meunier was right. Surely guards would be posted if they were prisoners . . .

Monsieur Liotot was nearly across the courtyard. Pierre hurried to catch up. In the shelter of the trees, he began to run, his moccasined feet silent on the path.

Soon he was breathing hard. His shoulders ached from the weight of the bundle, and his head began to pound with the pounding of his feet. They were out in the open now, skirting a newly broken field. Then, ahead, was a meadow with dark shapes moving in it.

The surgeon halted at the edge of the meadow, his finger to his lips.

Pierre moved up beside him and leaned over to catch his breath, his hands on his knees. He had been too long cosseted by Na'-ta-ty!

Liotot seemed to be watching the shapes in the meadow—horses, a dozen or more. One of them snorted softly. Liotot put his hand on Pierre's shoulder and motioned. They were to reconnoiter the meadow, make certain the horses were not guarded.

Pierre shrugged the heavy bundle of guns and ammunition from his back, as he saw the surgeon do, and crept away through the brush. Every few paces he paused to listen. Once a bird called, high in some tree. Once something rustled in the undergrowth, and Pierre remembered his terror early on the march, when he had feared the creatures of the swamp. Wild things were the least of the threats of this expedition, he knew now. He heard the heavy flapping of wings and saw a shadow plummet to the earth. There was a squeak, then the owl was beating upward, something in its claws. Pierre's breath sounded in his ears, so loud he had to hold it to listen. He heard his own heart. That was all.

When he retrieved his bundle, the surgeon was waiting. The horses still grazed peacefully, tethered, for they had not moved far.

The surgeon motioned forward.

Pierre ran behind him toward the horses. He chose one whose white spots shone through the darkness. He caught its mane with one hand. The horse shied and whinnied. The sound carried, loud as a scream, and Pierre expected Hasinai to fall upon him, expected their cries and the sound of their running feet. But the horse quieted, sidestepped, tripped on its tether.

Pierre's hands shook as he unfastened the tether. At his side the surgeon was swinging himself onto a horse's back. Pierre tried several times, his horse shying, before he was able to haul himself and his bundle up. But then he was on, clinging with all his might and digging his moccasined heels into its flanks. Ahead he heard the beat of the hooves of the surgeon's horse. His own followed without guidance.

Perhaps the Hasinai did not care if they fled. Perhaps they weren't in any danger, never had been in danger. But there was no going back now. Pierre hung on, leaning forward to relieve his shoulders of the weight of his bundle, and rode into the night.

They rode west—in the direction of the settlement—and it seemed, for a time, that they rode into a void. Where were those Indians who would help them as Monsieur Liotot had said? They came upon no road, no village, not even an encampment. There seemed no human beings in the empty landscape. Pierre's spirits sank lower and lower. He was a fool. Meunier had been right. Except . . . they *were* headed toward the settlement. They were not just running away. They were going back as Pierre intended.

Pierre glanced sideways at his companion. The surgeon's face was set toward the horizon, but he seemed to feel Pierre's gaze upon him. He turned his head and met Pierre's eyes.

"It will not be long before we find help, my boy," he said, and his voice was so warm, so reassuring that Pierre nodded, and for the moment, was eased.

On the third morning after the flight from Nabedache town, Pierre woke with a start. The black eyes of a tattooed warrior stared into his. Pierre reared up.

The warrior knocked him flat. "Who are you, ghost-boy?"

Through the pounding in his head, Pierre realized he could understand the words. They were not Hasinai, but very like it. Were these the people the surgeon sought?

He rolled his head to see Monsieur Liotot held in the grip of two more warriors. The surgeon did not struggle. He bowed his head in submission.

"Tay'sha," stammered Pierre, swallowing his fear. It was not only his Hasinai name, but the word most of these people used for friend. Pierre hoped it was true.

The warrior sat back suddenly on his heels. "They are harmless," Pierre thought he said to his companions. "Let the old one go."

Pierre sat up. Monsieur Liotot was rubbing his arms where his captors had grasped him. He was smiling—a false smile, Pierre thought and wondered if the warriors could see its falseness, too.

"We come in peace," Monsieur Liotot was telling them in signs. He was not skilled at signing, and Pierre began to repeat the signs correctly until Monsieur Liotot ceased trying and simply spoke.

"We come with our fire sticks to help you fight your enemies," he said, and reached toward his musket.

Pierre jumped when one of the warriors kicked it away, his eyes narrowed. "No fire stick!" he shouted.

"But we will fight on *your* side," Monsieur Liotot said. "We will help you defeat your enemies with our white man's power, if you will help us."

The warriors were of the Toho tribe, a war party searching for a band of Paouites, though the Hasinai were also their enemies, they said. All the rest of the morning they sat smoking beside Pierre's and Monsieur Liotot's fire, while Liotot demonstrated their weapons and begged to join them.

Pierre could see the Tohos did not believe Monsieur Liotot's promises of friendship. But when he told them he and Pierre had been prisoners at Nabedache—not exactly the truth, Pierre thought, but perhaps it must be told this way—suddenly the Toho leader nodded and rose, gesturing to his fellows. Pierre had counted a dozen squat, dark men in paint and feathers who rose now and stalked after their leader toward the horses.

Monsieur Liotot rose also. "I surmise this means we may have a chance to prove ourselves to them, Pierre," he said.

Was it relief Pierre felt as he got to his feet, or was it dread?

They did not go far. The sun had sunk only halfway to the horizon when a scout came riding back. The Toho leader reined in his horse, holding up a hand to halt the others. The two men conferred, then the leader turned.

"Here is a good place to camp," he told them. "The enemy is near. We will attack at daybreak."

Pierre looked at Monsieur Liotot. What enemy? Pierre remembered that Monsieur Liotot had gone with English Jem to battle Hasinai enemies. Tohos? Perhaps. But the enemies of the Hasinai, the enemies of the Toho were not *their* enemies. What were they doing, riding over these grassy plains in search of battle when they should be heading back to the settlement?

But when he voiced his thoughts that evening, lying beside the surgeon on the hard ground, Monsieur Liotot only grunted. "Don't be afraid, Pierre," he said. "I'll keep an eye on you."

Was that it? Was Pierre afraid?

"I am not afraid," he said. He hoped his voice sounded sure and strong. "I am not afraid."

He was not like Papa. Papa whom the others called coward. They had found him hiding in the bushes after an attack by the hostile coastal Indians shortly after their arrival in the New World, and he had never been able to live down the insults.

"We have the advantage," Monsieur Liotot was saying. "We have guns and the knowledge to use them. If we shoot a dirty Indian or two, it will put the fear of God into these savages. The Tohos will not dare to harm us, and we will be able to dwell with them in safety."

Dwell with them? But Pierre did not want to dwell with the Tohos. He wanted to get back to Maman and the children. He wanted no more killing . . .

That was another way that Pierre was different from Papa. Papa also killed men. Or at least, he boasted he had. He liked to tell of how he sneaked up on an Indian kneeling to drink from a spring and drew a knife across his throat. The others still scoffed. *Sure you did, Talon,* they said, sneering. Non, non, Papa would cry. *You should have seen the brute's face.*

Papa and Liotot. Both murderers.

Monsieur Liotot was snoring.

Pierre turned over, trying to find a comfortable place in the grass. Beneath him, it seemed, was a bed of sharp stones, of poking sticks. He hurt all over. He was unaccustomed to riding all day, to sleeping on the ground, to eating scanty rations.

At last he turned on his back and opened his eyes to gaze up at the faraway glittering stars. It was not stones and sticks that poked him. It was not the riding or the lack of food that kept him awake.

CHAPTER V

Pierre would have said he did not sleep that night. Yet when Liotot shook him, he found himself swimming up through layers of nightmare.

"It is time," Liotot said.

Around them in the darkness, the Tohos were renewing their paint, helping one another to smear streaks of it on faces and bodies. They moved silently in the starlight, stashing their provisions among some rocks. Pierre and Liotot also left their bundles, but took guns and ammunition.

"Is your firearm at the ready?" the surgeon whispered. "Stay near and follow my lead."

Pierre tugged his crimson cap down over his ears. The stock of his flintlock felt greasy in his hand. His stomach rolled. He cringed at the sound of his horse's hooves. The horse was wheezing, and the snorts of the other horses sounded loud in Pierre's ears. The sky was lightening. If they did not reach their prey soon, surprise would be lost. Pierre bit his lip. What was he doing?

Then suddenly the Toho leader wheeled his horse to face them, and Pierre scrambled to swing onto his own horse's back. From that height, he saw ahead of them, in a hollow out of the wind, the dark shapes of sleeping men around a banked fire. Beyond, two of the Tohos were creeping toward their enemies' horses. The Toho leader raised his hand, then slashed it down and dug his heels into his horse, shrieking a cry that made the hair on Pierre's neck rise.

Liotot rode forward, his flintlock in his hand. Pierre heard the gun thunder. The dust swirled, and Pierre found he, too, was riding forward, clinging to his horse's mane, his flintlock clumsy across its neck. There were shouts and screams. A woman ran in front of his horse, her face twisted in terror. There was a child in her arms. A woman, a child! This was not a war party they attacked!

Pierre's horse wheeled. He could not control it. He slid forward over its neck. Its head was down, its front legs crumpled beneath it. Pierre hit the ground. The musket flew from his hand. His horse struggled beside him. Something warm and wet sprayed over him, and Pierre realized it was blood. An arrow pierced the horse's neck. Pierre looked into its panicked, rolling eye and scrambled away from its flailing hooves. On hands and knees he searched frantically for Liotot. Another roar of musket fire, and Pierre turned toward the sound. The surgeon was riding toward him through the dust. Pierre could hear bloodcurdling screams and sobs of the wounded. A baby cried. Then, just as the surgeon's horse reached him, Liotot's hands flew up. The surgeon toppled, one foot caught in the reins. The horse was circling, sidestepping, trying to shake away the weight that dragged on its reins. Its hoof struck the surgeon. Liotot reached out, and Pierre saw the lance in his chest, the red blood welling from his mouth. Pierre grabbed the reins to disentangle the surgeon and saw him kick free.

Clutching the reins of the frenzied horse, Pierre knelt beside the surgeon. But Monsieur Liotot was pushing him away.

"Take . . . horse . . . run!" he gurgled.

Pierre saw him convulse, saw another upwelling of blood, saw his eyes stare at something Pierre could not see.

When at last Pierre could think, when at last his heart had slowed and he became aware of his hands—claws that clung to the reins as though to a lifeline—the horse had slowed, too. The wild gallop away from the battleground was replaced by a steadfast, purposeful walk. Pierre did not know where they were going, but the horse seemed to.

Monsieur Liotot was dead.

One by one, they died.

Pierre thought of what the men had said of Monsieur de La Salle—he leads us to disaster. Indeed, it seemed, all whom Pierre followed led him to disaster. Papa . . . no, truly it had been Maman who led them from New France to join Monsieur de La Salle's company. Maman, who had sent him on La Salle's last expedition. Then Monsieur de La Salle. And now, Monsieur Liotot . . .

Meunier had tried to warn him.

Yet Monsieur Liotot had thought of him with his last breath, had urged Pierre to save himself even as he died. Were all men such mixtures of evil and good?

Pierre dozed, finally, on the horse's back. When the horse stopped to drink at a stream, Pierre slid down to drink. When the horse grazed, Pierre dismounted and tethered it with the cord that tied his breeches. Then he lay down and slept.

In the afternoon, they moved eastward slowly, through grassy meadows and woods of oak and nut trees. Pierre saw no humans nor any animals at close range. His stomach ached with hunger. Why had he not thought to retrieve his musket? On the second day, he ate a few green nuts and some grass as the horse did, but his bowels were loosened and the pain grew worse. So finally he drank when the horse drank and slept when the horse slept and went forward with the horse through night and day and night until Pierre did not know how long he had been riding.

He was so weak he could barely cling to the horse's back, especially now, when it picked up its pace. He mumbled into its ear, "Slowly, slowly." It lifted its head and whinnied, as though in answer. Then Pierre heard another whinny. He squinted in the sunlight's glare and saw ahead of him a meadow full of horses. Beyond were beehive-shaped houses, golden in the morning sun. Someone came out of one and gestured. Then there were more people, running toward him. The meadow, the houses, the trees that grew among them, the roof of the temple on its mound were familiar to Pierre. It was Nabedache town. The horse had come home!

Pierre leaned forward and patted its neck, even as he felt himself slide into darkness.

When he awoke, he could smell wood smoke, roasting meat, and maize, even before he opened his eyes. Beneath him was the comfort of a willow bed, the softness of well-tanned hides. Voices rumbled, speaking Hasinai. It was as though he had never left.

"He may abide here, in my lodge," a voice was saying. "My wife is fond of him. She will tend him as her son."

"But he went with that other, that killer of his own kind," said another voice. "How can we be certain he is worthy?"

"We cannot be certain," said the first. "But he is young. He came back to us, bringing back one of the horses. Mun says he is worthy."

Mun. Pierre turned his head and opened his eyes. They were

speaking of Meunier, but he did not see him. There were only a handful of Hasinai men squatted about the fire pit in the center of the house. Pierre remembered one face from the river, another who had come to bid them to the field clearing. One man, a sturdy, pale-skinned elder, was seated above the others on a bench—the Caddi! Pierre had not been this close to him before.

This was not the house Pierre and the other Frenchmen had shared. It was larger, but it had the same kind of willow beds about the walls, these screened from one another, the same kind of storage baskets and shelves.

"My sons have lodges of their own," the Caddi was saying, "and my lodge is empty of young men. I will soon discover his worthiness."

"I am not worthy." The Hasinai words burst from Pierre's lips, spilling his shame. He wanted to sob.

The men turned. Then the Caddi rose and came to stand over him. Pierre pulled himself up, leaning on one elbow. He needed to tell them.

"I did not bring the horse back," he said. "It brought me. But I wish to be worthy." He tried to keep his voice steady. "I wish to learn to be strong and brave."

The black eyes stared at him. There was no friendliness in them, but neither was there enmity. They regarded him, considering.

His words kept coming. "I have no father," Pierre said. "I have no leader. I must learn to lead myself. Teach me."

The Caddi stepped closer. He laid his hand on Pierre's head and looked into his eyes.

"You may dwell in my lodge," he said. "I will teach you."

"Why do you keep this boy talking when what he needs is food?" It was Na'-ta-ty's voice.

Pierre craned his head. "T'ahay-ti-ti," he said. "Elder sister."

"Tay'sha," she said. "Why did you leave us? Our hearts have wept for you."

She bustled forward, pushing her way between the men, who stepped aside to let her pass. She carried an earthen bowl in her hands. "You must drink. You must eat, Tay'sha. You must regain your strength. Have I nothing to do but nurse you?"

Already she was holding the bowl to his lips. Pierre tasted the strengthening drink.

"Let us leave him to my wife," said the Caddi.

The others nodded and turned to go.

Pierre was choking on his drink. Wife? Na'-ta-ty was wife to the Caddi, to this old man?

But she was calmly wiping away the spilled drops with her hand. "Yes, go, husband. Leave this boy to me. When he is stronger, you may counsel with him all you like."

Chapter VI

Only days later, Pierre sat cross-legged in the hot sunlight outside the house of the Caddi and Na'-ta-ty, which was his house now. In his hands he turned the crimson cap Maman had knitted for Papa before they set sail from France. He remembered clearly her setting it on Papa's head, its bright color and jaunty angle proclaiming that here was a French Canadian, citizen of the New World, on his way home. Papa had laughed and grasped Maman about the waist, whirling her.

"I will make my fortune yet, Isabelle," he had boasted. "I have not been defeated!"

Maman had smiled and smoothed her skirts.

"But of course," she had said in her calm, determined way. "That cap will bring you good fortune, *mon mari* . . . and courage to prosper for your family."

Good fortune . . . and courage.

The cap had faded to a dull brick color, stained and frayed and shrunken so that now it barely fitted. It had not brought good fortune, or courage, to Papa. Had it brought them to Pierre? But he could not throw it away. He must keep it to remind him of Maman, of the family. He must not forget them, for one day soon he must go back to the settlement to try to rescue her, her and the children. It would not be deserting them to stay with the Hasinai for just a little while, learning all he could from the Caddi . . . Not desertion to be, for a time, part of the Caddi's family . . . Surely that was not desertion . . .

"You are looking grim, *mon brave*," said Meunier, sitting down beside him. "What do you think of? How to mend your cap?"

"It is past mending," Pierre said. He poked a finger through a hole in the cap. "Meunier . . . do you ever think of your family?"

The smile on Meunier's face faded.

"I think of them," he said. "But it is no use. I was young when my mother died, but my father . . . I thought to make him proud. I thought to increase his fortune. But I fear I have brought him only grief. My elder brother will inherit our land, and my younger brother . . . I see no way to get home to France again."

Pierre smoothed the cap on his knee. He *would* go back to his mother . . . someday.

The house of the Caddi was different from any home Pierre had ever known. For one thing, there were more people there, even though the Caddi's first wife was dead and her sons grown and living in lodges of their own. There was the Caddi, of course, and Na'-ta-ty, his wife, newly wed, Pierre had learned, shortly before Pierre came to Nabedache. There were the Caddi's old parents, and the Caddi's brother and his wife and four giggling young daughters so alike that Pierre could not tell one from the other. There was a toothless old uncle whose food was chewed and brought to him every day by his daughters and a widowed cousin and a cousin with only one hand who told stories so thrilling that neighbors came often in the evening to listen by the fire.

Yet with all these people living so closely together, Pierre seldom heard quarreling. Not like Maman and Papa surely, whose wrangles had woken the neighbors and disturbed their children's rest. Not like Pierre's brothers and sisters, who fought over food and clothes and the nearest place to Maman until she smacked them all soundly and cursed them to silence. Not like Monsieur de La Salle's followers.

The house itself was large, and each person had a bed and a storage space, in addition to the communal living area around the fire and the platform and bench of the Caddi.

All day long elders came and went from the house, to ask advice, to seek justice in cases of dispute, to sit on the Caddi's platform and visit, or plan the affairs of the town. Women dropped by to gossip. Children ran in and out. There was a constant noise and bustle, and yet it seemed to Pierre there was a kind of quiet, too. A kind of tranquillity.

"If you would be men of the Hasinai," the Caddi said one day to Pierre and Meunier when a number of townsmen had gathered in his house, "you must wear our tribal tattoos."

Pierre looked up from where he and Meunier squatted on the bare-swept floor in front of the Caddi's bench. The Caddi wore a turkey feather cape and a headdress of bird skulls. His tattooed face was painted, vermilion on one side and white on the other. The women of the house took delight in bedecking him thus, and he looked, in a barbarous way, regal. Like a king.

Pierre felt a thrill of honor and dread. The Caddi had chosen him as a foster son. Of course he must be marked for this distinction. Would it hurt?

Meunier bowed his head immediately.

"I will wear the Hasinai tattoos with pride," he said.

Pierre also bowed his head.

"Yes," he said. "I, too."

The Provençal sat among the townsmen, and from the corner of his eye, Pierre saw him nod. The Provençal had been tattooed long ago.

Even babies were tattooed, both boys and girls. Pierre had seen their swollen little faces and heard their irritable cries. It was done soon after birth, as soon as the Conna, the shamans, thought it likely the child would live, and the marks were added to throughout life when important events took place. Pierre had seen the contempt the People showed for a child who cried too loudly when it was tattooed.

"That one is a whiner," he had heard when a little one screamed and struggled as his face was pricked by the tattooing thorns. But a baby who only whimpered was much esteemed. "She will be valiant," they said.

So he must not cry when he was tattooed. If a baby girl could bear the pain, surely *he* could.

The Caddi was consulting his advisers.

"The time of the harvest festival is an auspicious occasion," said an old man with flapping earlobes weighted by bones and shells.

The others murmured assent.

"The harvest festival, then," said the Caddi. "Let the Tammas carry the news to all the houses of Nabedache. When we celebrate the second harvest, the People will welcome these two, Tay'sha and Mun."

But the discussion was not at an end, though Pierre grew restless. The Hasinai talked until everyone had spoken and agreed, even about such a thing as the day of a festival. Sometimes it took a long time. Why did the Caddi not simply tell his followers what to do, as Monsieur de La Salle had? He was their leader, after all.

"We will not have the maize gathered before the moon waxes," said one of the younger men now.

Pierre sighed.

"We must," said an old man, his wattles trembling.

"It will not be ripe," the young man insisted.

"When the moon is full, the maize will be ripe. It has always been so," said another.

"How many days until the full moon?" said the Caddi.

The old men put their heads together, murmuring.

"Twenty days," they finally agreed.

"Is not twenty days sufficient?" asked the Caddi. "The sun is hot. There is no sign of rain."

The young man nodded, his brow furrowed with thought.

"It is a long time," he agreed. "Perhaps the harvest might be accomplished by then if we hurry."

The old men made approving sounds.

"There are many strong young men and women in this town," said the old man with bones in his ears. "It will be accomplished."

They had forgotten Pierre and Meunier and the tattooing. Pierre cast a sidelong glance at Meunier, and Meunier looked back and yawned behind his hand. The sun slanted low through the doorway of the house and crept below the rolled-up wall mats. Pierre could smell squash and beans cooking outside over open fires. Sweat dripped down his sides. It was many hours since his morning bath, and he felt hot and sticky. His mouth was dry. The Hasinai men talked on.

"Will you talk all night?" It was as though Pierre had spoken aloud, but it was the old woman, the Caddi's mother, stooping through the doorway. "It is time for food," the old woman said. "If this is not a council of war or some other vital business, it should come to an end. The food is cooked. Your wives wait to serve you."

"Go away, old mother," said the Caddi sternly.

She turned away, grumbling, but she did not seem cowed by her son.

"The food is cooked," she repeated over her shoulder as she retreated.

Pierre sneaked a look at the Caddi to see if he was angry with her. His face was stern beneath its paint, but his eyes were smiling.

"In fifteen days' time, the Tammas will announce the harvest festival," he said, sweeping the townsmen with his eyes.

They were moving restively, stretching their backs and necks. They seemed eager for their food.

No one disagreed now, and Pierre wondered—if Monsieur de La Salle had listened to his men as the Caddi did, would he still be alive?

"The food is cooked," the Caddi announced, as though the news had come to him from the heavens. "Our council is at an end."

Chapter VII

The temple courtyard was filling with people. Pierre watched them flow in so that he did not have to watch the Conna, who was busy with his pestle, crushing the charcoal of walnut wood that would stain the incisions of the tattoos. Beside Pierre in the temple doorway sat Meunier, a comforting presence, though Pierre did not look at him, but stared straight ahead as he had been instructed. The Conna set the crushed charcoal to soak, and the grand Chenesi, the most revered of the Connas, laid out his thorns on a creamy piece of tanned skin. Again, Pierre looked away. He could not bear to see the long, sharp thorns, their wicked points glistening in the early morning sun.

Pierre felt light-headed. All night long the Connas and the old men had chanted and danced, and he and Meunier had been obliged to sit motionless in a place of honor, watching.

"Do not cry out, Tay'sha," Na'-ta-ty had warned him yet again when the sun rose, and she brought him water to drink. She need not have reminded him. The memory of his cowardice on the Toho battlefield was still bitter in his mouth. He had told no one, not even Meunier. He could not shame himself again.

All about Pierre and Meunier the townspeople stood or squatted to watch. The grand Chenesi chanted, swaying with his eyes closed above the soaking charcoal and the waiting thorns. Pierre's palms sweated, and he wanted to wipe them on the breechclout he had taken to wearing since his return. But he did not. He tried to sit perfectly still, his hands on his knees. He could not keep his eyes still, however. They flicked from face to face and back again to the thorns. Pierre fought down a shudder. Which of them would be first?

He touched the crimson cap tucked into the waist of his breechclout.

The Chenesi knelt before Meunier and took up a thorn.

Pierre slowly let out his breath.

Beginning at Meunier's hairline, the Chenesi pricked a line of cuts, one after another, to divide Meunier's forehead. Pierre saw tiny red beads well from the pricked skin. The Chenesi wiped them away when they began to flow down Meunier's face. Meunier did not wince or cry out. Pierre saw that his eyes were closed, and from time to time a shudder ran through him.

Pierre felt his gorge rising. If he had eaten that morning, he would have vomited. Faintness washed over him, and he tried to turn his eyes from Meunier's bleeding face. But he could not look away.

The townspeople murmured in admiration.

"He shall not shame the People," someone said.

Would Pierre?

The Chenesi was rubbing soaked charcoal into the cuts he had made. He began another line of cuts beside the first. The blood flowed faster down Meunier's face.

When the lines had reached the bridge of Meunier's nose, the Chenesi rose and hobbled around him six times, chanting. Pierre saw Meunier draw in a deep, trembling breath. The Chenesi's hand descended to the top of Meunier's head and stayed there a moment.

Then he came to kneel before Pierre. He took up another thorn.

Pierre caught his breath. Again he touched the crimson cap. He closed his eyes and tried to remember a prayer. He felt the first prick of the thorn.

It did not hurt much. Relief flooded him. Then there was another prick, and another and another and another . . . The pain began to sear itself into his forehead. Wetness rolled down his face. Sweat? Blood? Pierre did not know, and it took all he had in him to keep from cringing away from the relentless prick of the thorn. He steeled himself against each prick. His head began to throb. Tears rose, and he could not keep them from spilling. His hands were slippery when he gripped his knees. He clenched his teeth.

Holy Mary, he said to himself. Holy Mary, Holy Mary, Maman, Maman, Maman!

But he did not cry out.

For a night and a day and a night, Pierre lay, his face hot and painful, in the house of the Caddi. Whenever he opened his eyes, Na'-ta-ty and the Caddi's old mother hovered over him. They petted and praised him. They brought him choice tidbits to eat and cooling drinks.

"You are a brave boy, Tay'sha," said Na'-ta-ty, her eyes shining. "Now you are truly my brother, or . . . perhaps you are my son?"

Pierre could not but smile at this, though it made his face hurt more. For all she was the Caddi's wife, Na'-ta-ty was scarcely older than Lisette had been. Nowhere near so old as Maman.

"I am your brother, T'ahay-ti-ti," he said, moving his mouth carefully, the tattoos around his lips aching.

On the second day, when Pierre awoke, the Caddi stood over him.

"It is time to arise, my son," said the Caddi. "We must gather the last of the corn and prepare for the festival. It is time to feast with your people."

"Mun?" said Pierre.

"Arise and come greet him," said the Caddi.

Outside, Pierre looked at Meunier with astonishment. It *was* Meunier. Yet it was not Meunier, for now a black line ran from his forehead to his chin.

Did Pierre look like someone else? He put his hand to his own face. Did he look like a Hasinai now? Like a man?

"Tay'sha!" Meunier said.

Was Pierre Tay'sha now, no longer Pierre Talon? Was he now the son of the Caddi, and not the son of Lucien Talon? Then— Maman would not know him. His heart sank.

But Meunier was laughing. He slapped Pierre on the back and capered. The Caddi and the Tamma, Bah'din, Meunier's foster father, looked on, smiling. Pierre began a jig to match Meunier's. But somewhere, deep inside him, he heard Maman.

Remember your family.

The Caddi taught Pierre the ways of the Hasinai.

A man of the Hasinai must be able to run for long distances. Every day the boys and young men practiced running. Pierre was proud that he could keep up with the boys, and as autumn and winter passed, he found he could run faster and faster. He began to catch up to the men.

A man of the Hasinai must be able to swim. Each morning, no matter how chill, Pierre went with the men to the river. Each morning the Caddi put his hand beneath Pierre's chest while he instructed him how to move his arms and legs. Little by little he led him deeper into the water, while Pierre struggled to keep from sinking, tried to lie upon the surface without flailing, tried not to show how he trembled.

One morning Pierre realized that he had slipped from the Caddi's supporting hand. He was swimming!

In his excitement he took a gulp of water. He rose sputtering and saw the Caddi was a distance away. Pierre gasped air into his burning lungs and put his face into the water again. He reached with a hand and kicked . . . and felt himself glide through the water.

A man of the Hasinai must hunt. On rainy days Pierre sat with the Caddi and the Caddi's old father and learned to fashion his own bow and arrows. Pierre worked the bright heartwood of the osage orange limb with his iron knife, and the old father murmured in admiration at the ease with which it shaped the wood. Pierre could see, when he tried the same task with one of the Caddi's flint knives, why the natives so treasured the cheap blades of the French and the Spaniards.

Once that winter, Pierre and Meunier were allowed to go with a bear-hunting party. Pierre learned how to search out and recognize bear signs, how to creep silently downwind, how to rise on a signal from the hunt leader and loose his arrow. The maddened bear rose up roaring, and Pierre fell backward in surprise. He scrambled toward safety when the bear lumbered in his direction, swinging its head as though bewildered. Then it crumpled to the ground, bleeding from a dozen wounds. Not one of the arrows protruding from its hide was Pierre's. He found his arrow in a clump of grass nearby.

"But see," Meunier said, coming to put a hand on his shoulder, "there is blood on the tip. You did better than I, for you nicked him."

A man of the Hasinai must fish. The Caddi's father showed Pierre how to make a harpoon. When the weather warmed, the whole town moved to a camp beside the lagoons that formed when winter's high water receded. There Pierre learned to watch for a silvery flash in the water. Again and again he hurled his harpoon. Again and again he retrieved it, empty. But on the last evening in the fishing camp, Na'-ta-ty cooked a fish Pierre had speared. It tasted better to him than all the fish he had eaten, brought home by other men.

A man of the Hasinai must work. When it was time to clear the ground of the Caddi's field, all the men were called by the Tammas to help. Pierre thought of that day last year when English Jem and Rutre had died.

We may raid other peoples and defend ourselves from enemies, he thought as he took up his buffalo bone hoe, but we do not murder one another.

Thus, the time slipped by until two summers and two winters had passed. Pierre lived in the house of the Caddi of the Nabedache Hasinai. His skin browned in the sun. His muscles grew strong. His legs, longer than those of any man in the town, longer even than Meunier's or the Provençal's, could carry him swiftly and far. He could swim and hunt and fish and work in the fields and build houses. He could make weapons and tools by the fire when the rain fell.

He tucked the tattered crimson cap in a deerskin pouch Na'-ta-ty sewed for him. He tucked away in his mind—so deeply that he only remembered in those last unguarded moments before sleep—thoughts of returning to rescue his brothers and sister, to rescue Maman.

CHAPTER VIII

The People of Nabedache had been bidden to a feast at Neche. Pierre was close behind the Caddi, walking toward the welcoming Neche delegation. Behind them came other men of Nabedache, elders and warriors, and behind them the women and children. Almost the whole Nabedache town had come, painted and dressed in their finest.

Ahead of them the Neche men were also clad in painted buffalo robes, the women in the long black deerskin skirts Pierre knew had been softened almost to velvet. Pierre caught the eye of a Neche maiden, who blushed and dropped her gaze to the ground. He would try to find that one again, after the feasting.

"Talon! Pierre Talon!"

Who was calling him by name? By his French name?

"Meunier!" cried another voice.

Two men came hurrying forward, out of the crowd of Neche townspeople. The sun caught the lightness of their hair, and Pierre saw that one of them bore no tattoos. There was something familiar about his rolling gait, something sailorlike . . .

"Grollet!" Pierre shouted.

Meunier had already run forward to embrace L'Archevêque.

They had heard reports of two Frenchmen seen with the Paouites. Then, someone claimed they were living with the Tohos, and once Pierre heard they hunted with the Nasoni Hasinai. But this was the first time the four had met since Grollet and L'Archevêque disappeared after the murders of English Jem and Rutre.

Pierre thought Grollet was much changed, and so was L'Archevêque. Their hair was dressed in the native fashion, shaved except for a long scalp lock trimmed with shells and feathers. But it was not their hair, or their native robes and breechclouts. It was something more subtle, an ease perhaps with the natives, a loss of the despair that had for so long marked the faces of La Salle's followers, a new confidence.

Was Pierre so changed?

"You have grown tall," L'Archevêque said. "Tall and brown. Your tattoos are quite as handsome as mine."

When at last the four Frenchmen were alone, Pierre once again felt that he was still French, and these men were his comrades. French words rolled easily from his tongue, and there was much to say. *Where have you been? What are you doing here? Have you news of those who went toward New France?*

"I am shamed we ran away the day of the shootings," L'Archevêque admitted. "We were afraid."

"In your wanderings," Pierre said, "have you chanced upon news of our people at the settlement? Have you been there?" He leaned forward.

"There is nothing for us at the settlement," said Grollet. "They must fare as well as they can until Joutel returns for them."

Pierre sat back and let out his breath. He should have returned to the settlement himself by now.

L'Archevêque was silent, but later he touched Pierre's hand. "I will watch and listen for word of your family, Talon," he said.

Grollet and L'Archevêque had not heard of the death of Liotot, but they did not seem surprised.

"There are not many of us left," said L'Archevêque with a sigh.

Pierre caught his eye. "Will you not come back to Nabedache with Meunier and me?" he asked the young man. L'Archevêque would make a good companion, and together they might have a better chance of finding their way back to the settlement.

L'Archevêque cast a glance at Grollet, then lowered his head. "I am well enough as I am," he said.

Pierre could not persuade him, and he did not even try to persuade Grollet. In truth, he was not sorry to leave Grollet in Neche when the feast was over and he returned with the People to their own town, but he regretted leaving L'Archevêque.

Back at Nabedache, Pierre and Meunier talked about leaving for the settlement at last. But they were needed first for the harvest, and then it was winter, not a good time for journeys . . .

In the third spring that Pierre lived in Nabedache town, Grollet and L'Archevêque returned.

This time it was Pierre who ran first to greet them. He grabbed the reins of L'Archevêque's horse.

"Yah-cooh!" He greeted him with his Hasinai name.

When L'Archevêque swung down to stand beside him, Pierre stroked his face, rather than kissing his cheeks.

"It is good to see you, *mon vieux*." Every day the French words felt stranger to Pierre's tongue. Not even with Meunier did he still speak the language of his birth.

But L'Archevêque did not smile in answer, nor exclaim on how tall Pierre had grown. He avoided Pierre's eyes.

Grollet had dismounted and was greeting the people who had come out to meet them. He did not greet Pierre.

"We have news, Talon," said L'Archevêque in a low voice.

Pierre's heart froze.

"Where is Meunier?" Grollet asked.

"Here," came a voice from behind them. "Yah-cooh, Grollet, it is good to see you well."

"We must talk," said Grollet.

"We have been to the settlement," said Grollet when the four of them were seated together in the house of the Caddi. Pierre held his breath. Na'-ta-ty and the other women had gone to prepare food. The Caddi and his father and the other important men of the town sat in a ring around the Frenchmen, listening and grave.

But Grollet spoke rudely in French. "We have been to the settlement."

Pierre's hand trembled.

"They are gone, *mes amis*," said L'Archevêque, still avoiding Pierre's eyes.

"Gone?" Pierre's voice was a croak. "Have they been rescued? What do you mean, gone?"

"There was a battle with the Clamcoëhs," said Grollet. "Our people were killed."

"Battle?" said Meunier. "You mean massacre. Our people had no soldiers to protect them—"

We were not there to protect them, Pierre thought.

"—They were women and children, priests, and the sick."

"All?" whispered Pierre. He could hear the puzzled murmur of the Hasinai, who did not understand what they were saying. But the room seemed to have shrunk to the small circle of Frenchmen.

"The Toho say the Clamcoëh women carried off the children."

Pierre's heart started beating again.

"What is the matter, my son?" said the Caddi.

But Pierre could not answer him.

"All of the children?" he said in French.

L'Archevêque looked at him for the first time, sympathy in his eyes. "Four boys and a girl, they said. We did not see them."

A girl and four boys. Magda, Jean-Baptiste, and his two baby brothers, Pierre counted. Who was the other? Then he remembered Eustache Bréman, the paymaster's orphaned son, the only other child left at the settlement. He drew a deep breath.

"Then they are alive. My family is alive."

He concentrated on the image of Jean-Baptiste and Magda and the little brothers alive with the Clamcoëhs. But his thoughts kept veering toward the question he could not bear to ask.

L'Archevêque pulled from his pouch a soiled blue rag and handed it to Pierre.

"We buried what bones we could find," he said.

Pierre took the cloth in his hands. His throat closed and he shut his eyes.

It was the neckerchief Maman always wore.

Chapter IX

"There is more important news," said Grollet.

Pierre focused his eyes on him. More important news than that Maman—He could not say it, even in his thoughts.

He turned the faded scrap of fabric in his hands. What was this stain? He rubbed it, and the cloth gave away beneath his fingers. It was rotted, he saw, the threads barely clinging together. He lifted it to his nose and sniffed, but he could not smell Maman. She was not here, in this piece of cloth. Not here . . . or anywhere? His mind turned the thought as his hands turned the cloth.

Perhaps Grollet was mistaken! Perhaps Maman, too, had been taken captive.

He lifted his eyes and saw the pitying look Meunier cast his way.

She was not captive.

"They will meet us at the village of the Tohos in three days' time," Grollet was saying.

Who? Who would meet them?

"Who?" he said.

"The Spaniards!" growled Grollet. "Have you heard a word I said?"

Meunier put his hand on Pierre's arm.

"Spaniards are near," he repeated. "They search for survivors of La Salle's party. We are some sort of threat to their sovereignty over this country, they think."

"But this is Hasinai country . . ." Pierre objected.

"They think it theirs, as we thought it ours when La Salle laid claim to it. Now that they know La Salle is dead, they are willing to take us away from this country, they say."

"To a country of civilized men," L'Archevêque said. "To New Spain."

There was a disturbance at the door, and Pierre looked up to see the Provençal pushing his way between the Hasinai elders.

"What is this talk of civilization?" the Provençal said, speaking the Hasinai tongue. "The People are civilized enough for me."

Pierre saw the Caddi's lips twitch, and two or three of the elders murmured. Grollet paid them no heed.

"Stay, then," he said in French. "We are going with the Spaniards."

"But the Spaniards are our enemies," said Pierre. "Monsieur de La Salle warned us—"

"That was when we represented the French crown," said Meunier. "I do not think, when they see us, they will think us enemies."

"But the Spaniards are savages . . ." Pierre realized Grollet was looking at him with scorn.

Meunier spoke gently. "It is what is said of enemies, Pierre."

Pierre noticed he called him by his French name.

"We French say it of Spaniards. No doubt Spaniards say it of us, as the Hasinai call the Paouites savage, the Paouites call the Tohos . . ."

Pierre nodded.

"Spaniards are at least Europeans," said Grollet. "From New Spain, we might find passage to Spain—"

"And Spain," L'Archevêque interrupted, "is not far from France, I have heard it said. Not far from home!"

But Pierre wondered, Where was home?

"Ay'shah!" cried Na'-ta-ty. "What troubles you, my brother?"

Pierre had dragged himself away from the council to sit, in the warm still dusk, by the river. He watched the eddying water, his mind drifting with it, and fingered the yarn remnants of his crimson cap.

At Na'-ta-ty's voice, he straightened his shoulders and tucked the yarn back into his pouch with the fragment of blue neckerchief.

"They say the Children of the Sun are near and you will go away with them. Is that why you are sad, Tay-sha?"

Pierre shook his head.

"No," he said. "I have word of my family . . ."

Na'-ta-ty squatted before him and ducked her head to look into his downcast eyes.

"You have not spoken of family," she said. "I thought *we* were your family. Am I not your elder sister? Your mother?"

Her tone was teasing. Na'-ta-ty often called herself his "mother" when she wished to order him about. But Pierre could not smile.

"I have an elder sister," he said, "and brothers who are captives of the Clamcoëh. I—I had a mother. I thought to go to her some-day . . ."

"But you did not go, Tay'sha," said Na'-ta-ty gently.

It was true. He had not gone. The days, the months, the years had passed, and he had not gone . . .

"Where is this mother of yours?" Na'-ta-ty said.

Where was she? In purgatory, as the priests would say? In heaven, as Meunier said his mother was? Pierre could not imagine his mother among the angels in heaven.

"She is dead," he said.

"Ay-shah!" breathed Na'-ta-ty.

Pierre put his face in his hands.

Na'-ta-ty swayed before him. She tore her fingers through her braids, loosening them, and seizing handsful of dirt, she streaked her cheeks with it.

"Ay-shah!" she cried. "Tay'sha's sorrow is mine."

If only she would put her arms around him. If only he could weep, as she was weeping. But Pierre sat gazing over her head at the river, and his eyes were dry.

It was not until the depths of the night that sobs suddenly shook him. He wanted to shriek aloud as he had shrieked when he was a child, but he shoved his fist into his mouth. He tasted salty blood before he felt the pain of his teeth biting into his flesh.

He was not a child. He was thirteen years old, a man of the Hasinai. If he cried, no mother would comfort him, not even Na'-ta-ty. It was what he had wanted, was it not? To be a man.

Even before he heard the first birds, Pierre knew it was morning. Spent with weeping, he could scarcely find strength to climb from his bed. There was pain in his head. His mouth tasted bitter. As he cracked open the thatched door, the light of the rising sun hurt his eyes.

But he knew what he must do.

Remember your family, Maman had charged him. He could not go with the Spaniards, nor stay in Nabedache, so long as Magda and the boys remained with the Clamcoëhs. It was his duty. Had he stayed at the settlement . . . Had he gone back later . . . He might have kept them from capture . . . Well, perhaps not by himself, but he might have been able to save Maman.

Pierre had thought to be first at the river, for he could not have borne the good-natured banter of the townsmen. But as he emerged from the trees near the water's edge, he saw someone was there before him. Brown arms stroked through the water toward the shore, and Pierre saw the top of a sleek head. Then the arms ceased stroking; the head lifted. It was Meunier.

Meunier tossed his wet scalp lock from his eyes and rose from the water. He ran his hands across his head. He was breathing hard.

"Mon brave!" he said, recognizing Pierre with the old affectionate name. "You are awake early."

Pierre waded out to sit on a rock, and Meunier pulled himself up beside him.

"I will not go with the Spaniards," Pierre said. "I must find my family." He dipped his hands into the water and splashed his face.

Meunier nodded.

"This must be farewell," Pierre said. "You have been a firm friend. I am grateful."

But Meunier was grinning.

"Hold on, Tay'sha," he said. "Do not think to rid yourself of me so easily. Are you not my clumsy brother?"

Pierre cocked his head, looking deeply into Meunier's eyes.

"But—" he said.

"I think Grollet and L'Archevêque could as well end up in a Spanish dungeon as at home in France." Meunier was suddenly serious. "I am content with my lot as Bah'din's foster son. Soon, indeed, I may become his son-in-law, if his daughter will have me."

Pierre's eyes widened.

"If you are my clumsy brother," Meunier was saying, "then your brothers and sister are mine also. Why not go in search of them together?"

Pierre felt Meunier's hand on his shoulder. He turned away his head, so Meunier might not see the wetness in his eyes.

Chapter X

Once again, L'Archevêque and Grollet left Nabedache without Pierre and Meunier.

"It is your choice," Grollet said, as Monsieur Liotot had once said to Meunier. Meunier had been right then. Pierre hoped they were right this time.

But they did not stay long. They began their preparations to leave almost at once, though first there were many councils with warriors who had gone to Clamcoëh country before them, many maps drawn in the dust, or on skins with burned sticks, and committed to memory. The women of both lodges, the Caddi's and the Tamma Bah'din's, set to work to sew new deerskin breechclouts and robes for them, to dry maize and meat and berries. The Caddi and Bah'din chose three horses from their herds and presented them to Pierre and Meunier.

Spring passed, and full summer was upon them before at last the Caddi deemed them ready, and the Connas had pronounced a day auspicious for setting out.

When they were ready to leave, their families walked with them to the edge of the town. The Caddi put his hands on Pierre's shoulders and looked deeply into his eyes.

"You will make the People proud, my son," he said. "Of that I am certain."

Pierre wished *he* were certain.

Suddenly Na'-ta-ty was weeping. Bah'din's daughter wept to see Meunier go, but Pierre had not expected this of Na'-ta-ty.

"Do not go, Tay'sha," she cried.

"I will come back," Pierre said, and he remembered when he had said those same words to a weeping Magda. He *would* come back this time. He did not want to leave Na'-ta-ty. He wanted to put his arms around her, clasp her close. She was sister, friend . . .

He turned away abruptly, snatching from her hands the woven-reed panniers she had packed with food.

"I will bring my sister, Magda, to help you with the cooking and the tanning of hides and the tending of the fields," he said. "I will bring my brothers to hunt for you."

Na'-ta-ty touched him on the arm, and something melted in him. He trembled. Na'-ta-ty put her fingers softly on his cheeks and stroked them. The strokes were like pain.

"Walk in safety, my brother," she said.

It was early fall when Pierre and Meunier came back to the settlement they had left more than three years before. It was here that the search for Pierre's family would begin, for doubtless the invading Clamcoëhs dwelled nearby.

The buildings were above the creek, as Pierre remembered, at the top of a steep bank, which stretched away from the stagnant tidal stream in a broad, flat expanse where the colonists had planted their garden. Now all that remained of that garden was the remnant of a picket fence and a few scattered cornstalks. As they approached, Pierre could hear the wind buffeting the plank walls of La Salle's headquarters, which still stood solid, though the doors gaped. There was no movement about the building, or about the smaller, mud-plastered huts. The buffalo-hide roofs of the huts had fallen in.

"They are truly gone," Meunier said.

Pierre could not speak.

He urged his horse forward. Broken chests and bottle cases lay scattered among the shattered furniture and ruined pots and bottles. The Clamcoëhs had destroyed everything they did not carry away. He wondered if Maman's sea chest was there somewhere, smashed beyond recognition. Doubtless her wedding sheets now adorned some Clamcoëh woman, the baby dresses of his brothers some Clamcoëh child.

Then, near a hut, he saw a rough cross, erected above a mound of dirt—a grave. Pierre slid from his horse, but at the edge of the grave his legs gave way beneath him, and he sank to his knees. He sifted the sandy soil through his fingers.

Was Maman in this crude grave? Who had dug it? L'Archevêque and Grollet? We buried what bones we could find, L'Archevêque had said. Or was it the Spaniards? It was said by the natives that the Spaniards had also visited the abandoned settlement. Spaniards were Christian men.

Pierre realized that some part of himself had not believed Maman was dead. He had continued to see his family in his mind's eye as he had left them—the children growing, no doubt, as he had grown. Jean-Baptiste doing his sullen best to take Pierre's place. Magda helping with the little ones. Maman, surely wakened from her stupor of grief, seeing they were fed and warm and safe from harm . . . But Maman had not been able to keep them safe.

Pierre felt Meunier's hand on his shoulder.

"Come, *mon brave*," Meunier said. "There is nothing for us here."

Twice that autumn as Pierre and Meunier searched the countryside, they were told of sightings of white children—now two boys, in another place a girl and a boy. The children were with bands of roaming Clamcoëhs, the natives said. That was the trouble. The Clamcoëhs did not stay in one place, especially as winter approached and food became scarce. They moved constantly in order to sustain themselves.

"If they would build a village and plant a few fields as we do," a Paouite elder said, "they would have maize and beans for winter. They would not need to wander in search of game and water chinquapin and nuts, starving half the time. But there is no accounting for the Clamcoëhs. They think it noble to go hungry and cold in winter, thirsty and hot in summer, to have no proper lodges or clothes. They are lovers of dogs. Their women are without virtue. I do not know why you even seek your kinsmen if they have lived long with the Clamcoëhs. They will have become barbarians also, with no proper manners."

Pierre tried to imagine Jean-Baptiste, Magda, and the little ones becoming so degraded. Would the little ones even remember by now that they were born sons of a French mother and father? Would they remember Maman, who once cared for them so fiercely? Would they remember their brother Pierre, who abandoned them?

In late fall Pierre and Meunier happened upon a small band of Clamcoëhs, spearing fish in tidal pools. Pierre used sign language to ask after the children.

The Clamcoëhs shook their heads—sullenly, it seemed to Pierre. Their eyes shifted.

"We know of no white children," the leader signed. "Perhaps you are mistaken. Perhaps the children you seek were taken by Tohos or Paouites. Perhaps they are dead."

Pierre lunged forward.

"If they are dead, it is Clamcoëh dogs who killed them," he signed, his hands slashing the air.

The Clamcoëhs reached for their weapons.

Meunier's restraining hand was on his arm.

"My friend mourns his kinsmen and knows not what he says," Meunier signed to the Clamcoëh leader, who menaced them with a spear.

Then he turned Pierre toward his horse. His voice was urgent.

"Let us go, Tay'sha," he said.

The weather was chill when Pierre and Meunier gave up the search and accepted the hospitality of a Toho winter camp near where the children were last reported seen.

Though Pierre well remembered the Toho war party he and Monsieur Liotot had joined, none of the men in this camp looked familiar. They treated him and Meunier with courtesy so long as they joined the hunts and did their share. And none of the Tohos seemed to recognize Pierre.

Of course, he had changed. He was not the weak and fearful child who had followed Monsieur Liotot.

He was a man of the Hasinai.

"Tay'sha!"

Pierre lifted his eyes from the bear tooth he was shaping into an arrow point.

Meunier sprinted toward him from the direction of the Toho

camp. "Tay'sha, Spaniards have been seen in this country again. It is said they have burned the settlement."

Pierre sat back on his heels. He had come to this quiet place in the rocks because the rough good humor of the Tohos put him out of sorts. As spring came on, and the Toho camp readied itself to move with the buffalo, their plans and jokes and pranks seemed only noise and clamor to him who could not join them. More and more, he wanted to be alone. Not even Meunier's company soothed him. He wanted to brood on his family, to cast his mind back to that long ago time in the cabin in New France when he was just a little boy, cared for and at home. He wanted to remember the hope-filled voyage to France, the jubilation of procuring passage with Monsieur de La Salle's expedition. He liked to think of Maman's face then, call to mind the children, one by one. He did not know where to search for them next.

Now it took a moment to understand what Meunier was shouting. Spaniards? Burned the settlement?

"Why would they do that?" he said as Meunier dropped down beside him in the dust. "Why burn it now? They left it standing before."

Meunier shrugged. "I don't now. But they have come back and burned it this time. Do they look for us, do you think?"

Pierre thought out loud. "No doubt L'Archevêque and Grollet told them about us. But why would they want us enough to search us out?"

"If they do," said Meunier. "Perhaps they have come for some other purpose. Still, I do not want to chance falling into their hands. Shall we return to Nabedache?"

Pierre hesitated. Abandon the search for his family?

"Only for a while," Meunier said as though reading his mind.

"We could come back soon to continue our search, but for now, while the Spaniards haunt this country—The hunting party that leaves tomorrow will travel in the direction of Nabedache . . ."

Pierre rose, dropping the half-finished point and his shaping tool into the pouch at his waist.

"Then let us go with them as far as we can," he said.

Meunier grinned. "I would not mind a visit to the house of Bah'din," he said.

Pierre laughed, thinking of Bah'din's daughter. He winked. "You are as fond of your foster father as I am of mine." And his heart leaped at the thought of seeing the Caddi and Na'-ta-ty once more.

PART III

PEDRO

CHAPTER I
May 1690

Pierre and Meunier were on their way to Nabedache early the next morning, riding with the hunting party, a band of rowdy young Tohos. Meunier rode ahead with two others, and the set of his shoulders was jaunty.

Pierre rode a little behind. It would be good to visit Na'-ta-ty and the Caddi, the old father and the old mother, and yet . . . He had failed to find Magda and the boys. It seemed a little as though he were abandoning them once again to the lying Clamcoëh dogs.

His stomach tightened. He kicked the flanks of his horse, urging it forward. He had almost caught up . . . Suddenly, Meunier's horse lurched to its knees. It screamed. Meunier clung to its neck as it scrambled to regain its footing.

"Mun!" Pierre drew abreast and slid from his own horse's back.

Meunier dismounted, and so did the others, who helped calm the quivering horse. Pierre knelt and lifted its hoof. He had dropped the reins of his own horse, and the horse stood, taking the opportunity to tear up a mouthful of grass.

"What is it?" Meunier asked, panting.

"He stepped into a prairie dog's burrow, I think," said Pierre, running his hand over the horse's leg. "It's not broken . . ."

The Toho leader bent to inspect the leg.

"This animal is no good to ride," he said. "It was foolish of us not to bring extra mounts. Now perhaps you will wish to turn back, rather than hinder the hunt."

Pierre knew this was more than a suggestion, yet the natives did not order one another. Each man was expected to consider the good of the whole group.

"Is there not a town or village nearby where I might obtain a horse to replace this one?" Meunier asked.

"I will take you on my horse, Mun," offered a young man called White Buck. "There is a winter camp not half a day away. We will catch up to our friends easily, since they will be stopping to butcher the quantities of game they are certain to shoot." He winked.

"I, too, will go with you," said another man. "My sister lives in that camp."

A third also volunteered.

Pierre hesitated.

"Why don't you stay with the hunt, Tay'sha?" Meunier said. "I would not return to the People empty-handed. We will be back before you notice we are gone."

Yet Pierre's band did not find game as White Buck had predicted. The buffalo had not yet moved into the area from their winter grazing grounds, and though they saw deer and antelope in the distance, when they gave chase, the herds outran them.

The Tohos were good-natured about it. They had the food their wives and mothers had packed for them. They shot a few rabbits and birds. Pierre thought they dawdled, stopping that afternoon to nap, and camping early to gamble beside the fire. He would have been impatient had Meunier been with them, for he worried a bit about the Spaniards. But since Meunier would be racing to catch up, it was just as well.

Near noon the next day, Pierre heard a strange sound in the distance. Ahead an oak thicket rose above the tall grass. He reined in his horse and cocked his head to listen. The others halted beside him.

"Look!" cried their leader, pointing.

There was a brilliant flash of light. The May sun was shining on something . . . something advancing from the trees. A horse and rider, another and another . . . The riders wore the pointed helmets and armor of . . .

Spaniards!

Pierre wheeled his horse, kicking its sides. He heard the shouts and galloping hoofbeats of his Toho companions beside him. There was a low thundering on the hard-packed earth, the liquid sound of parting grasses, then—an explosion! Something whistled past Pierre's ear.

Musket fire!

The Tohos shouted and dove from their panicked horses. Pierre was alone, pounding across the plain, but someone was behind him. He glanced back and saw a Spanish soldier, lance raised, closing in on him. What a horse he rode! Its strides covered the ground in great leaps while Pierre's mount faltered. Pierre's horse's breathing was labored, and flecks of foam flew from its gasping mouth.

Pain splintered Pierre's skull. The lance clattered past him, glancing off the horse's shoulder. Pierre slid over its neck. He grabbed for the reins, the horse's mane. His hands closed on emptiness.

He was lying on the ground. The horse sidestepped away from him, its head flung up, its eyes white and rolling. There was thunder in Pierre's ears. He choked on dust. He rolled over, gathered his knees beneath him, scrambled to push himself up, to draw breath.

A shadow fell across him. His shoulder was seized. His eyes traveled up the length of two high, tooled boots, up soft leather breeches and tunic, up the hard, glinting surface of a breastplate, to the dark beard and swarthy face of a Spaniard.

Pierre was jerked to his feet, his arms pulled behind him and tightly bound.

"*Frances?*" his captor demanded, and though the pronunciation was strange, Pierre knew what he was being asked. How could the Spaniard guess? Pierre's skin was almost as dark as the natives, his face tattooed with the marks of his Hasinai clan. But then he remembered his hair, the dull brown of his scalp lock, instead of glossy black, his light-colored eyes, and his height. Through the haze of his pain he answered.

"*Oui,*" he said. "*Je suis Français.* I am French."

There was a triumphant cry. Pierre realized other men had ridden up. Some were still mounted, but others menaced him from the ground with their muskets. Two of the horsemen whirled and galloped away.

Pierre wanted to put his head in his hands. It was hard to stand upright with his head pounding so violently. He felt warm blood in his ear.

"May I not sit down?" Pierre asked in French, swaying on his feet.

They did not seem to understand. Pierre tried again, this time in Hasinai. They glared and jabbed their muskets at him.

Pierre remembered what the Caddi had taught him. A man of the Hasinai could bear any pain. He remembered what Maman had taught him. Her son did not give up. He pulled himself upright and fastened his eyes on the distant wood, from which the Spanish column was emerging.

The Spaniards numbered more than a hundred, Pierre estimated as he gazed at the column of dust approaching across the plain. He thought he saw priests among them, riding mules, and soldiers on horses, clanking, both men and animals, with armor. As they drew near he could hear shouting. Horses chuffed and whinnied. Carts creaked beneath their loads. He squinted at the sunglared helmets and muskets and armor. No wonder the Hasinai called Spaniards "Children of the Sun."

As his head cleared, he saw his Toho companions had been rounded up and herded into a straggling, dispirited group. Their hands were not bound, nor were they guarded as he was. They would drift away soon, one by one, if they could not persuade the Spaniards to give them presents. They might try to collect a reward for him, and he would not blame them if they did. They had not purposely led him into this trap, he was sure, and it did him no further harm if they profited from his capture. At least Meunier had escaped.

Another group of soldiers rode toward him. He lifted his eyes to the officer on the lead horse, who halted just in front of him. Pierre had to tip back his head to see the thin face beneath its shining helmet, and the movement made him dizzy. But the blue gaze of the officer steadied him.

A second man rode forward and dismounted. He came to stand beside the officer's horse. The officer spoke, and the second man spoke after him, in accented French.

"You are the prisoner of General Alonso de León, in the service of the king of Spain," he said. "What is your name and your country?"

Pierre stared, wordless. His name and country . . .

"I was called Pierre Talon," he said at last, answering French with French, though the words were clumsy on his tongue. "I was born in New France, but came to this country from France in the party of René-Robert Cavelier, Sieur de La Salle, who was an emissary of King Louis of France."

He looked into the blue eyes of the officer on horseback—General de León, the translator had said. The general's dark lids closed as he listened to the translator. When they opened, León was looking at Pierre with pity, and something inside Pierre loosened a little.

León spoke, his voice gentle.

"You are but a boy," the translator relayed. "The Indians have marked you like a savage, branded you like a beast."

The general was wrong. The Hasinai had treated him with honor, with kindness. They had made him one of them. But his head hurt, and it was hard to form the words that might explain.

Pierre was loaded into a supply wagon, and a priest—Padre Miguel, he called himself—climbed in with him. It was a painful, lurching ride, made worse by his bound hands. But the priest did not loose them. He only wetted a cloth from a sloshing water skin and roughly wiped away the worst of the blood—Pierre thought with longing of Na'-ta-ty's gentle hands. Then he tied up Pierre's head in another cloth and made the sign of the cross over him.

"By God's mercy you were struck but a glancing blow," Pierre thought he said, though his French was none too good.

He climbed from the wagon to resume his mule.

Pierre fell into a half sleep, jostled awake again and again, until he did not know whether he slept or woke.

Chapter 11

When Pierre stumbled into the light of the general's fire the next evening, León sat in a leather camp chair before his tent.

"Be seated," the general said through the translator. He waved a slender, long-fingered hand toward a place on the ground. "You are ill."

From the shadows beside the tent came a noise. A priest stood there, his hands folded beneath his cassock, his insolent sneer visible in the flickering firelight. This priest would not have let him sit down were it up to him, Pierre knew at once.

The general followed Pierre's glance.

"Fray Damián Massanet," León said, and the translator repeated in French, "this is Pedro Talon, whom we have had the good fortune to rescue from *los indios*."

"You did not rescue me," Pierre protested. "You took me prisoner." He held up his hands, still bound at the wrists, as proof.

The general frowned and spoke to Pierre's guard, who stepped forward and released his hands. Pierre sank to the ground.

"You will not run away, will you, Pedro?" the general said.

Pedro. Pierre had been given another name. He rubbed his wrists. He did not answer the general. The place on his skull where

133

the Spanish lance had broken his scalp sent thudding pains through his head. He felt sick. No, he would not run away . . . yet.

The translator was called Captain Martínez. He spoke fluent, cultured French. Like a French gentleman, Pierre thought.

"It is the activities of le sieur de La Salle the general would like to know," Martínez said, "and the activities of the other Frenchmen from the North."

"Monsieur de La Salle is dead," said Pierre. "I know of no others from the North."

Again the priest, Fray Massanet, made a noise, an incredulous snort, as Martínez translated.

"I am glad you confirm La Salle's death," said León. "But there *are* others. *Los indios* report that Frenchmen have come overland from the North. We cannot allow French incursions on Spanish territory. Spain is at war with France."

Pierre groaned. Frenchmen from the North. Was it the rescuers sent by Joutel, arriving too late? He thought of the pitiful sandy grave at the settlement. What did he care about war? What did he care about France, for that matter? He cared only to stay alive . . . and find Magda and the boys, he reminded himself. He closed his eyes and felt the heat of the fire at his back.

"I know of no others," he repeated.

"Do not lie to the general!" The priest stepped forward. He loomed over Pierre, threatening, and Pierre would have known what he said without Captain Martínez's translation.

León spoke. His tone was placating, and the priest stepped back into the shadows again.

"I have told you all I know," Pierre said. "I was a child when we sailed from France five—perhaps six years ago. We landed and built a settlement on the Gulf. You know it, for you burned its remnants not many days hence." He saw the general and the priest exchange glances as Martínez translated.

"Where are the soldiers from the settlement? Where are your ships?"

Pierre looked at León, who was regarding him with a sharp blue gaze. This man would know if he lied. But what was the point of lying? He looked back steadily and spoke directly to León. "I am sure L'Archevêque and Grollet must already have told you," he said. "The ships are sunk in the bay. The soldiers are dead."

"All? All dead?"

Pierre looked at the ground. He felt somehow ashamed.

"I am alive," he said. Perhaps L'Archevêque and Grollet had not mentioned Meunier and the Provençal. Pierre would not betray them. "The men who surrendered to you are alive, if you have not killed them. A few of our party journeyed toward New France. I know not if they succeeded in reaching it. But Monsieur de La Salle is dead. Most of his men are dead. The women and children—" Had L'Archevêque and Grollet told León about his brothers and sister? He took a chance. "—the women and children are dead," he said.

"Women and children," the general repeated in Spanish, shaking his head. He looked tired. The lines about his eyes were deep. "We did not kill your comrades who surrendered," he said. "They have gone to Mexico City with some of my men." He paused. "How many of you came from France?"

"Perhaps two hundred," said Pierre.

"Two hundred? All dead?"

"Most," Pierre said, looking again straight at León. "We

failed," he said. "Whatever it was Monsieur de La Salle had in mind to do, we failed. You need not fear us."

The translator sneered the words as he repeated them to the general, but León did not sneer. He turned away.

"We have never feared the French," he said.

Pierre thought *that* was a lie, for the general had not been able to look at him as he said it.

They remained the next day in that same camp beside a river. After the morning meal, Pierre was allowed, under guard, to bathe, and the cool water seemed to wash away the ache in his head and soothe his cuts and bruises.

He was stumbling out of the river when he heard a shout. Four riders were galloping toward the camp, yipping a cry of greeting. Pierre's guard started forward, then remembered his duty and jerked Pierre in front of him. Pierre squinted at the riders. They were Tohos, he saw, surprised, for the last of his Toho companions had departed the day before. He heard his name.

"Tay'sha! It's me!"

Meunier.

Pierre's heart leaped at the sound of his friend's voice, then plunged. Was Meunier mad to come thus boldly into the Spanish camp? They would take him prisoner, too!

Spanish soldiers ran forward, pointing muskets at the newcomers. Meunier held up his hands, and the Tohos reined in, making the sign for peace.

Pierre and his guard hurried forward, the guard jabbing Pierre's naked back with his sheathed sword, and when they were near enough to hear, the guard brought the sword down hard on Pierre's shoulder and yelled, *"¡Basta!"*

Meunier held out his hands, crossed at the wrists as though to be bound.

"I surrender myself to the king of Spain," he said.

"How could I leave you alone in the hands of Spaniards?" Meunier said when at last his Toho companions had ridden away, their horses laden with Spanish gifts, and he and Pierre were left to await León's pleasure.

"I am scarcely alone," Pierre said, squatting in the shade of a wagon. He glanced at his guard, who lounged beside a nearby cook fire, chaffing the cook. "I have not been left alone two minutes together since I was captured."

"Precisely why I could not rescue you any other way. Together we may be able to get away if we watch for our opportunity."

"But you were away free!"

Meunier looked at the ground beneath his crossed legs. "Together you and I have survived many a narrow escape, *mon brave*," he said. "But without one another . . ." He shrugged.

Pierre sighed. It was for him that Meunier had sacrificed his freedom. He should be grateful . . .

His gaze swept the trampled campground, the soldiers snoring or gaming beside tents and wagons, with their filthy uniforms and lousy hair. "Oh, my friend, you should have returned to the house of Bah'din to wed that pretty maiden there. Who knows what will befall us in Spanish hands?"

"I will return there," Meunier said, "when you and I make our escape."

But it seemed the Spaniards were not so cruel as Pierre had feared. Meunier was questioned, and that evening when they were taken to the general's tent, León seemed satisfied with his answers.

"You came to us of your own will," he said to Meunier. "It was well done. I invite you both to join us as *compañeros*." He paused while Captain Martínez repeated his words in French. "Our priests wish to build a mission among *los indios*. Will you guide us to the *ranchería* of the Hasinai?"

Pierre glanced at Meunier, who met his glance with an uplifted eyebrow. The general was not so much asking their help as commanding it.

"You have my word as a gentleman that we will not bring them harm," said the general. "We bring only the blessings of Mother Church to these lost ones."

Pierre's thoughts were racing. He could see that Meunier, too, was thinking fast. Home again at Nabedache, surrounded by their friends and with the influence of their foster fathers behind them, they might persuade the Spaniards to let them go. Was there much hurt the Spanish priests could do to so powerful a people as the Hasinai? Meunier was looking at him, the same question in his eyes. Pierre shrugged imperceptibly.

"Very well," Meunier said, and Martínez did not need to translate, for assent was in Meunier's nod.

"It is well done," León said through the translator. "Padre Miguel and Captain Martínez will begin at once to instruct you in our language, so you may confess and be shriven. After so long without the consolation of the sacraments, I know you are eager."

Was he eager to make confession? Pierre had fallen out of the habit of prayer and observance, and he had not missed God. He had shown respect for Ayo-Caddi-Aymay, as the Caddi had instructed. He supposed it was the Hasinai god who had protected him in Hasinai country. Was God even needed there? And he did not feel sinful, or needful of absolution. The only guilt he felt was for abandoning his family, and that was not a sin, so far as he knew, for he had followed the orders of his leader, whom God had set above him.

But he said nothing. General de León would be shocked to know his thoughts. So would Monsieur de La Salle have been . . . and Maman.

It would not hurt to know a few words of Spanish, nor would it hurt to appease God.

CHAPTER III

Captain Martínez said the general had once been a fierce Indian fighter. "He allowed his captives to confess and be shriven . . . before he hanged them," said Martínez. "The general is a merciful man."

Something inside Pierre quivered. He thought of the general's concern for his own confession.

"Are we acting wisely?" he asked Meunier when they lay side by side in their bedrolls beneath their tent's canvas.

"The general needs us at present," said Meunier. "I think we are safe, at least for now. And as to the People . . . the Spaniards have roamed from New Spain for a hundred years or more. They have left the People to themselves all that time. Why would they harm them now?"

Pierre was thinking of the way Monsieur de La Salle had treated the Clamcoëhs near the settlement. He had stolen their canoes, and when they complained he sent soldiers to kill them as though they counted for nothing. But those *were* Clamcoëhs, not Hasinai.

Still . . . How would Fray Massanet treat the People if they refused his religion? Pierre hoped the Caddi would allow the Spanish priests to build their mission.

*　*　*

As they topped a rise and saw before them the scattered golden houses of Nabedache, Pierre felt a sudden warmth rise in him—then drain away, leaving him chilled and shaking. If only it were Magda and his brotherrs he was bringing to the People!

Then the Caddi was striding toward them, his arms wide and welcoming. Behind him trooped the rest of the townspeople, important men first, then the rest, the women and children following after, calling glad greetings.

León had left behind the bulk of his force, camped less than half a day's ride away. He brought only the priests and translators and a handful of officers, with Pierre and Meunier riding in front to dispel any uneasiness the Hasinai might feel. But the Caddi knew where every Spaniard camped or rode, Pierre was sure.

He saw the Caddi's eyes flick toward the Spaniards. He spotted a few young men ranged among the trees, their weapons at hand. The Caddi was no fool.

"Tay'sha, my son!" the Caddi called in his deep, resonant voice.

Pierre slipped from his saddle and ran forward. As the Caddi's arms closed around him, he felt at home and an intruder at one and the same time.

Na'-ta-ty wept again when she greeted him, touching his face as though she were blind, and murmuring, "I feared we might not meet again."

Something stirred in him at her touch. "I told you I would return, T'ahay-ti-ti," he replied, and though she did not ask, he saw her looking behind him for his brothers and sister. He defended his failure to bring them. "We have brought these Children of the Sun," he said. "They have gifts for the People. Their Brown Robes wish to live among us for a time and teach us of their god."

He should not be telling this news to a woman before even the Caddi knew it, but Pierre wanted her to think well of him.

Na'-ta-ty only smiled. "So long as they come with my brother," she said, "they are welcome."

At the welcome feast, Pierre leaned against the back of his bench and gnawed a rib bone, watching as Na'-ta-ty hurried to and fro with the other women, serving the foreigners. The platters were heaped with venison and quail. The women offered bowls of stewed beans and baskets of cornmeal bread. Even at this season, when the first crop of maize was not yet harvested, the Hasinai had abundant food, and the Caddi's wife was gracious as she led in sharing it.

Pierre looked about for Meunier. He was nowhere in sight, and Pierre thought he must have stolen away with the daughter of Bah'din. He saw General de León beckon.

"Pedro!" the general called.

Pierre rose to his feet and made his way to the fire, where the elders sat with the general and his officers and Fray Massanet.

"We need a translator," said Captain Martínez in French.

"But the feast is not yet over," Pierre said. "Council should wait until hunger is satisfied."

The priest made an impatient gesture when this was translated.

"Fray Massanet wishes to speak now," Martínez said.

It was very rude, but Pierre did as he was bidden.

"Pardon, my father. These foreigners have no manners, but their discourtesy must be excused. They are ignorant of proper conduct. The Brown Robe wishes to speak."

The Caddi laid down his meat and wiped his fingers in his hair.

"Let him speak, my son," he said.

Pierre looked toward the priest, who did not conceal his impatience. Fray Massanet spoke in Spanish, and Martínez repeated his words in French. Pierre translated to Hasinai.

"The Brown Robe says, my father, that he brings a great gift to the People."

The Caddi's eyes lit up, calculating, Pierre was sure, what this gift might be.

Pierre paused, trying to think how to explain. "It is the gift of the Spaniards' god, Jesus, who sacrificed his life so men may live forever."

Pierre could see the Caddi's disappointment, but the Caddi slapped his knee and laughed out loud with goodwill, repeating Pierre's words to the elders as though they had not heard. The elders laughed.

Fray Massanet jumped to his feet, shouting. The general reached out a restraining hand, and the Caddi sobered immediately.

"Are these Spaniards mad, my son?" he asked. "No man lives forever. We all must die, else the world would soon be too full of people. There would not be enough maize or game to sustain us."

"I think, my father, the Brown Robe means that Jesus brings life after death. He says if we accept the gift of Jesus, we will go to a place called heaven, where maize and game are abundant."

Fray Massanet was still making a disturbance, despite León, but Pierre and the Caddi ignored him, as they would a noisy child. The Caddi pursed his lips.

"If we live bravely and well, providing for our families and our town and the People, and bringing harm to no one but our enemies, Ayo-Caddi-Aymay has promised much the same," he said. "Why have we need of this Spanish god?"

"I know not, my father," Pierre said, "but I must tell you that

Jesus is not the god of the Spaniards only. The French also worship him, and I think that other nations do, too. The English and—"

"I have heard that tribes to the south and the east have taken up this new god," said the Caddi. "During the dry season last year, my brother Caddi of the Neche Hasinai had council with a Brown Robe. Perhaps it was this one, for he also was rude, I was told. The Brown Robe promised to send teachers to the People so we might learn the sources of the white man's strength."

By now, Fray Massanet's impatience could not be contained.

"In God's name, tell us what their chief is saying," implored Captain Martínez.

"He says he has heard of Jesus from the Caddi of Neche."

Martínez translated.

"That good man implored me to send him priests," said Fray Massanet to Martínez, who was translating as quickly as he could. "If we cannot build our mission here, we will build it at Neche."

Pierre told this to the Caddi and saw his face change as he considered whether the priests were more apt to bring prestige than trouble to Nabedache.

"So, the Brown Robe would build a house in our town and teach us . . ." he said.

"Yes, my father, but . . ." Pierre did not know why he felt uneasy.

"It would be good to know about the weapons of their warriors," said the Caddi to his elders, signaling to Pierre not to translate.

The elders murmured.

"It is said the Brown Robes have powerful medicine against sickness," said the Caddi's father.

The Caddi nodded. "If they do not live here, they will go to some other town," he said. "It might be well to have them under *our* eyes." The Caddi was coming to a decision. "If the elders approve," he said, turning to Pierre to translate, "these Children of the Sun may leave a Brown Robe or two to live with us. We will give them food and help them to build their house, and they may teach us in return. Tell them this is my decision unless, after proper council, the elders disagree." He reached to take up a roasted quail leg, and Na'-ta-ty came forward to refill his gourd cup. "Now," he said, "let us eat this good food."

Chapter IV

"Tell me, my son . . ." The voice of the Caddi came softly out of the darkness of the sleeping house. ". . . What of those you went to search for?"

Pierre turned on his willow bed toward the voice and propped himself on one elbow. It was good to sleep again in the house of his foster father, and León had not objected. Pierre assumed he was still a Spanish prisoner, for all the general's talk of *compañeros*, but for now he was soothed by the sight of the coals glowing in the fire pit, and by the presence of the Caddi and Na'-ta-ty in their own beds against the far wall. The snores of the Caddi's old parents comforted the night.

"I did not find them, my father," Pierre admitted. "The Clam-coëh dogs seemed to know where I would be and kept them out of sight."

Na'-ta-ty murmured, then the Caddi voiced her question. "Are you certain they still live?"

"Yes!" Pierre's answer came without thinking and louder than he intended. "Yes," he repeated more quietly. "Many have seen them."

"Will you search for them again?"

Pierre flopped over on his back. It was a question he had been asking himself. "I am still a captive of the Spaniards," he said, "though they pretend I am not. I do not know if they will allow me to continue my search. Can you obtain my release, my father? Mine and Meunier's?"

The Caddi grunted. Then a silence deepened around Pierre, despite the soft snores of the old people. Pierre's heart beat in his ears, and the blood rushed to his temples. Perhaps the Caddi would not want to jeopardize the tentative alliance with the Spaniards by challenging them to release an adopted son.

"If the Children of the Sun are friends of the Nabedache Hasinai, they will not make a prisoner of the Caddi's son, nor of any man of our town," the Caddi said.

Tears flooded Pierre's eyes.

"Then, yes," he said when he could control his voice. "I will search again for my brothers and sister when the Spanish general has gone."

Again Na'-ta-ty murmured. The murmuring continued a long time, with now and then a word from the Caddi. Pierre strained to hear, but they talked too softly.

"You may wish," said the Caddi at last, "to consider whether you wish to be freed. My wife points out that the Spaniards have fire sticks and many warriors. The Clamcoëh dogs fear them above anyone. It could be they would aid you in your search and in the release of your family. The Spaniards found and captured you. They might likewise find and capture your brothers and sister."

What the Caddi said was true. The People would not want to war over a handful of foreign children, however fond of Pierre they were. But General de León seemed set on locating all of La Salle's survivors. If he knew of Magda and the boys, likely he would leave no stone unturned to find them.

Pierre would have his family back. The Caddi might then bargain with the Spaniards for them all.

The Caddi was still speaking. "My son, there is one thing more you must know," he said.

Next morning Pierre hurried down the path to the oak grove, brushing past others curious to see what the foreigners did there so early in the day. The Spanish priests were ahead, in their dark robes, gathered near the sprawling oldest tree. Padre Miguel stepped back from its trunk, where he had just nailed a crucifix.

Was Meunier in the gathering? It was he Pierre wanted to find.

The priests, the general, and his officers were bowing their heads. They made the sign of the cross, and Fray Massanet began to intone a prayer for the dead.

It was a prayer for English Jem and Rutre, Pierre realized. The crucifix on the tree was for them, too, to mark the place where they had been buried. Fray Massanet had insisted last evening that their graves must be marked, as befitted Christian men.

Christian men! They were scoundrels and murderers. Many a worthy Christian, or heathen for that matter, lay in an unmarked grave. Monsieur de La Salle . . . Maman . . . even Papa was more deserving of this ceremony than those rascals. But Pierre thought it must have been these priests who erected the cross at the grave in the settlement. Perhaps Maman's grave *was* marked . . . if the cross had not burned with the rest of the settlement.

Pierre spotted Meunier, standing a little away from the Spaniards, as though to separate himself from these unfitting rites. Pierre stared at him hard and, as though in response to the stare, Meunier looked up. Pierre caught his eye.

Fray Massanet finished his prayer. He and the other Spaniards turned away from the tree, crossing themselves again. Pierre found that he, too, was touching his forehead, his belly, his shoulders, and the gesture seemed as familiar as though he had done it every day of his life. Indeed, he did until—When *had* he ceased his prayers?

It didn't matter. What mattered was to tell Meunier the news. He hurried forward against the flow of people following the Spaniards back toward the temple. The Hasinai were enjoying the show the strangers put on. Then Meunier was just ahead of him, and Pierre jerked his head, motioning him out of the press of people. They fell into step and hung back.

"There are Frenchmen nearby," Pierre said in a low voice, speaking French, when they were alone.

"Frenchmen?"

"Aye. It is as General de León said—Frenchmen from the North. Three who may be of Joutel's party, come back from New France, and a man with but one hand."

"Tonti," Meunier said. "That would be Henri Tonti, who was a great friend of La Salle in Canada. But why only four men? Do they search for La Salle?"

Would not Tonti know that La Salle was dead? Surely Joutel would have spread the news.

"How do you know this?" Meunier asked.

"The Caddi. On the very day he got word the Spaniards approached Nabedache, he received a message from the Frenchmen. They were three days' journey to the east. They wished to come to Nabedache, to bear witness to their friendship."

"The Caddi refused them?"

"He knew you and I were with the Spaniards, and that French and Spanish must not meet."

Meunier nodded. He stopped and looked hard at Pierre in the

filtered light of the pathway. They were about to come out into the sunlight of a small clearing, where a beehive-shaped house stood near a field of maize.

"If we wished to return to civilization, the Spaniards might be a better choice than four Frenchmen who may be lost," Meunier said. "Who is to say they will survive to return to New France?"

Pierre stared at him. "If we wish to return to civilization?" he said. "What do you mean? I thought we were agreed that this is our home."

Meunier began walking again, and Pierre followed.

"I have decided to stay awhile with General de León," Pierre admitted. "But it is not so I may return with him to civilization. The Caddi thinks the Spaniards, with their soldiers and arms, may be able to obtain the release of my family."

"Four Frenchmen could not do that," Meunier agreed.

"But I will bring them back to Nabedache," Pierre said. "I do not wish to go to New Spain, nor do you, I thought."

Meunier did not look at Pierre. "I have changed my mind," he said.

"What of the daughter of Bah'din?" Pierre felt as though he had been struck in the belly. What he wanted to say was, what of *me*?

"Ah!" Meunier shrugged and chuckled mirthlessly. "Ah, yes. I am told the daughter of Bah'din is to be wed . . . to the son of a Tamma of Nacono."

Now it was Pierre who stopped dead.

"Oh, *mon ami*!" he breathed.

But Meunier kept walking, more swiftly now, past the rustling field of maize. He raised an arm to greet a group of women, bending among the stalks.

Pierre watched his retreating back.

Meunier could not leave him. He would change his mind again when his disappointment was not so bitter. Perhaps, by the time the children were found, he would want to return with them to Nabedache . . .

In any event, Pierre would not tell General de León of the Frenchmen from the North.

CHAPTER V

But the Caddi had different advice.

"Tell General de León of the Frenchmen when you tell of your brothers and sister," the Caddi advised, "and say they search for your family. Then he may be more zealous to find and ransom them himself."

"You should have told me sooner, Pedro!" the general exclaimed. "Of course we must find your family and bring them away from the savages. These Frenchmen from New France would not be able to rescue them. My orders are to find the remnants of La Salle's colony, so four newcomers do not interest me. They pose no threat to Spain, I think, if there are only four of them. We shall know it from our priests at the mission here if they get up to any mischief."

Pierre saw how eager León was to be on their way to find the children. As the Caddi said, competition made him more keen.

Why was Pierre not as eager to leave as the general? It was *his* family they would search for, but to do so meant once again leaving Nabedache. Once again leaving Na'-ta-ty . . .

And then, one day, as he hurried toward where Na'-ta-ty stood on a rise, silhouetted against the paling sky, Pierre stopped suddenly to look at her more carefully. She stood in just such a way that, beneath her black skin skirt, he saw the way her belly curved, the way she put her hand to her arching back as though it ached. Na'-ta-ty was with child! He blinked, to push away the knowledge, but even as he did, he remembered how plump her cheeks had grown of late, how, bending over her mortar, a sweet, inward-looking smile seemed to touch her lips. She was quieter . . . softer . . .

Pierre turned abruptly and hurried away, hoping she had not seen him coming. His heart was thumping in his chest as though it might burst through his skin.

Na'-ta-ty would be a real mother now.

By the time of the first harvest, the Spanish column was moving westward again, leaving Padre Miguel and two other priests behind in Nabedache, with three soldiers to protect them. Pierre was relieved Fray Massanet was not one of them.

What changes would the priests bring to the People? Pierre wondered as he and Meunier rode out behind the general. They had bidden farewell to their Hasinai families once more. Pierre noticed, as they rode away, that the daughter of Bah'din was nowhere to be seen. He heaved a sigh of sympathy for Meunier.

But there was a pain in his own heart, too. A pain that not even Meunier knew about. When he saw Na'-ta-ty at the side of her husband, weeping, he turned his eyes away.

Days later, Pierre and a small party of Spaniards rode into the main camp of the Clamcoëhs. Pierre and Meunier had been here before, and it was as dirty and poor as Pierre remembered. But it was here that General de León had been informed that his sister and brothers were held. Were they hidden somewhere inside these hovels scattered along a murky inlet?

Disheveled women and toothless old people squatted before the dwellings, many of them almost naked. Near the farthest hut stood a company of men, the Clamcoëh leader and his elders. They were taller and more powerfully muscular than Hasinai men, with darker skin. Their faces and bodies were not only tattooed but scarified and pierced.

Pierre peered into the faces of the skinny children who ran shrieking beside his horse. What would Jean-Baptiste and the babies look like now? Would he know them?

General de León pulled up before the Clamcoëh leader. León had brought only a dozen or so men, including Pierre and Meunier, so as to appear unthreatening, and these now halted behind him. But the Clamcoëhs looked ferocious, ready to raise their war clubs at any moment. Had the general been wise?

León motioned to Captain Martínez and Meunier to come forward to translate and sign, but he gave Pierre a warning look. Pierre was to stay in the background, watching for the children.

Pierre dismounted. The horses were led aside. Now was the moment when at last Pierre might know the fate of his family. Would the Clamcoëh dogs lie to the Spaniards as they had lied to him?

Pierre listened and watched, catching now and again a word or phrase of Spanish and still more of the native sign language. The general caused the pack horse to be brought forward and unloaded on the ground. The faces of the Clamcoëh leader and his men lit up at the sight of the cheap metal blades, the beads, and hatchets spread before them. Though the leader did not deign to examine the gifts, his men could not restrain themselves. They fingered the things and cried aloud in delight.

Then it was the turn of the Clamcoëhs to show their hospitality. The women were commanded to bring food, and though it was but poor and scanty—ash-coated seed cakes and water chinquapin roots and a few half-cooked oysters—the general and his men squatted and ate. Even Fray Massanet took a few bites, though he made a sour face.

Pierre could not swallow the food for the tightness in his throat. He was looking closely into the faces of the serving women, hoping to see the flash of hazel eyes. Would Magda be as old as any of these? How old *was* she?

He was fourteen, he knew, for the day of his eleventh birthday, the day when he learned of Monsieur de La Salle's murder, was three springs ago. Magda was older. Perhaps sixteen?

The serving women had breasts. Would Magda have breasts by now? It was difficult to imagine Magda with breasts—skinny Magda with her tight braids and worried face.

Pierre glanced toward the general. Why was he taking so long to ask about the children? Pierre longed to be as ill-mannered as Fray Massanet. He felt he could not wait much longer to see what answer the Clamcoëh dogs might give.

"We have come on a small matter that may be to your profit," Captain Martínez translated for León just then.

Pierre was instantly alert.

Meunier turned the French into sign language.

"It is the matter of a few useless foreign children, who are your captives," Martínez said. "We would take them off your hands."

The shadows cast by the Clamcoëh hovels grew long, and still the council dragged on. General de León sat with the Clamcoëh leader on skins thrown down before his hut. Around them were ranged half a dozen elders and most of the Spaniards, including Fray

Massanet. A few women moved or sat among them, offering food or drink from time to time, squatting to listen, then wandering away. Children ran and played at the edges of the gathering.

The general seemed unperturbed, but Pierre could not match his patience. His anger seethed as the Clamcoëhs haggled and hedged.

Perhaps they had seen foreign children in the camp of their neighbors . . . Captive children were not uncommon . . . But no, those were not French children, but Pauoite, and their people had come to ransom them. It had been a sizeable ransom. Anyone would covet such a ransom . . . *If* they held captive children. They, for instance, this very band of Clamcoëhs, had need of many things the Spaniards might give them. The Spaniards were rich, and they were poor, as the Spaniards could surely see. They needed horses and knives and iron pots. With such gifts, perhaps, they might persuade someone to give the children up. *If* someone held the children . . . Who could tell? Who would notice so insignificant a thing as foreign children in the camp of a neighbor? What good were children anyway, of whatever nation? Horses, now . . . Horses were of value. Who could tell what a gift of horses might do to soften the hearts of people who held captive children? *If* there were such people . . . *If* there were such children . . .

When General de León said he would trade horses for white children, Pierre saw the Clamcoëh leader beckon to two young men with pieces of cane thrust through their lower lips. The young men sprinted away.

Three or four of the Spanish soldiers had drifted away from the group squatting before the leader's hut. They were courting young women, Pierre saw, trying to lure them into the thicket nearby. The Clamcoëh men did not seem to notice, but Fray Massanet frowned, his attention distracted from the council. The voice of an old woman rose querulously. She was dickering for a buckle a soldier held out, while a young woman peeked giggling from the doorway of her hut. Fray Massanet leaned forward to speak to the general, but León brushed him away.

"How many horses?" the Clamcoëh wanted to know.

"How many children?" León asked.

Fray Massanet flushed and leaped to his feet. He stalked over to the soldier who was haggling with the old woman. He barked a reproof, and the soldier slunk away.

There was a stir at the edge of the circle of people. Pierre glanced back at the council, then looked again hard. The voices of the bargainers fell silent.

Some Clamcoëh children were being led forward. They were naked and filthy, their faces darkened by the crude tattoos of their tribe. Pierre thought of the tattoos on his own face.

A young woman stepped out from behind the children. Her hands were crossed over her bare breasts, and her head was bowed. Her hair glistened darkly with alligator grease. Ornaments of bird bones dangled from her ears. About her hips was a skirt of Spanish moss. As Pierre watched, breath held, the woman lifted her head to stare with emotionless eyes at the Spaniards. The staring eyes were a clear greenish gray.

Magda?

Pierre felt the shock of it deep in his belly. Magda of the skinny brown braids and worried frown—a woman, tall, thinner even than when he had bade her farewell, half naked and bedecked as a Clamcoëh. But it *was* Magda!

Chapter VI

Pierre forced back a cry. General de León had been firm. There must be no sign that anyone cared much about the outcome until the ransom was completed.

He wrenched his gaze away from Magda's face and looked again at the children in front of her. All boys. One. Two, three. Four. The two older boys must be Jean-Baptiste and Eustache Bréman. He searched their faces for some remembered feature and found none. The little ones were surely his baby brothers, but they were babies no longer. Pierre swallowed hard. He shrank back where the children would not spot him. Though . . . would they recognize him if they did?

He had not recognized them. They looked—they did not look like French children at all, but like natives, like Clamcoëhs. What had he expected?

Pierre could not tear his eyes away from the thin, dirty faces. They were silent, even the little ones, and no feeling was evident in their expressions. The little boys clung to Magda's moss skirt, as once they clung to the skirt of Maman. Their eyes were huge and blank. Jean-Baptiste and Eustache stood on either side, motionless. Only their eyes moved, glancing first at the general and then at the Clamcoëh leader, who gestured toward them with a casual hand.

"Are these the ones you seek?" the leader signed, and when this was translated, León looked at Meunier.

"Jean-Baptiste Talon?" Meunier questioned, and the heads of the older children jerked in his direction. "Marie-Magdelaine Talon?"

Pierre saw one of the older boys nod. Then Magda nodded. Her lips formed the word *oui*, but Pierre heard no sound.

"These are the French children," Meunier assured the general.

"Five horses," General de León offered. "A horse for each of them."

"Six horses," the leader signed. "The female is a woman grown. One of my warriors would give me two horses at least for her. And ten knives, ten pots, more beads."

"We have already given you knives and beads," said the general. "Six horses is too many."

Give him the horses, Pierre wanted to shout. Give him the horses and let us be gone. But he pressed his lips together.

"Six horses," signed the leader.

From behind the hut at his back stepped a dozen or more naked warriors, their faces and bodies painted, their scalp locks bristling with feathers and shells. Each held a long cedar bow, its cane arrow at the ready.

From behind him, Pierre heard a cry. A woman was screaming. A soldier shouted in Spanish.

"Six horses," signed the Clamcoëh leader with a slashing motion. He leaped to his feet. "Six horses, or we will kill you and keep the captives."

Even as he spoke, his warriors loosed a rain of arrows. The Spaniards scrambled out of the way, running for their tethered horses. General de León did not move, and Pierre heard the impotent clash of arrows against his armor.

Pierre started forward, toward the huddled children. Four Clamcoëh warriors ran past, shooting after the retreating Spanish soldiers. One or two soldiers emerged from the thicket, firing their muskets. As the Clamcoëh leader grappled him from behind, León was shouting orders. Men ran forward to snatch up the cowering children. One burly sergeant, with the little boys under his arms, was struggling onto a horse. Fray Massanet mounted and rode away. Four or five Clamcoëhs lay bleeding on the ground, one with a shattered skull.

A soldier raced past with Magda clinging to his saddle. The little boys clutched their sergeant around his brawny neck. Jean-Baptiste and Eustache were flung across the saddles of two more mounted soldiers. There was nothing more Pierre could do for them. He wheeled toward the horses and snatched at the tether of one that trampled a wounded mare beside it. The mare was down, kicking, an arrow through her eye.

Pierre pulled the sound horse away and swung himself into the saddle. Ahead of him, Spaniards were galloping through the encampment, trampling over the flimsy huts, while Clamcoëhs screamed and scattered. He saw General de León mount a steed at last, assisted by his aide.

Pierre leaned forward, digging his heels into his horse's sides, and fled.

Across the campfire, the five children crouched together. Pierre watched the flames play on their faces.

They had not spoken, even when Meunier coaxed them in French. They had eaten, ravenously, whatever was offered them. They had slept, fitfully. They had ridden, uncomplaining, until dark yesterday and all today until León's party caught up at last with the main body of soldiers at their camp on the river the Spaniards called Guadalupe.

Each of them was now garbed in a Spanish shirt, which, on the smallest boys, reached to the ground. Magda clutched hers to her throat with one hand and, with the other, stroked the bony back of the youngest boy. Baby Robert, that would be. Magda's slowly moving hand reminded Pierre of the way Maman used to rub his own back when he was small. But that was all Pierre could see of Maman in the tattooed faces of his sister and brothers.

"Are you never going to greet them?" Meunier said, lowering himself to the ground beside Pierre. "They are your family, whom you have sought for so long, and yet you do not rejoice in them. You do not even acknowledge them." His voice was accusing.

Pierre pulled his knees to his chest and rested his forehead on them. "They do not seem like my family," he muttered. "They do not act like them, or look like them—"

"But . . ." Meunier reached out his hand and tipped up Pierre's chin until he had to look him in the eye. "You do not look much like Pierre Talon yourself. In those Spanish breeches and coat, you do not look much like my friend Tay'sha either. In fact, you look every day more like the general's Pedro. Does that make you Pedro?"

Pierre Talon. Tay'sha. Pedro.

Who *was* he?

Pierre looked again through the flames of the campfire. Jean-Baptiste was glaring at him in a way that brought back a memory.

I want to live with the Indians, he had said, glaring in just that way.

Pierre pushed himself to his feet. He took a deep breath.

As he walked around the fire toward them, the little ones cringed against Magda as they did when anyone approached. Jean-Baptiste and Eustache moved closer protectively. Pierre reached into the pouch that hung from a thong around his neck, the pouch that held the remnant of Papa's crimson cap and Maman's neckerchief.

"Don't be afraid," he said in French, but his words did not seem to reassure them. Jean-Baptiste was measuring him suspiciously. "Petit" Lucien closed his eyes as though to shut him out.

"We are not afraid," said Jean-Baptiste, but Pierre thought his voice quavered.

"Don't you know me?" Pierre said, squatting.

Magda cocked her head and looked hard at him. She frowned.

"Your tattoos say you are Hasinai," said Eustache.

"But you wear the garb of the Spaniards," said Jean-Baptiste.

"So do you," reminded Pierre gently. "Magda?" he said, holding out the tattered crimson cap. "Do you remember when Maman gave this to me?"

"Maman . . ." she said.

"I am your brother Pierre."

"Pierre is dead," said Jean-Baptiste, his voice hard.

But tears were shining in Magda's eyes. "*Non,*" she whispered, reaching out to touch the cap. "*Non,* our Pierre is not dead." She pushed the little boys aside and leaned forward to clasp him about the neck. "Pierre, *mon frère!* You said you would return."

Pierre was weeping. He had not wept since the news of Maman's death. A man of the Hasinai did not weep. But the tears flowed nonetheless, wetting his cheeks, and Magda's, too.

Chapter VII

Pierre and the children sat beside the dying fire late into the night, while Meunier and the Spanish soldiers slept around them, and they talked. That is, the older ones talked. The little ones knew no French, Magda said. In the year they had lived with the Clamcoëhs, they had forgotten their native tongue.

"We did not speak French," she said.

"They punished you if you did?"

But the three older children shook their heads.

"They favored us above their own children," said Eustache. "My Clamcoëh mother would give me food when her other sons went hungry."

"Mine also," said Magda. "*C'est vrai*, during the attack on the settlement, the warriors were cruel. They murdered even our priests, our sick, our women. Maman—"

"I know," said Pierre.

"But the women—" Jean-Baptiste said.

"The Clamcoëh women," said Magda, "would not let the warriors kill *us*. They said we were sent to them to bring good fortune."

"We brought them death," said Jean-Baptiste. "Back there at the camp, the Spaniards—"

"The leader said," Magda put in gently, "so long as we kept out of the way, the women could have us."

"The women were kind," said Eustache.

Kind. It was something for Pierre to ponder. He thought of Na'-ta-ty and the Caddi, the old parents and the Nabedache townspeople. It seemed one could meet with kindness anywhere. Or cruelty.

"Maman was ill," said Jean-Baptiste, his voice surly. "She would not have lived in any case."

Pierre whirled on him, his hand uplifted to strike. "She would have! She would have lived—"

Jean-Baptiste's eyes were hard. "If La Salle had come back to rescue us, as he said he would," he said, "perhaps . . ."

Pierre's arm dropped.

"Monsieur de La Salle is dead," he said in a low voice. "He could not rescue even himself."

"And Maman *was* ill. She was never the same after Lisette died," Magda said quietly. "The young ones do not remember her as we do, Pierre."

"Magda took care of us," said Eustache.

"We know you would have come for us," Magda soothed. The little boys had fallen asleep beside her, and she took both his hands.

He could not meet her eyes.

"We know you came for us as soon as you could, but—"

"But you came with the Spaniards. Our enemies! Will they put us in prison?" Jean-Baptiste wanted to know. "Will they kill us?"

Pierre looked across the dark camp to the candlelight glowing from the tent of General de León. The general was also awake, it seemed, writing perhaps to his superiors in New Spain.

"I knew of no other way to obtain your release," he said. He thought of the pitying way the general had looked at the children when they were brought to him after the wild ride from the Clamcoëh camp. "No," Pierre said. "I'm certain they will not harm us, but I don't know what they plan to do with us. The general has vowed to me that he will give us a home until the Spanish viceroy makes provision for us. But I have it in mind to escape the Spaniards and return to Nabedache, where I am of the People there."

"Nabedache? The Hasinai town?" Magda said.

But when Pierre nodded, Jean-Baptiste spoke out angrily. "Hasinai? The Hasinai are our enemies, too!"

Shouts and the creaking of harness. Cart wheels thudding over uneven ground. The clang of a spoon against a pot.

Pierre opened his eyes as faint light streaked the sky. He was curled in blankets with his brothers and sister near the dead fire. The coolness of morning touched his cheek, but against his back, he could feel the bony warmth of Robert—or was it "Petit" Lucien?

Gently he extricated himself from the sleeping children, rose to his knees, and looked about him. The camp was breaking up.

Pierre stood up and stepped over Jean-Baptiste. Meunier was striding toward him.

"*Mon brave!*" he said, and Pierre thought Meunier must approve of his reunion with his family because he used the old, affectionate name. "You must waken them," Meunier said. "We have orders to move out in less than an hour."

"And where do we journey?" Pierre asked, half dreading the answer. "Do we return to Nabedache?"

"Did you think León would return there? He has finished what he came here to do. He has gathered up La Salle's remnants and established a mission for the People." Meunier was shaking his head. "No, we go to New Spain. The Spaniards are jubilant to be going home."

Pierre realized that, all around them, soldiers were laughing and joking as they tore down tents and rolled blankets. It was as he had feared.

He lowered his voice. "Then we must slip away," he said. "We must flee to Nabedache." Even as he said it, he saw the stubborn look that settled on Meunier's face.

"Perhaps you will find a way to flee in a few days. The main body of soldiers will be traveling slowly, with the carts of provisions, and you and your family will stay with them. I am to go with the general, ahead of you, to report to Mexico City."

"He is separating us?" Pierre felt a hollow open someplace in his belly. "Did you not tell him we must stay together—"

Meunier put out a hand.

"I will not go back to Nabedache, Pierre," he said. "There is nothing for me there."

"But what is there for you in New Spain?"

There was no time, no time to think, no time to persuade Meunier. What will I do without you? Pierre wanted to say. How can you leave me now? You have always been there for me. Me, me, me . . .

Pierre looked into Meunier's eyes and saw there a depth of despair he had never seen before. Had all his bravura been only a sham? Or was this something new, something to do with the daughter of Bah'din? Something like Pierre's feelings for Na'-ta-ty?

"Did she mean so very much to you?" Pierre said.

Meunier did not answer. "I am not Hasinai, Pierre," he said. "I am French."

"But—"

"Waken your family, Pierre. You are lucky to have them. Waken them and care for them as best you can. Perhaps we will meet again . . . in New Spain . . . in France . . ."

He turned on his heel and walked swiftly away.

Pierre stood frozen, empty, looking after him.

Nabedache? New Spain? France?

He looked back at the children. Magda was sitting up now, combing her fingers through her matted hair. Robert had crawled into her lap and leaned against her, sucking his thumb. Care for them . . . How best to care for them? And where?

"We must ready ourselves to ride, *ma soeur,*" he said to her.

Magda nodded, unquestioning, and bent over the others to wake them.

Chapter VIII

In the green valley below were perhaps twenty mud-brick houses, of a style Pierre thought must be Spanish. Some distance away from them, down the stream that meandered through the valley floor, was a native town, smaller, but much like Nabedache. Smoke rose into the late afternoon sky from its cooking fires. It was the town that looked welcoming to Pierre, not the Spanish houses. But it was not to the town that they rode, but to the Spanish settlement—San Francisco de Coahuila, General de León's ranch. They would refresh themselves there, Captain Martínez said, before going on to New Spain.

Now a body of horsemen rode up the dusty track from the ranch. León's second in command, who had been left in charge of the Spanish column, rode forward to confer with them. Then he waved the line of Spanish soldiers and carts forward.

In the past days, they had traveled farther and farther from Hasinai country, from Nabedache and Pierre's friends there. Yet Pierre had seen no opportunity for escape. It was not so easy a thing to slip away when one had others to think of—Magda, who was truly a young woman now, and the boys, who seemed so young. "Petit" Lucien was afflicted with boils on his buttocks and legs, so that riding was a misery to him, and to all who must ride with him, listening to his plaintive cries. Jean-Baptiste remained surly and uncooperative. Pierre almost wished he could leave Jean-Baptiste behind, but, of course, he could not. He was responsible for all of them.

Now Magda urged her horse up beside Pierre's.

"Is this the place where we will rest?" she asked.

Pierre nodded and saw how she expelled a deep, tired breath.

"*Bien,*" she said. "Good."

They were given a room in the house of the general's *capataz*, his foreman. It opened onto a central courtyard, with a little fountain. There, to the courtyard, the wife of the *capataz* and her maids brought their sewing. There, at the other end, Pierre sat on a bench in the sun, his head leaned back against the mud-brick wall, and tried once more to decide what to do.

The Spanish women were shy with Pierre and Jean-Baptiste and Eustache, but they had petted the little boys, fussing over "Petit" Lucien's boils, cleaning and dressing them. The little boys played now at their feet with a kitten and a ball of string.

Magda emerged from the house, wearing the bodice and skirt and pretty, soft blue shawl they had given her. Her feathers and bone ornaments were gone. Her hair was washed and braided. Her step was hesitant.

"¡*Pobrecita!*" the women cried when they saw her, and Pierre wondered if she knew they called her "poor little thing." But the women were clustering around her. The wife of the *capataz* reached out and gently touched her tattoos.

Magda drew in a breath. She put her own fingers to her cheeks. She snatched the shawl over her face and broke away from the women.

Pierre stumbled to his feet. He ran after her into the house.

He found her in their room, flung across her pallet. In the dim light that filtered through the window, Pierre saw that her shoulders heaved, but she made no sound.

"Magda," he said.

No answer.

"Magda."

She shuddered, her face turned to the wall.

"I forgot," she said. "For a moment, wearing these pretty things, I forgot that I am branded."

Pierre sat down beside her, cross-legged, his hands clenched in his lap.

"Do you want to go back?" he said after a moment.

She turned her head to look at him. "Back?"

"Back to the natives. I keep thinking I might be able to contrive our escape. There would be a place for us in Nabedache. I have friends . . ." It didn't seem right to say he had family there.

She shook her head.

"To the Clamcoëhs, then?" Perhaps it had been a mistake, taking them from the Clamcoëhs.

"*Non!* Even with these tattoos, I am not Clamcoëh."

I am not Hasinai, Meunier had said.

Magda's voice hardened. "I cannot forget what they did to Maman."

She pulled herself up and looked at him, her eyes hopeless. She did not look like a young woman now, but like a child, afraid.

He had been afraid, too—marching away from the settlement all those years ago. When Monsieur de La Salle was murdered. When he rode into battle with Liotot.

Pierre fumbled with the thong tied around his neck. He unfastened the deerskin pouch Na'-ta-ty had made for him and took from it the remnant of Papa's crimson cap. It was tattered and full of holes. He began unraveling the wool and plaiting the strands together.

Magda was watching. He could feel her gaze on his hands. "Papa's crimson cap," she said at last.

"Maman knitted it for him in France before we sailed, remember? Remember what she said? 'For good fortune and courage.' "

"*Oui,*" she whispered.

"She gave it to me when I set out with Monsieur de La Salle, and I have kept it ever since," said Pierre, finishing. As he leaned forward to tie the plaited yarn onto her braid, he searched for words.

"Magda," he said. "We *are* branded, you and I. Not by our tattoos, but by our sufferings. I am proud of that. I am proud that we survived, that we are strong, that we are—"

Magda tilted her head, looking into his eyes.

"We are Marie-Magdelaine and Pierre Talon. We have brought honor to our name, and we have shown courage, as Maman wished us to. With courage, we can make our own good fortune."

Magda nodded. She reached up to touch the yarn in her hair.

Pierre tried to picture her in Nabedache. Would she be content as a Hasinai woman? Or did some other future await her, await *them*?

Magda put her hand on his arm.

"Maman never looked backward," she said.

"You do not wish to run away from the Spaniards?" he asked.

She shook her head. "Running away is no use."

Pierre straightened his shoulders. No one in Nabedache needed him now as Magda and the boys needed him. As he took a deep breath, he felt something within him break. It hurt. Leaving always hurt. Maman had known that, but she had sent him away nonetheless, toward an unknown future. Still, it was a future . . .

"Then," he said, "let us go forward."

After

There really was a boy named Pierre Talon who accompanied the famous explorer La Salle on his last expedition, was left with the Hasinai Indians, and was captured from them by Spaniards. Accounts of Pierre's life are incomplete and sometimes contradictory. Nonetheless, as I wrote this story, I tried to be as true as possible to what really happened. In places, I simplified events or left out confusing aspects. And writers can seldom know what went on in the minds and hearts of the real people upon whom we have based our characters. We can only guess and imagine their thoughts and feelings from what the historical record says they did.

All of the European characters in this book are based on real people.

Because the Native Americans of seventeenth-century Texas left behind them very little information, what we know about them is mostly gleaned from European accounts. The Native American characters in this book are purely imaginary. With the help of Cecile Elkins Carter, herself descended from Caddo Indians (the confederacy of tribes that included the Hasinai), I have tried to honor what little is known, including fragments of the Caddo language.

What Happened Afterward

Readers may be interested in knowing what happened to Pierre Talon, his family, and others in this story.

For the purposes of the story, I made one material change in events. General Alonso de León brought only Pierre, his sister Marie-Magdelaine (I called her Magda), and his two youngest brothers "Petit" Lucien and Robert, along with his companion Pierre Meunier, out of Texas on his expedition of 1690. It was not until the following year that the remaining Talon brother, Jean-Baptiste, and Eustache Bréman were located by the Spaniards and ransomed.

Pierre and his sister and youngest brothers arrived in Mexico City in the late summer of 1690. Pierre was fourteen; Marie Magdelaine was about sixteen; Lucien was eight; and Robert was barely six. They became household servants of the Spanish viceroy, Conde de Galve, and were treated kindly, by all accounts.

When the viceroy and his wife returned to Spain six years later, they took Marie-Magdelaine and Robert with them. Eustache Bréman remained in Mexico. Pierre, Jean-Baptiste, and "Petit" Lucien were enrolled as soldiers on a Spanish vessel bound for Spain. But their ship was captured by a French warship near Havana, Cuba. They were taken to France, where Pierre and Jean-Baptiste were impressed into the army, and "Petit" Lucien, only fourteen, was placed as a servant. Here history loses track of "Petit" Lucien Talon.

It was while Pierre and Jean-Baptiste were in the French army, shortly after their return to France, that they were questioned by French authorities eager to learn all they could of the La Salle venture and the lands of Texas and Mexico. The questions and their answers are known today as the Talon Interrogations.

Although Pierre and Jean-Baptiste asked to be reunited with

their sister and younger brothers, they were instead shipped back to North America in 1699 to take part in French expeditions of exploration from the French colony of Louisiana. They were in their early twenties, and their previous experiences among the natives, their knowledge of native languages and customs, and their familiarity with the terrain made them valuable guides and translators.

They returned to France in 1702, and two years later were reported to be in the "prisons of Portugal," though we don't know why they were imprisoned or when or why they were later released.

Pierre, however, reappeared in 1714 in the company of his youngest brother Robert on the banks of the Rio Grande. They were guides to yet another French expedition. By this time, Pierre would have been thirty-eight and Robert thirty. For the next two or three years, records indicate the Talon brothers were active as guides to French exploration. I like to think that, on these or some earlier journeys, Pierre may have met once again with his Hasinai friends. It is said that the tattoos of the Talons acted as passports among the natives.

Jean-Baptiste Talon was reported to have settled in what is now Louisiana.

Robert Talon, the baby, was listed in a 1721 census at Mobile, now in Alabama, where he was married and had two children. He was a carpenter by trade.

Meanwhile, Marie-Magdelaine somehow made her way from Spain to France where, despite her tattooed face, a liability in seventeenth-century Europe, she found a husband, Pierre Simon of Paris. She gave birth to a son in 1699 when she was about twenty-six years old. It is thought she eventually returned to Canada, the place of her birth, where her son was married in Charlesburg in 1719.

Pierre's companion, Pierre Meunier, did not go back to

Europe. His name is last recorded in 1699 in New Mexico, where Jean L'Archevêque and Jacques Grollet also settled.

The party led by Monsieur Joutel did succeed in getting to Canada and from there to France, where Joutel published his journal of the expedition. No rescue party was ever sent back from Canada, and the four Frenchmen reported seen by the natives were searching for La Salle, ignorant of his death. They were not of Joutel's party.

General de León died the year following his expedition to found missions and search for La Salle's survivors. He was partially in disgrace with his government, because his leadership had been called into question by Father Damián Massanet.

Pierre Talon died in France at an unknown date according to one source.

Today you will not find Clamcoëh (Karankawa) or Cenis (Hasinai) people living in Texas. The Karankawas were hunted to extinction by white Texans in the early nineteenth century. It is probable that the Hasinais had been decimated even earlier by the disease and disruption of their culture brought by contact with Europeans. Their well-organized towns disappeared; their systems of religion and politics were mostly forgotten. Today only about four thousand men, women, and children can trace their ancestry to the once-powerful confederation of tribes that counted the Hasinais among them.

The History

The larger historical context of Pierre Talon's story is the competition between France and Spain in the late seventeenth and early eighteenth centuries for control of the southern portion of the

North American continent—notably what is now New Mexico, Texas, Louisiana, Mississippi, Alabama, and Florida. The Spaniards had been established in Mexico for some time, and French exploration of the North American South was viewed by them as a threat to Spanish sovereignty. When Spain became aware that La Salle had landed on the northern gulf coast of what is now Texas, they set out to find the interlopers and expel them. They did not know that La Salle's expedition had met with disaster practically from its start.

Unaware, the Spaniards continued to search for La Salle until their location of the remnants of his followers finally convinced them that the La Salle expedition was no threat.

How Do We Know About Pierre Talon?

Two primary sources were used for information about René-Robert Cavalier de La Salle's last expedition and the events of the life of Pierre Talon: a reprint of the first English translation of the journal of La Salle's lieutenant, Henri Joutel, and a translation by Ann Linda Bell of *Voyage to the Mississippi through the Gulf of Mexico*, commonly referred to as the Talon Interrogations. Joutel published his journal in part to contradict the account of La Salle's murder published by Chrétien Le Clerq in the name of Father Anastase Douay. Joutel's journal is generally accepted as the most reliable narration of the La Salle expedition.

The Talon Interrogations, seventeen questions put to Pierre and Jean-Baptiste Talon in 1698 by representatives of the French government and their paraphrased answers, contain all we know of Pierre's years among the Hasinai. They also tell of Jean-Baptiste's experience of the massacre of the French colonists and his subsequent time spent among the Clamcoëhs (Karankawas). A tantalizing and incomplete document, the Talon Interrogations suggest much, but leave even more untold about the boys' extraordinary experiences.

Where the Talon Interrogations disagree with Joutel's Journal, I chose to rely on Pierre's version of events, since this is his story.

Ellen Howard
Salem, Oregon 2009